Simply LAURA LEA

Simply LAURA LEA

Balanced Recipes for Everyday Living

LAURA LEA

Certified Holistic Chef + Creator of *LLBalanced.com*

Foreword by **SEAN BROCK**

BLUE
HILLS
PRESS

Publisher: Matthew Teague
Editor: Candace Floyd
Design: Lindsay Hess
Layout: Jodie Delohery and Lindsay Hess
Photography: Laura Lea Bryant and Anna Haas
Hair & Makeup: Nissi Lee
Index: Jay Kreider
Proofreader: Lelan Dunavant Davidson

Blue Hills Press
P.O. Box 239
Whites Creek, TN 37189

ISBN: 978-1-951217-22-8

Library of Congress Control Number: 2019955723
Printed in China
10 9 8 7 6 5 4 3 2 1

ACKNOWLEDGMENTS

For my best friends—Chelsea, Adi, Lily, Leanne, Frances—my chosen family, my soul family, my backbone, and the lights of of my life. I am grateful daily that the universe brought us together.

For my parents, who continue to show up and love me unconditionally through the darkest and lightest of times. Thank you, Mom, for being the best sous chef.

For Lelan, without whom this book would never have come to life. Lelan's brilliant mind and diligent work ethic were irreplaceable when it came to editing and testing these recipes, as well as offering some of the best tips and tricks in the book!

For Jordan, who makes me look at lot more professional than I am! Jordan is the reason I'm able to get this book into so many hands so quickly.

For Jack and Will, my brothers, simply because they love and support me and know me in a way that no one else ever will.

For Sean, who never ceases to amaze me with his combination of unparalled talent, graciousness, and zest for life. It is an honor of a lifetime to have him write the foreword for this book, and I am forever grateful.

For Matthew, for taking another chance on me with these big clunky things we call cookbooks. I'm so lucky to have established both a friendship and a mutual professional respect with you.

For Candace, for turning her brain into applesauce editing this, my second-born child. Her attention to detail and kind communication made the process so smooth and successful.

For Alice, who continues to champion me from afar, and who instilled a confidence in me early on that I carry throughout every work endeavor.

For the whole team at Blue Hills Press, as well as my incredible photographer Anna—they make the real magic happen, and the amount of work they put into this project does not escape me.

For all of my readers and the LL Balanced community. None of this would exist without you, period. Thank you for trusting me and thank you requesting more from me!

Contents

Recipe Directory

Foreword

by SEAN BROCK

"I don't know how she does it," I think as I shake my head from side to side. This is the reaction I have every time I'm lucky enough to eat something that Laura Lea puts in front of me. From baked goods, to hearty breakfasts and snacks, and creative lunch and dinner entrées, Laura Lea has achieved delicious, executable, and nutritious recipes.

She painstakingly tests these recipes over and over, seeks feedback from lucky friends and family, and perfects them through trial and error. Even in the restaurant world, I don't know many chefs who work as diligently and prolifically to develop reliable recipes quite like Laura Lea. One of the things that I admire about her is that she is always "working on it," determined to make the most delicious recipes she can with the home cook in mind. I love making her recipes. In general, I never, ever follow recipes, but Laura Lea's are different. I follow them because I've tasted the results and wouldn't even know where to start to create the things that she does. She takes the time to understand every little nuance of an ingredient, what it is made up of, what its capabilities are, and how to make it sing.

Her food is designed to make you feel good. As we know, "healthy" food hasn't historically been thought of as the most delicious. But the level of deliciousness she achieves with food that is good for both your body and soul takes tremendous drive and skill. I find myself craving her food. A lot. Laura Lea's cooking is not simply for sustenance—it makes you feel something. It also directly reflects her sunny, nurturing, and enthusiastic personality. You can taste the love and passion she has for her craft. In *Simply Laura Lea*, she shows us that we can take better care of ourselves while still enjoying the pleasure of something very delicious and satisfying. In our house, we refer her food as "Laura Lea treats." I am so excited for you to try these recipes and witness for yourself why I am such a huge fan.

—**Sean Brock** has won James Beard Awards for
Best Chef: Southeast, for American Cooking, and
for his first book, *Heritage*. His latest book is *South*.

Introduction

When I my began my first cookbook, *The Laura Lea Balanced Cookbook*, I sought out the opinions and advice of everyone I knew who'd written a book. While I received a variety of stories, cautions, and encouragements, there was one shared sentiment: you'll never do it again, or you'll fall in love—you'll fall deeply, feverishly in love with the blood, sweat, tears, and triumphs that make up this wild journey. And you'll know you want to write books as long as you can cobble words together and find just *one* person to read them.

I fit effortlessly in the latter camp. Writing my cookbook was the most exhilarating and exhausting experience of my life, and I adored every moment of it. While I am incredibly grateful that my book was well-received, I know in my bones that I would have written a second cookbook regardless. Just as I know that I'll write a third and a fourth and, Lord willing, more.

Not only does the process itself light me up—the creating, testing, photographing, typing, deleting, and typing again—but there's always so much left to share. More has changed in the three years since I wrote my first book than I could possibly begin to describe. In the birds-eye view picture of my life, yes, just about everything is different. More importantly, though, my knowledge of ingredients has expanded,

The LL BALANCED APPROACH to FOOD

1

Focus on whole, fresh foods that make you feel great.

2

Ditch any preconceived idea of what you should eat,
and listen to your body; it is your best wellness guru.

3

Indulge in moderation and, occasionally, not in moderation!

4

Have fun and don't take yourself or your food too seriously.
Enjoy food in a relaxed atmosphere and in the company of dear ones.

5

Above all, practice self-love and patience in the kitchen.
It will translate to the rest of your life.

my techniques have streamlined, new research has come out (and comes out daily), and earlier studies have been discredited. My own body has healed and aged and become more flexible *and* less yielding in myriad ways. I feel like I have thirty-four years of new information and experience that I *need* to share. One practical example is my use of avocado oil. When I wrote my first book, I'd never heard of avocado oil, and I didn't have a great substitute to offer for inflammatory vegetable oils. Now avocado oil is one of my most-prized pantry possessions, and I use it multiple times per day (more on page 17 for why it's so great). A less concrete but equally impactful example is my deeper understanding of bio-individuality—the concept that because of our uniqueness, we cannot appropriate another person's diet and assume it will work for us. This understanding led me to rekindle a romance with dairy, because I realized that it actually works for me (more on this on page 21). At least for now!

Writing these books also affords me the opportunity to answer your requests directly. You told me you wanted more vegetarian recipes, so I doubled the vegan and vegetarian entrées section. You were befuddled by your Instant Pots (leaving many still in their boxes), so I created recipes that will make your purchase worthwhile and save you

time. (P.S. I implore you to tell me what else you want to see in future books, even as you are getting to know and using this one.)

I'll tell you a little secret. Despite my intense cookbook-writing love affair, I almost put the kibosh on this one. Last year, I went through one of the most difficult periods of my life, and I could barely eat or sleep for weeks on end let alone birth a book-baby. I even considered throwing together a twenty-recipe paperback to give you *something* while keeping my workload light. But the idea of nothing or something "less than" sat more heavily in my gut than the emotional pain I was in. So here we are.

And you know what? Creating this book healed me. It healed my aching gut and glued my heart back together and softened the muscles in my braced shoulders and put the good kind of butterflies in my belly. It affirmed the incomparable therapeutic power of a well-loved and well-used kitchen. It ignited a confidence in my—our—ability to grow alongside and in spite of pain. And I've never been happier.

Over the last thirteen months, I've been asked almost weekly "What's the theme of your new book?" While it would have been easy to be able to say "Laura Lea Holiday" or "Laura Lea Keto," the truth is that there is no ostensible theme. More accurately, the themes that course through the veins of this book are the same as the first: ingredients and recipes that are approachable, family-friendly, familiar with a twist, comfort-food inspired, and which offer something for everyone, at any meal, for any occasion. My goal with this book wasn't to reinvent the wheel, but to provide more of what you've told me adds value to your life.

I cannot wait to hear how you (hopefully) enjoy these dishes, make them your own, and come up with ways I can do it better the next time.

SPECIAL RECIPE SYMBOLS + LABELS

V	Vegetarian	🕐	1 hour or less
Vg	Vegan	💧	Soaking required
DF	Dairy-Free	❄	Chilling required
K	Keto-Friendly	⬆	Marinating required
GF	Gluten-Free	⊕	Secondary recipe
P	Paleo	🍚	Instant Pot & Crock-Pot

Chapter 1

The LL BALANCED APPROACH to FOOD

I have allowed myself more indulgences over the past year and a half than I did in the previous six. And yet, I have felt more vibrant and comfortable in my skin, have slept better, and have experienced less anxiety than in those previous years. Don't get me wrong; I've eaten all of the nourishing food in this cookbook and enjoyed every healthful bite, but I've also been more flexible.

What does this mean? To me, it is a reminder that more important than the tangible food "stuff" is the mindset with which we approach food and ourselves. We must come from a place of self-compassion, from the understanding that there is no "right," "wrong," "good," or "bad" when it comes to food. There are foods that make us feel better and foods that make us feel less so, and that varies from moment to moment. When we make space for what seems like imperfection and trust that our bodies, brains, and hearts know what we need, we cannot go wrong. As you progress through this book, I invite you to approach each recipe with playfulness and curiosity. My hope is that the experience of doing so will echo into every other aspect of your life, because you deserve it.

The THREE STEPS *to* ACHIEVING *the* LL BALANCED APPROACH *to* FOOD:

1. Fill your pantry with nutrient-dense, whole foods.

2. Properly supply yourself with the basic kitchen equipment and ingredient staples.

3. Create a relaxed and happy eating environment.

1

Fill your pantry with nutrient-dense, whole foods— *including these awesome new ingredients.*

I had so much fun coming up with a list of new, fabulous, and unique ingredients to include in this cookbook. (For a quick review of the ingredients in my first book, see Stocking Your Pantry, page 348.) While I want y'all to have the vast majority of ingredients already in your pantry, I feel that it's my responsibility and privilege to introduce new, healthy foods and flavors to you. In my first book, you learned about gooey, caramel-y medjool dates; crunchy, fiber-filled chia seeds; utterly versatile almond flour; and so much more. I have loved seeing y'all incorporate those gems into your weekly cooking routines, and I know you'll feel the same way about these wonderful ingredients. To read more about their health benefits, see Sources for Nutritional and Dietary Information (page 350).

Coffee

Oh goodness, the coffee controversy! While I included coffee in a smoothie recipe in my first book,

I didn't go into any depth about this famous and infamous beverage. Here's the deal: I *love* coffee—the flavor, the aroma, the experience of holding tight to a warm, frothy mug first thing in the morning. However, I am more caffeine-sensitive than most, so I have to limit my consumption. Most people can enjoy a moderate amount of coffee every day ("moderate" will vary from person to person), while feeling steadily energized and maintaining a regular sleep schedule. In addition, responsible intake of high-quality coffee can indeed be a boon to your health. Consuming coffee has been shown to have a beneficial impact on cardiovascular disease and chronic liver disease, and it is antioxidant-rich. I highly recommend consuming organic, fair-trade coffee, which is free from pesticides and supports humane labor practices. There are countless brands that fall under this umbrella, with a variety of roasts and strengths. I do not recommend consuming excess coffee when pregnant (but go with what your doctor says). Otherwise, I say enjoy your Joe in moderation, periodically checking in to make sure it's still working for you. Signs that it's not might include feeling jittery or restless, having trouble sleeping, having unusually intense sugar cravings (a sign that your hormones might be out of balance), or feeling like you can't start the day without it. Note: I chose to use cold-brew espresso in this book's recipes, simply because the work is already done for you, and it has a concentrated flavor, so a little goes a long way.

Avocado Oil

It utterly blows my mind that avocado oil wasn't a *thing* when I wrote my first cookbook. I'm sure it existed, but I'd certainly never heard of it. I actually can't pinpoint when I first learned about this phenomenal oil, but I immediately fell in love. Avocado oil is simply the oil extracted from avocado flesh, but the magic lies in what components make up this beautiful fruit (yes, avocado is technically a fruit, as it has a seed). Avocado is a fantastic source of potassium and vitamins A, C, D, and E, benefiting everything from your skin to your eyesight to your immune system. In addition, avocado and its oil may help our bodies better absorb nutrients such as antioxidant carotenoids. Perhaps most importantly, unlike vegetable oils, which have an inflammatory and damaging fatty acid profile, avocado oil is a great source of heart-healthy, anti-inflammatory oleic acid, a monounsaturated omega-9 fatty acid. Enjoying moderate amounts of avocado and its oil can improve signs of aging, reduce skin damage, promote joint health, and have a positive impact on cholesterol levels. Not only is avocado oil great for us to consume, it has a high, stable smoke point of approximately 520° F, compared to 320° to 350° F for olive oil. It also has a relatively neutral flavor. As a result, it is an ideal substitute for traditional vegetable oils and my go-to choice for any high-heat cooking, especially searing or pan-frying. It even does well in baked goods, as you will see!

Chives

Does it seem silly for me to include chives in my "unique ingredients" section? Hear me out: Onion chives are the variety found in most grocery stores, but I don't see them in many cookbook recipes or across the Internet. But in my opinion, chives should be a pantry staple for their health benefits and versatility. They're a member of the allium family, which also includes garlic, shallots, onions, leeks, and scallions. While they share the hallmark pungency of this class of vegetables, chives are milder and sweeter than most alliums, much like shallots (another favorite of mine). I mean, they make ranch dressing *ranch dressing* (and I have a healthy recipe in this book, page 339). The National Cancer Institute has identified chives as having cancer-preventive properties due to to their concentration of phytochemicals, flavonoids, and carotenoids, among other compounds. Garlic chives, also known as Chinese chives, have a slightly stronger flavor, but they also offer antimicrobial and antibacterial benefits. Both types are a wonderful way to add brightness, zest, complexity of flavor, and beauty to almost any savory dish. I love keeping them in my fridge, wrapped in a damp paper towel, to snip on eggs, avocado toast, cooked grains, seared salmon, grilled chicken—you get the idea. When you try them in this book's recipes, I think you'll agree that they add an irreplaceable *je ne sais quoi*!

Farro

Farro, how do I love thee? Let me count the ways! I have been itching to put farro in a cookbook since before my first book was a reality. Why? First, because it has my favorite texture of all grains. Chewy, nutty, and deeply satisfying, farro stands up to countless flavor profiles and pairs beautifully with almost any herb or vegetable (or fruit, for that matter). I chose not to use it in my first book, only because I wanted to limit the number of unique or less-familiar ingredients. But now that we've tackled and mastered ingredients like nutritional yeast, tahini, coconut flour, and more, it's time to add farro. It's important to note that farro is *not* gluten- or wheat-free. Technically, "farro" refers to three different strains of wheat grains, but the one we typically find in the US is emmer wheat (we'll call it "farro" in the book). Farro is a source of free-radical-fighting antioxidants, as well as soluble and insoluble fiber, which can benefit digestion. Farro offers zinc, B vitamins, and magnesium, which aid various functions within the body. Magnesium can improve heart health, PMS symptoms, and metabolic syndrome conditions like diabetes. In the world of grains, farro takes a bit longer to cook, but it is worth the time. I know you will fall in love with farro too!

Frank's RedHot

Here's another ingredient you might not have been expecting. But here's the deal: the original Frank's RedHot sauce includes the following: aged cayenne red peppers, distilled vinegar, water, salt, and garlic powder—real ingredients you can pronounce, which come together in a magnificent combination to create a powerful flavor base for recipes. While I love to make healthier versions of condiments (see: Ranch (page 339), Caesar (page 339), and Italian (page 340) dressings in this book), I'm not above using something store-bought, if I approve of the nutrition. Frank's RedHot is especially helpful when attempting to please those who may subsist on foods like fried wings, fake-cheese queso, and vegetable-oil laden potato chips. Likely, they will be familiar with the signature flavor of Frank's and will be willing to give your dairy-free chicken dip or buffalo tempeh a try. In addition, consumption of chili peppers has been linked with decreased mortality and protection against obesity and metabolic syndrome. Much of this is attributed to capsaicin, the phytochemical in chili peppers responsible for their spiciness, because of its anti-inflammatory effect on adipose (fat) tissue. I love to pair the heat and acidity of Frank's with healthy fats, such as tahini and coconut milk, and it's lovely on both animal proteins and vegetables. Feel free to add a drop or two of Frank's into some of the other savory recipes in this cookbook—just start slowly!

Miso

Hands down, miso paste is the ingredient I am most excited to share throughout the pages of this book. First things first: What the heck is miso? Miso is a fermented paste that's created by inoculating or culturing soybeans with a mold called koji. Over a period of time, ranging from weeks to years, koji enzymes interact with organisms in the surrounding environment to break down the beans into a savory, rich, earthy paste—miso! In this book, we'll be using a mild, white miso paste (called "mellow" or "Shiro"). It has a fairly short fermentation time, which results in a lighter, brighter, and less pungent flavor than its darker counterparts. Brown or red miso pastes are the result of a longer fermentation period, and they tend to be quite strongly flavored and salty. According to the Japan Miso Promotion Board, there are more than 1,300 different kinds of miso. Personally, I haven't met a miso I don't like, but I find that mild, white miso enhances other ingredients, adding umami (the fifth taste next to sweet, savory, salt, and acid), without overpowering them. In addition to being a cook's best secret weapon, miso paste is incredibly healthful, full of vitamins E and K, folic acid, and more. Miso is a fermented food, and it is rich in probiotics that may be beneficial to your gut microbiome. Medical studies have shown that miso may help protect against a variety of cancers, strokes, Irritable Bowel Syndrome, and more. It can also help modulate immune system function and manage allergies.

Kimchi

I'm telling you, Asian cuisine has the best ingredients! Or, I should say, the best foods for providing dynamite nutrition and flavor in one go. I've been enjoying kimchi as a side dish for years, but I only recently started integrating it into recipes, such as my 5- Ingredient Kimchi Coleslaw (page 163) and my Cashew Kimchi Lettuce Cups (page 137). Like miso, kimchi is the result of fermentation alchemy. It begins as cabbage (usually), and it becomes a probiotic oasis, teeming with gut-friendly life and

fabulous flavor to boot. Consumption of kimchi has been linked to health benefits such as improved immunity and cardiovascular disease, as well as anti-aging effects. There are countless varieties of kimchi, all with their own spice and heat profiles, and even under the same label, jars will vary slightly. As a result, I highly recommend trying several brands until you fall in love with one (and I'm sure you will). But what every kimchi I've eaten shares is a signature sour-savoriness and crunch that pairs beautifully with eggs, soup, meat, seafood, vegetables, and even peanut butter. Kimchi is one of my absolute favorite ways to douse my inner ecosystem with bioavailable "good" bugs, and I encourage you to keep a jar in the fridge at all times.

Unsweetened Almond Milk

Most of you are probably familiar with the concept of nut "milks," and almond milk seems to be the most popular among them. Simply put, nut milks are the milky-looking and -tasting liquid created by blending nuts with water, and then straining out the resulting pulp. They're delicious, relatively affordable, and make for a fantastic smoothie or latte base. So why didn't I include nut milk in any of my recipes in my first cookbook? Because when I wrote it, I couldn't find brands that didn't include a whole host of gums, oils, and preservatives in the ingredient list. In fact, it seemed that the "nut" component was the least prevalent in these dairy-substitute liquids. Thankfully, in the last few years, several companies have started making nut milks with much shorter and cleaner ingredient lists, and I feel good about recommending them to you. When purchasing an almond or other nut milk, look for ingredients you recognize and can pronounce. Ideally, you want to see "almonds (or whatever nut), Himalayan salt, filtered water." Another brand I can easily find contains "organic almond milk (water, organic almonds), organic acacia gum, sea salt." Acacia gum is a natural source of soluble fiber, so I don't mind consuming it in this particular brand. In addition, almonds contain antioxidants, which play a

crucial role in combating free-radical damage. I still absolutely love canned coconut milk, and I continue to use it throughout this book. But variety is the spice of life, and I'm glad to be able to offer more options! You might be wondering about dairy milk, so please see the "Dairy" section for details. Overall, I approve of consuming high-quality cow's milk (from pasture-raised cows with no added sugar) in moderation, if it doesn't cause allergic or food-sensitivity reactions. If you're not sure how you respond to cow's milk, I suggest working with a doctor or dietitian.

Chickpea or Garbanzo Bean Flour

Ohhh, I was so happy to add a new flour to the LL Balanced pantry for this book, and I knew immediately that chickpea/garbanzo bean flour would be the winner. Also known as "besan" or "gram" flour, chickpea flour is made from ground chickpeas, usually raw, but sometimes roasted. It is used to make a thin flatbread, known as *socca* in French cooking and *farinata* in Italian. Chickpea flour is also a staple in Indian cooking, where it is used to make *pakoras, papadums,* and more. It is naturally gluten-free and rich in plant protein, fiber, iron, vitamin B-6, and magnesium. Research indicates that compared to wheat-based flour, chickpea-based flour results in less of a glucose and insulin response. I have found that chickpea flour recipes are very satiating, keeping me full for quite a long time. That said, the main reason I fell hard for chickpea flour is its texture. Using it creates a dense and moist but still light crumb, and it is simply delightful to consume. This is why I chose to include chickpea flour in recipes such as my Double Chocolate Avocado Blender Muffins (page 107) and my Lemon Almond Pound Cake (page 309). As the British would say, recipes with chickpea flour are just "moreish." In addition, chickpea flour has a natural binding property, so it tends to hold baked goods together well.

Macadamia Nuts

I really try live in the present. And yet, I often regret not including macadamia nuts in my life much earlier. They are ridiculously delicious. They offer a satisfying crunch that quickly turns into creamy liquid gold, with a mildly sweet, nutty flavor. Forget about it! As with cashews, macadamia nuts are notably versatile. They can be soaked and blended to mimic dairy products, but they're equally at home as a crust for tuna steaks or a crouton replacement for salads. Macadamia nuts contain more fat than most nuts and seeds, 80 percent of which is high-quality monounsaturated fats (think: *energy*). Indeed, moderate consumption of macadamia nuts can favorably alter one's fatty acid profile, potentially improving cardiovascular health. A source of calcium, magnesium, iron, zinc, potassium, fiber, and phytochemicals, macadamia nuts also have a particularly low carbohydrate content. Thus, they are a great nutrient-dense snacking option for someone pursuing a lower-carbohydrate lifestyle.

Whenever you're purchasing nuts or seeds, keep them tightly sealed in a cool, dark place; otherwise they may oxidize and go rancid quickly (although macadamia nuts never last long enough in my pantry for that to happen). I also recommend freezing to extend shelf life. I know that these little beauties are on the pricier side, so I buy mine online at Thrive Market (www.thrivemarket.com), which makes them much more affordable.

Dairy

Now for the elephant in the room—okay, maybe not for y'all, but for me. When I wrote my first cookbook, I stayed away from almost all dairy. I used butter and yogurt in a few recipes, but otherwise, I came up with dairy-free substitutions. The reasons for this were twofold: 1) I wanted to offer creative, dairy-free solutions to some of your favorite cheesy, creamy dishes, and 2) I didn't feel that the pros of dairy consumption outweighed possible downsides. I noted the following:

- Many people are allergic to dairy, in which case their bodies react negatively to the protein casein.
- Dairy intolerance to the milk sugar lactose is also common.
- Most factory-farmed dairy is the result of inhumane practices that I don't want to support
- Many of the industrial dairy animals are injected with hormones.

I still stand by all of the above. However, while dairy is not for everyone, research and experience has led me to believe that consumption of high-quality dairy in moderation is welcome in a healthy lifestyle. Again, this doesn't apply to those with allergies, sensitivities, or intolerances to all dairy, and I highly recommend working with a medical professional to determine if you have any of these conditions.

When I was almost through with the first book, I created a recipe that required yogurt and another that I wanted to garnish with some cheddar cheese, just for looks. At the time, I barely ate any dairy at all. The only plain, full-fat, grass-fed yogurt I could find was a large container, so I resigned myself to eating it slowly over a few weeks. Similarly, I couldn't find anything smaller than an 8-ounce block of 100 percent grass-fed cheddar cheese. And something magical happened. As I slowly spooned and nibbled my way through the yogurt and cheese, my digestion began to improve and regulate in a way I hadn't experienced in years. I also felt less bloated after fibrous meals, which had been an ongoing source of frustration.

It was very clear that dairy was to be thanked for these health improvements, specifically, the beneficial probiotics that it contains. Our gut health is directly linked to the health of our gut microbiome, which is simply the compilation of microorganisms in that particular environment. Probiotics are considered "good" bacteria, because when they populate our microbiome, they aid in digestion, combat inflammation, and can even improve responses to chemotherapy. I believe that my gut needs the types of probiotic strains that are bio-available in dairy, and I have included

high-quality dairy in my diet ever since that yogurt/cheese experiment.

When I began this book, I dedicated time to learning the science behind the health benefits of dairy, but I also wanted to dispel some common myths about the "downsides" of dairy—most importantly, the misconception that the saturated fat in all dairy products is harmful. As researcher Charles Benbrook noted in an article in *PLOS One*:

> Dairy products contribute significantly to dietary intakes of saturated fat in the United States and Europe, which has led to widely endorsed recommendations to limit consumption of whole milk and other high-fat dairy products, in favor of low- and non-fat dairy products. However . . . they give little or no consideration to the cardiovascular disease-risk reducing components in milk fat, especially omega-3 fatty acids, conjugated linoleic acid . . . protective minerals, and a beneficial effect on serum HDL ("good") cholesterol.[1]

We must consider that milk fat with a high omega-3 fatty acid content, which is found in pasture-raised dairy, may actually help combat cardiovascular disease. Here are a few research excerpts that describe possible benefits of grass-fed dairy:

- Milk from cows consuming significant amounts of grass and legume-based forages contains higher concentrations of omega-3 fatty acids (FAs) and conjugated linoleic acid than milk from cows lacking routine access to pasture and fed substantial quantities of grains, especially corn.[2]
- Daily consumption of grass-fed dairy products could potentially improve U.S. health trends. In addition to the well-established metabolic and cardiovascular benefits of omega-3 fatty acids and conjugated linoleic acid, there are additional benefits for pregnant and lactating women, infants, and children. Various forms of omega-3

fatty acids play critical roles in the development of eyes, the brain, and the nervous system. Adequate omega-3 intakes can also slow the loss of cognitive function among the elderly.[3]
- Our dietary modeling scenarios show that replacing recommended daily servings of conventional dairy products with grassmilk products and avoiding some foods high in linoleic acid (LA) could substantially decrease historically high dietary [omega 6: omega 3 ratios]. . . . Such decreases have several potential health benefits.[4]

While I consider plain, full-fat dairy from 100 percent pasture-raised cows to be ideal, I know that it is not accessible for everyone. That said, organic dairy is increasingly available in most grocery stores, as well as Target and Walmart. What "organic" means

THREE TIERS OF DAIRY QUALITY

1. "Grassmilk" cows receive an essentially 100 percent organic grass and legume forage-based diet, via pasture and stored feeds like hay and silage. . . . [G]rassmilk provides by far the highest level of omega-3s.

2. "Organic" cows receive, on average, about 80 percent of their daily Dry Matter Intake (DMI) from forage-based feeds and 20 percent from grain and concentrates.

3. "Conventional" cows are fed rations in which forage-based feeds account for an estimated 53 percent of daily DMI, with the other 47 percent coming from grains and concentrates. Conventional management accounts for over 90 percent of the milk cows on U.S. farms.[5]

---

[1] Charles M. Benbrook et al., "Organic Production Enhances Milk Nutritional Quality by Shifting Fatty Acid Composition: A United States–Wide, 18-Month Study," *PLOS One* 8, no. 12 (2013): e82429, https://www.ncbi.nlm.nih.gov/pmc/articles/PMC3857247/.

[2] Benbrook, "Organic Production."

[3] University of Minnesota, "Forage-Based Diets on Dairy Farms Produce Nutritionally Enhanced Milk: Markedly Higher Levels of Health-Promoting Fatty Acids Reported," *Science Daily* 28 (February 2018), https://www.sciencedaily.com/releases/2018/02/180228085349.htm.

[4] Charles M. Benbrook, et al., "Enhancing the Fatty Acid Profile of Milk Through Forage-Based Rations, with Nutrition Modeling of Diet Outcomes," *Food Science & Nutrition*, February 28, 2018, https://onlinelibrary.wiley.com/doi/full/10.1002/fsn3.610.

[5] University of Minnesota, "Forage-Based Diets."

varies from company to company, but it is still a better choice than conventional. If you're not sure about the quality of the dairy you're purchasing, I suggest reaching out directly to the company offering the product.

As you can see, there is a generous amount of research that supports including high-quality dairy in one's daily food routine. In this cookbook, I use cheese, butter, and sour cream, which are fermented, probiotic rich forms of dairy that can be easier to digest than milk. Many adults are lactose-intolerant and have Primary Lactase Deficiency, in which case the production of lactase, the enzyme responsible for the digestion of lactose, declines over time. This typically begins around age two, but symptoms may not appear until later in childhood or even early adulthood. However, some pepople do fine with cow's milk on a regular basis. Note that I offer a non-dairy substitution in most recipes, but not all. That said, the majority of my recipes are still dairy-free.

Soy and Tofu

I didn't include a single tofu recipe in my first cookbook, for two primary reasons: 1) I didn't enjoy eating it, and 2) I had the option of including tempeh as a soy-based source of protein. Tempeh is always fermented, which can make it easier to digest. While I still absolutely adore tempeh, I have also fallen in love with tofu. I don't remember when I began my tofu affair, but I do remember immediately running out to buy more and start experimenting. I also began to dive into the controversial research about tofu.

Much of the conflict surrounding soy, and particularly tofu, centers on its high concentration of isoflavones. Isoflavones act as phytoestrogens, or plant-derived estrogen, in mammals. As a result, when we eat sources of isoflavones, such as soy, our bodies may respond as if human endocrine system estrogen were present. This has led certain studies to conclude that consuming soy may negatively impact hormone-driven illness, particularly estrogen-dominant breast cancer. On the flip side, a Japanese study found that the consumption of soybeans may reduce the risk of breast cancer.

What's the deal? Well, it all depends on *context*. Factors such as age, hormone levels, ethnicity, the type of soy, and countless qualifiers about the studies themselves can all impact an ultimate conclusion about soy intake.

When I synthesized all of my research, I came to the conclusion that consuming moderate amounts of tofu, tempeh, and miso paste can be a beneficial part of one's diet. As Jie Yu notes in an article in *Nutrients*: "[Soy] isoflavones exhibit impressive anti-inflammatory properties in various animal models, and even in humans, through increased antioxidative activities."[6]

Of course, this is barring any specific conditions that have led your doctor to caution you to limit or omit soy. As usual, I cannot say what is "moderate consumption" for you, but I enjoy tofu or tempeh two or three times a week and miso paste five or six times a week (in very small quantities). I also love organic edamame as an appetizer or snack every month or so. I urge you to do your own research if you're still unsure about your stance on consuming soy, or if you're simply interested in learning more.

A WORD ABOUT VEGETABLE OIL

Vegetable oils are inflammatory due to their undesirable ratio of omega 6 to omega 3. They oxidize easily, which means they can more easily go rancid. In addition, vegetable oils are heavily processed, making them an all-around no-go for me. If you're going to spend the time and money to buy high-quality dairy (also applicable to meat, seafood, and eggs), please prioritize quality oils as well, such as extra virgin coconut oil, 100 percent first cold-pressed olive oil in dark glass bottles, and avocado oil.

Stevia and Monkfruit

Stevia and monkfruit are non-nutritive sweeteners, which means that they contain zero calories, or very close to zero. In addition, neither has an impact on blood sugar levels, with a Glycemic Index Rating of 0. Pure stevia comes from the stevia plant, which is part of the Asteraceae family (related to daisy and ragweed), and it originally hails from Brazil and Paraguay, though it grows all over the US now. It is significantly sweeter than table sugar, approximately 100 to 200 times, so a very little goes a very long way. As researcher Margaret Ashwell concludes, "Stevia is a natural-origin sweetener that is increasing the options for reduced sugar and reduced energy foods and beverages. Stevia shows promise as a tool to help lower energy intakes, which may lead to the reduction and prevention of obesity."[7]

While stevia leaf is a natural herbal sweetener, the stevia found at your grocery store (liquid or powder) is a relatively processed form. As such, many brands include additives and fillers. I look for organic brands, where the only ingredients are "purified water, organic stevia leaf extract, and natural flavors." While "natural flavors" is not ideal, it doesn't concern me in such small quantities. I also prefer liquid stevia over powder, because I find it easier to control the sweetness. Some people notice a somewhat unpleasant aftertaste to stevia, but I find it easy to mask by layering flavors. Anecdotally, I've have also heard that stevia consumption can result in Irritable Bowel Syndrome symptoms. However, one randomized, double-blind, placebo-controlled long-term study reported in the *Regulatory Toxicology and Pharmacology* describes: "No side effects were observed in the two treatment groups. . . . [Stevia compounds] taken as sweetener are well tolerated and have no pharmacological effect."[8]

USING STEVIA AND MONKFRUIT SWEETENERS

Stevia (cold stuff)*: Monkfruit tends to have a gritty texture when it is not heated, even when blended into smoothies. Thus, I use stevia when I want a sugar-free substitute in salad dressings, smoothies, puddings, and ice cream. You'll note that I use stevia throughout the beverage chapter. You could use monkfruit instead of stevia in the hot beverages (add to taste), but I just use stevia to keep it consistent.

Monkfruit (hot stuff)*: I use monkfruit in recipes where it will dissolve at high temperatures, such as baked goods, roasted foods, skillet dishes, and, of course, soups or stews.

Note: I rarely use stevia or monkfruit as a substitute for dates, because the texture and volume of dates are often crucial to the recipe. However, if there is a recipe where a substitute is appropriate, I usually follow the above guidelines regarding hot or cold in choosing between the two non-nutritive sweeteners.

*There are exceptions to these "rules," but this is generally how I use them.

Monkfruit extract comes from a melon-like plant called luo han guo, native to southern China and Thailand. Pure monkfruit is also significantly sweeter than sugar, but most granulated brands are comparable in sweetness, as it is mixed with erythritol. Erythritol is a sugar alcohol that naturally occurs in some plants, but which is now typically synthesized in a lab. It is also a non-nutritive sweetener that does not have an impact on blood

[6] Jie Yu et al., "Isoflavones: Anti-Inflammatory Benefit and Possible Caveats," *Nutrients* 8, no. 6 (June 2016): 361, https://www.ncbi.nlm.nih.gov/pmc/articles/PMC4924202/.

[7] Margaret Ashwell, "Stevia, Nature's Zero-Calorie Sustainable Sweetener a New Player in the Fight Against Obesity," *Nutrition Today* 50, no. 3 (May 2015): 129–34, https://www.ncbi.nlm.nih.gov/pmc/articles/PMC4890837/.

[8] L. A. Barriocanal, "Apparent Lack of Pharmacological Effect of Steviol Glycosides Used as Sweeteners in Humans: A Pilot Study of Repeated Exposures in Some Normotensive and Hypotensive Individuals and in Type 1 and Type 2 Diabetics," *Regulatory Toxicology and Pharmacology* 51, no. 1 (June 2008): 37–41, https://www.ncbi.nlm.nih.gov/pubmed/18397817.

sugar. The only downside I have heard is that consuming excess erythritol can cause digestive distress (similar to stevia), but a study published in *Food and Chemical Toxicology* says otherwise: "Following extensive safety evaluations . . . it has been concluded that erythritol is well tolerated in humans and does not cause any toxicologically relevant effects even following ingestion of larger quantities."[9] Thus, I have no problem using a brand of monkfruit that includes erythritol. Monkfruit may also have some notable health benefits. Mogrosides, the compounds that give monkfruit its sweetness, are also free-radical-fighting antioxidants and anti-inflammatory. Studies have found monkfruit to have anti-carcinogenic (anti-cancer) properties, as well as the capacity to improve diabetic conditions. Per the latter, a Chinese study notes that one of the monkfruit mogrosides "can provide a positive health impact on stimulating insulin secretion."[10]

Why Lower-Sugar and Lower-Carb Recipes?

I didn't consciously set out to include lower-sugar and lower-carb recipes or recipe alternatives in this cookbook. As I noted in my first book (and as I do often on social media), natural sweeteners such as honey, maple syrup, dates, and coconut sugar are still sugar, and they should be treated as such: enjoyed small quantities, viewed as indulgent.

Why? Because all sugars (and carbohydrates) break down into glucose, the simple sugar that our body then uses for energy. Doesn't sound too bad, right? The problem comes when we consume more glucose than our body needs. Not only does the body then begin to store glucose as fat, high amounts of glucose and high sugar intake cause a pro-inflammatory state, which can contribute to cardiovascular disease and a host of metabolic diseases, such as type II diabetes. Even armed with that knowledge, I found myself eating increasing amounts of these natural

sweeteners in the fall and early winter of 2018, probably due to the stress of writing a book. The result? I noticed that my sugar cravings began to control my life, and I found myself eating half a batch of cookies or an entire bar of dark chocolate instead of my usual single-serving portion (okay, sometimes double). It seemed that my blood sugar was on a daily roller coaster.

To combat my growing sugar addiction, I began swapping the natural sweeteners for non-nutritive sweeteners such as monkfruit and stevia. I also substituted some of my complex carbohydrates, such as quinoa, chickpea pasta, sweet potatoes, and fruit, for non-starchy vegetables, such as zucchini, broccoli, cauliflower, bell peppers, and leafy greens. I began to include more healthy fats in my meals, snacks, and even beverages. Some of my favorite fats are avocado and avocado oil, coconut oil, coconut milk, butter, beef, yogurt, and cheese from 100 percent pasture-raised cows, wild-caught salmon, nuts and seeds, nut and seed butters, and olives.

When I made these simple swaps, my sugar cravings quickly diminished—in approximately ten days. I felt incredibly satisfied throughout the day, and I didn't experience "hanger" (that *gotta have food hungry-angry feeling*) as often. My overall mood improved, and I stopped having afternoon energy crashes. In addition, my palate changed, and I now find foods much sweeter than before. This makes it easier to satisfy a sweet tooth when it does crop up.

After a few months of following these changes consistently, I began bringing more complex carbohydrates back into my diet (because what is a world without sweet potatoes?) when I felt like I needed them. You might be wondering, what does that feel like? Well, for me, I need a few more complex carbohydrates when I am eating plenty of healthy fats, protein, and non-starchy vegetables, but I am *still* tired and sluggish throughout the day,

[9] I. C. Munro et al., "Erythritol: An Interpretive Summary of Biochemical, Metabolic, Toxicological and Clinical Data," *Food and Chemical Toxicology* 36, no. 12 (December 1998): 1139–74, abstract, https://www.ncbi.nlm.nih.gov/pubmed/9862657.

[10] Y. Zhou et al., "Insulin Secretion Stimulating Effects of Mogroside V and Fruit Extract of Luo Han Kuo (Siraitia Grosvenori Swingle) Fruit Extract," *Yao Xue Xue Bao* 44, no. 11 (November 2009): 1252–7, abstract, https://www.ncbi.nlm.nih.gov/pubmed/21351724.

or I'm having trouble sleeping, or I'm doing more high-intensity anaerobic cardio exercise. (Sometimes I have carbs *just because*, and not always the healthy kind, and that's okay, too.) A few of my favorite foods to add to a meal when I'm feeling carby are quinoa, farro, root vegetables, fresh fruit, dates, or any of my homemade baked goods.

I love knowing that I have this "tool" in my wellness arsenal should my sugar cravings go haywire again. This was such a great learning experience for me that I wanted to share it with y'all as well as offer lower-sugar and lower-carb recipes in this book. I hope they help those of you who feel that you are in a similar situation with a headstrong sweet tooth that just won't quit.

Please note that I am not a medical professional of any kind, and I highly recommend working with one if you think you're experiencing blood sugar imbalances. Leanne Vogel of Healthful Pursuit (www.healthfulpursuit.com) and Diane Sanfilippo of Balanced Bites (www.balancedbites.com) are fabulous resources, in addition to a medical professional, if you're interested in experimenting with a low-carb, high-fat diet.

Properly supply yourself with the basic kitchen equipment and ingredient staples—*welcome to the Instant Pot!*

One of the aspects of this cookbook I am most excited about is the addition of Instant Pot recipes. Not only was this highly requested, I personally have enjoyed using my Instant Pot the last few years to make meal prep easier. If you're not familiar with the Instant Pot or you want to learn more about it, I'm sharing the 411 here. The following information can help you decide if you want to invest in one, and if not, that's totally cool. I have a cooking alternative for every Instant Pot recipe in the cookbook.

What Is an Instant Pot?

An Instant Pot is a multi-cooker that does the job of a slow cooker, electric pressure cooker, rice cooker, steamer, yogurt maker, sauté and browning pan, and warming pot. It can also sterilize canned goods or pasteurize milk.

What Are the Benefits?

- Cooks more quickly than most other methods
- Offers multiple uses in a single appliance so there is less to store
- Can quickly thaw frozen meat and veggies
- Makes homemade broths and stocks without the smell or worry of leaving them simmering on the stove unattended
- Preserves nutrients: lack of air exposure means nutrients don't oxidize

Who Is an Instant Pot Right For?

- Someone looking to make large batches of food to enjoy throughout the week
- Someone who (or whose family) doesn't mind leftovers
- Someone who (or whose family) is okay with "softer" food textures. The Instant Pot doesn't really do crispy or crunchy.
- Someone who loves "set it and forget it" meals
- Someone who sometimes needs last-minute dinners for a group or family

There are two primary types of Instant Pot. I have the Duo, which is the original Instant Pot model, and the instructions in this book refer to the Duo model. I have used the Ultra model, and I do not find it as user friendly. It is also more expensive, and I'm not interested in the extra features it offers (such as sterilizing jars and sous-vide functionality). That said, I highly recommend that you do your own research before choosing your model. If you do have the Ultra, the instructions in this book should easily translate. Keep your manual in the kitchen just in case.

Getting Started with the Instant Pot

- Make sure the float valve and sealing ring are clean and in the right place and that the lid is properly placed.
- Don't fill to the max if making something that expands, like oatmeal or pasta, as it can overflow.
- The sauté function is great for browning and caramelizing before cooking, and you can set it to low, medium, or high. You have 10 seconds to adjust before it starts. Press "Cancel" or "Keep Warm" to stop sautéing.
- When you're ready to pressure cook, turn the lid clockwise to the locked position.
- Venting versus Sealing: "Sealing" means the pressure cannot escape; "Venting" means it is releasing pressure. Make sure it's on "Sealing" when you start cooking.
- The Instant Pot has pre-set modes to guide you for certain kinds of dishes.
- With rice, ignore the initial number it shows. The Instant Pot will adjust based on the volume. With all other functions, the Instant Pot will show the

most common time, but you might want to adjust based on what you're cooking. With these, you can also choose between "Less," "Normal," and "More" (25 minutes, 30 minutes, and 40 minutes).

■ Alternately, you can choose "Manual" and use the plus and minus signs to choose your own time setting.

INSTANT POT TIPS

■ The rice paddle that comes with your Instant Pot can be used to switch the release valve from "Sealing" to "Venting."

■ Don't use the Instant Pot directly under shelves or cabinets. The steam that's released from the pot can cause damage.

■ I use the 6-quart Instant Pot, and I suggest 1 quart for every person in your home (5-, 6-, and 8-quart models are available).

■ It can take 10 minutes or so to reach cooking pressure. While pressure is building, the read-out will say "On." When it changes to numbers and the pressure indicator pops up, it's starting to cook.

■ Don't panic if you see steam coming out during the cooking process. As long as it's sealed, you're good.

■ There are two ways to release steam: 1) manual/ quick-release method or 2) natural pressure release. If using the manual method, place a cooking mitt or towel over the release valve or use the rice paddle to turn the valve to prevent burning. The manual release can take 30 seconds to 2 minutes. You'll know it's safe to open the lid when the pressure indicator falls down.

■ With the Duo model, the Instant Pot will switch automatically to "Keep Warm." With the Ultra, you can choose whether to use this function. The "Keep Warm" setting will run up to 8 hours.

3

Create a relaxed and happy eating environment—
practice intuitive eating!

This section is particularly near and dear to my heart. Learning how to have a truly healthy relationship with food can be a lifelong journey, and it's one that I'm still on! But I have figured out something *crucial* in the last few years, which is that our behavior around food *isn't about the food. It's about the way we approach the eating experience, and it's about our perspectives in relation to food.* Once I digested this (pun intended!), I realized the importance of becoming an intuitive eater, which allows me to focus on what my body really needs, instead of what my brain *thinks it should* or *wants it to* need. Below you will find my top tips and tricks for intuitive eating.

It is very difficult to become an intuitive eater when you're purchasing most of your food through Postmates or grabbing it already packaged up in shiny plastic. On the other hand, when you cook your food from scratch, you can constantly tweak and adjust and try new things, which is the best way to know what works for you and your body. And if you've struggled with your mindset around food, you might also struggle with your mindset about cooking. So I've included a list here of the top "Cooking Mindset Myths" I've heard throughout my career, as well as the truths that debunk them.

Intuitive Eating

A lot of us have heard of it, and pretty much all of us like the sound of it . . . I mean, it's a good thing, right? Right. But the real question is, what does it mean? What the gosh-darn-heck does it mean to "eat intuitively"?

"Intuitive eating" is the reliance on physiologic hunger and satiety cues to guide eating. Studies have shown that the practice of intuitive eating is correlated with improved mental health and appropriate BMI (Body Mass Index).

Our culture has become increasingly distant from real food and its origin. We grab our produce cleaned, packaged, and presented on glossy supermarket shelves; that is, when we even reach for produce at all. Packaged "convenience" foods have become so popular since the 1960s that now we have a tough time determining what real food even is. I'd wager than many people consider most packaged foods to be "real" food.

But most are not. Most packaged foods are full of additives, chemicals, and synthetic ingredients. In addition, most are completely devoid of nutrition. Quite the double whammy, huh?

Even with the blessed rise of health-consciousness in the US, which has led to a prevalence of health-supportive packaged foods, there's still a catch. I'm sometimes *more* inclined to grab these boxed and bagged items *because* they aren't terrible for me. Unfortunately, however, my body doesn't respond to such products in the same way as it does to real foods. I don't feel satiated and often want to keep eating even if I've already consumed a high-calorie meal. Many people are now overfed and undernourished. Hunger and malnutrition are no longer just the result of a calorie deficit, but instead can result from a poor-quality diet.

Two decades into the 21st century, I believe that "intuitive eating" has become a buzz phrase because we're recognizing this problem. The dieting culture and encouragement of powders, pills, and bars seem to have made it more difficult to know when we're truly nourished.

If this resonates with you, please know that you haven't done anything wrong. You've been set up for this struggle, and there's no blame game allowed, only baby steps to proceed. Here are my top tips for learning to tune into your body, tune out the social media noise, and learn how to notice, decipher, and trust your hunger cues.

Eat primarily high-quality whole foods: This includes colorful produce, pastured and wild-caught proteins, whole-fat dairy from pastured animals, beans, grains, and fats (pick and choose depending on what works for you). Why? Because the healthy fats, fiber, proteins, and nutrients in these foods will help your hormonal signals work properly, letting your brain and belly know that they're satisfied and you can stop eating.

Minimize packaged foods, even the healthier ones: This tip is based on personal experience and has been corroborated by discussions with my cooking class students. Even if a bar or bag has the same number of fiber grams as an apple, often it's just not as filling and satisfying as the apple. Perhaps this is why scientific studies have indicated that consumption of processed foods is correlated with the increased risk of obesity and weight gain.

Do away with the notion of "appropriate" times to eat: You don't have to eat breakfast if you're not feeling it. Lunch can be at 10 a.m. or 3 p.m. Before you reach for your next grub, ask yourself if you're truly hungry. If not, wait until you are. If you're not sure, drink some water, distract yourself with a walk or phone call or book, then check back with your body.

Know what true hunger feels like: Learn to recognize hunger signals:
- The desire to eat gets stronger over time.
- Your stomach starts to growl.
- Most food sounds appealing, even or especially nutritious foods. When I am craving something sugary or carb-laden or salty-crunchy, but I have no interest in tuna salad and roasted broccoli, I'm usually anxious or stressed instead of hungry.

If you notice these signs but you're still not sure you're hungry, first drink a glass of water and wait fifteen minutes. If you're definitely hungry, prepare a meal or snack.

Track your diet: Try writing down what you eat and how it makes you feel, every day for one month. You will start to notice patterns in your hunger and cravings, as well as when you were particularly bloated or uncomfortable after eating. Consistency is key here, and it takes less than five minutes.

Sample Entry: *Today I ate oatmeal for breakfast, tofu tacos for lunch, an apple dipped in yogurt for a snack, air fryer broccoli plus kabobs for dinner, and ice cream with 3 or 4 spoonfuls of almond butter for dessert. I felt great—energetic, happy, and satisfied until after dinner. I ate my ice cream quickly, then I kept going back for almond butter. My stomach was a little bloated and gassy, and I felt overly full.*

Caveat: If you have struggled with an eating disorder or disordered eating, this might not be the right tactic for you. Work with your therapist or medical professional to determine if tracking is a good fit.

Work with a professional: Dovetailing on the above, if you have developed "food rules," work through them with a licensed therapist, dietitian, or other medical professional. Many people who have a tumultuous relationship with food choose meals according to their own self-generated food rules. I have personal experience with this. When I had an unhealthy relationship with eating, I had a rule that I couldn't have fruit in my breakfast *and* mid-morning snack; it had to be one or the other. I also had a rule that if I had almond butter with my breakfast, I couldn't eat any other nut butters throughout the day. I could eat more almond butter; I just couldn't eat peanut butter or cashew butter. As ridiculous as this may sound, these rules felt very real to me, and they prevented me from eating intuitively. I cannot recommend strongly enough that you seek professional counsel and help if you feel that you have a disordered relationship with food.[11]

[11] Disclaimer: I am not a medical professional. All information I share has been gathered through my own experience and research. Please consult a medical professional before making any changes to your diet and wellness routine.

Practice mindful eating: Researcher Ingrid Elizabeth Lofgren writes, "Mindful eating is a nonjudgmental acceptance of physical and emotional feelings while eating or in an eating environment."[12] Studies indicate that mindful eating is associated with weight loss, increased fiber intake, and lower transfat and sugar consumption. To practice mindful eating, give yourself time and space and as few distractions as possible when you eat. Eat slowly. Chew. Notice the flavors, the textures, any sensations associated with enjoying the food. Swallow and reflect on the experience. When I practice mindful eating, I have a much easier time noticing when I am comfortably full and stopping there.

Live in the present: When I allow what I've *been* eating to determine what I *will* eat, I often ignore my body's actual desires. Perhaps I've been on an indulgent vacation, so I feel that I "should" be craving a kale salad. And yet, my body wants something heartier and more substantial, like a burger and fries. In my experience, if I go for the kale salad anyway, I will be left unsatisfied, rummaging around the pantry grabbing handfuls of snacky foods.

As my favorite podcast-host Elizabeth Benton says, "Every choice is a chance." Don't focus on what you've done; focus on the moment you're in. Be gentle and forgiving with yourself—you are not the decisions you've made, and you're never stuck or "too late." Whether it is with food, your career, your relationships, or anything else, you *will* lose your way. You *will* make mistakes. Because you're human, and imperfection is knitted throughout the human experience. What matters is the perspective you *choose* to have every day. When I treat myself with grace and generosity, I am more likely to make a choice that is healthy for both my body and my mind.

---

12 Ingrid Elizabeth Lofgren, "Mindful Eating: An Emerging Approach for Healthy Weight Management," *American Journal of Lifestyle Medicine* 9, no. 3 (May 1, 2015): 212–16, https://journals.sagepub.com/doi/abs/10.1177/1559827615569684.

Breaking Down Cooking Mindset Myths

This is for all of you who bought this cookbook because food pictures are fun to look at, or because someone told you to, or because you love the *idea* of cooking, but you have no intention of actually making the recipes. As much as I appreciate your support regardless of intent, you now have the book, and I want you to get more out of it than a thirty minute flip-through.

In this section, I am going to break down some of the main mindset barriers that I see when it comes to cooking, one by one. (These aren't only from my perspective, but also from the perspective of clients with families.) If you purchased my cookbook with no plan of actually *using* it, my guess is that your reasoning falls into one of the following "Mindset Myths." And guess what? I had to work through these myths myself when I began cooking. So I switched my perspective and created new "Mindset Truths" about cooking, and it completely changed the game for me.

Cooking Mindset Myths:

- Cooking isn't sustainable.
- Cooking isn't fun.
- Cooking takes me away from things I'd rather be doing.
- Cooking is overwhelming.
- Cooking is too expensive.
- Cooking doesn't taste as good as takeout.
- Cooking isn't worth it.

Cooking Mindset Truths:

- Cooking is sustainable when I am willing to invest in pantry staples and equipment. Once I have that foundation, all I need to buy is nonperishables!
- Cooking is fun when I've practiced it enough that it has become easy and flexible and when I've created an enjoyable cooking environment. Music, a cute apron, kombucha (or wine!) to sip on, a clean kitchen, family corralled elsewhere . . . these things make cooking something I truly look forward to.

- Healthy cooking gives me more time for the activities I love, because it gives me energy, better sleep, and confidence to put myself out in the world.
- Cooking isn't any more overwhelming than anything else new that I decide I want to take on. "Easy is earned." (Thanks, E.B.!) If I've stocked my pantry and kitchen with the tools I need and applied some basic meal planning techniques, cooking becomes manageable—even easy!
- Cooking is way less expensive than eating out all the time, especially if you're thoughtful about it. There are plenty of ways to save money on meat and seafood (co-ops, Thrive Market, Costco, grocery store frozen sections), and there's zero need to buy any of the fancy "superfoods" out there.
- Home-cooked food tastes even better than takeout. Why? Because it can be 100 percent custom-tailored to *my* personal tastes. Plus, I have a whole fridge and pantry of condiments and seasonings that I can add to my meals to amp up the flavor. Also, fat can be incredibly healthy for you, and that's where all good restaurant flavor comes from . . . I can do that!
- Cooking is absolutely worth it, because I prioritize my health and my family's health over almost anything in the world—and that includes mental, physical, and emotional health. Cooking allows me to choose what I put into our bodies, so that we can have strong immune systems, excellent digestion, efficient metabolism, balanced hormones, and happy brains. In addition, cooking brings us together in a way that nothing else can. Free from the distractions and logistics that go into eating at a restaurant, we can come together in a peaceful atmosphere and connect in person. Cooking teaches my kids responsibility, because I ask them to help measure, stir, clean up, and more. While we're all running in million directions with varied interests, eating delicious home-cooked food is the one thing we *all* enjoy!

Chapter 2

COOKING TIPS *for* RECIPE SUCCESS

*W*hile this may not be the most exciting section of the book, it is arguably the most important. Friends, please take the time to read these cooking tips and tricks! They are meant to accompany and complement the tips and tricks in Chapter 1 of my first cookbook. Not only will they improve your experience in the kitchen overall, they also will help ensure that my recipes come out exactly as they should. These are the gems of information I've accumulated over six years of daily cooking, and I think you'll be amazed at what a difference they can make, in terms of time, ease, and fun. If you find yourself unsure of certain details such as what I mean by "standard loaf pan" or "aged" balsamic vinegar as you read the book, the answers are often in this section.

Tips for Prepping, Cooking, and Freezing

Gas versus Electric Stove: I'm addressing this first, in the hopes that more people will read it, because it is *important*. I cooked the recipes for my first cookbook on a gas stove, and I cooked these recipes on an electric stove. I had a team member, Lelan, cook most of this book's recipes on a gas stove, to make sure there wasn't a dramatic difference. There was not. You will get the same result cooking on a properly working gas stove as you will on a properly working electric stove. However, here's what you do need to know: electric stoves take longer to heat up—60 to 90 seconds longer. This means, achieving the "when the oil moves quickly around the pan" stage takes longer on an electric stove, and you do need to be patient and wait for it to reach appropriate heat. It also means that liquid might take longer to reach a simmer or boil than on an electric stove. However, once the pot or pan has reached the "marker," such as oil moving quickly or liquid simmering, recipes should cook exactly the same on gas and electric. If you have an electric stove, resist the temptation to crank it up to "high" to make things go more quickly—this will lead to burning and general inaccuracy.

Prepping a Recipe: First, a gentle reminder to *always read your recipes in advance*. That is probably the most valuable tip I can give you for cooking success! As you read through the recipes, you'll notice that some require a bit more prep, such as chopping, mixing, and measuring. It is very important to go ahead and prep the ingredients before you begin cooking. This is traditionally known as *mis en place* or "everything in its place," and it is absolutely key to a pleasant and victorious cooking experience!

Wet versus Dry Measuring: It's important to measure your wet and dry ingredients differently. Wet ingredients require a liquid measuring cup, which usually looks like a glass with a handle and markings that designate volume. Liquid measuring cups are specifically designed so that, if you squat down so that your eye is at measuring line level, you'll get an accurate reading. If you were to try to use dry ingredient measuring cups for liquid you would 1) likely spill some and 2) get a slightly inaccurate measurement. To properly measure dry ingredients, you want to scoop them so that they're a bit overly full, and then use a butter knife to scrape any excess off across the top. Before scraping, I suggest tapping the cup gently on the countertop, to remove any air and make sure you've actually filled it properly.

Making Sauces, Dressings, Seasoning Mixes, and Condiments: If an ingredient list includes a subsection for any of these, look for when to make them in the instructions. Often they don't need to be made first and instead can be made when something else is cooking or marinating or cooling.

HOW LONG CAN YOU FREEZE FOODS?

This chart assumes that the food you're freezing is fresh going into the freezer.

COOKED

- Bread, unfrosted cake or cupcakes & waffles: 1 month
- Burgers, meat patties, and meatballs: 1 to 2 months
- Casseroles and pasta-based dishes: 2 months
- Chicken breasts, thighs, & wings: 4 months
- Grains: 3 months
- Pancakes, quick breads, cookies, granola bars, & muffins: 3 months
- Soups, stews, marinara sauce, stock, & broth: 2 to 3 months
- Steak: 2 to 3 months
- Taco and Bolognese meat: 1 to 2 months
- Vegetables: 8 to 12 months

RAW

- Chicken pieces: 9 months
- Whole chicken: 1 year
- Citrus fruit: 3 months
- Other fruits & popsicles: 6 months
- Raw lean fish: 6 months
- Raw fatty fish: 2 to 3 months
- Ground beef, turkey, & chicken: 3 to 4 months
- Nuts: 3 months
- Shrimp & scallops: 3 to 4 months
- Steak: 4 to 6 months
- Vegetables: 8 to 12 months

DON'T FREEZE

- Dairy products: yogurt, cheese, sour cream, & milk
- Hard-boiled eggs
- Canned fish
- Fresh herbs (unless suspended in oil)
- Onions, peppers, artichokes, radishes, sprouts, & salad greens
- Uncooked rice
- Water-rich foods: lemon, lime, tomato, & cucumber

Oven Rack: I always use the middle rack. If I'm baking two things at once, I use the middle and bottom third rack and switch positions of the pans halfway through the cooking time.

Use Binder Clips for Parchment: When lining a loaf pan or other baking dish with parchment, this is a game changer—use small binder clips to hold parchment paper down around the edges of a loaf pan or baking sheet; you can keep them on during baking if they are metal. Other ways to manage your parchment include 1) greasing the dish before adding the parchment; 2) crumbling the parchment into a tight ball, then unfolding to make it more malleable; and 3) taping it down with regular adhesive tape—this will be fine in the oven.

Make Ahead: All casseroles can be assembled the night before and baked the next day, but they will need another 5 to 10 minutes baking time because of the chill.

Leftovers: All estimated lengths of time for keeping leftovers with meat assume the meat was fresh, not ready to expire, when the item was prepared.

Room Temperature Ingredients: Some recipes will specify room-temperature ingredients, and this is not to make your life more difficult! At room temperature, butter and eggs bond and create an emulsion that traps air. While baking, the air expands, which creates a light and airy texture. In addition, butter and coconut oil become harder when combined with cold ingredients, as they are saturated fats. If a recipe calls for melted butter or coconut oil, and you whisk it with a cold egg, the fat will solidify. I suggest taking ingredients out of the refrigerator at least 30 minutes and ideally 1 hour before baking. If you're short on time, microwave butter in 10 second intervals until just malleable but not melted or place eggs in a bowl of lukewarm water for 10 minutes.

Cooling Before Storing: No matter the recipe, I highly recommend allowing it to cool completely, uncovered, before storing in a sealed container, whether on the counter, in the refrigerator, or in the freezer. Any bit of residual heat will cause condensation inside the container, which will make your food mushy.

Tips for Freezing Food: Here are my tested tips and tricks for using your freezer to your advantage.
- Ensure that your freezer temperature is set to 0° F.
- Freeze fruits, vegetables and soups in sealable plastic bags.
- Use a silicone muffin pan or ice cube trays to freeze sauces. Once frozen, pop out the chunks, and store in a sealable plastic bag in the freezer.
- If you plan for an item to be in the freezer for more than one week, double bag or wrap in plastic wrap before placing in the bag.
- Label all your freezer bags with the name of the food and the date you froze it.
- Thaw food in the refrigerator, not at room temperature, to avoid the possibility of harmful bacteria.
- Freeze leftovers in individual portions, so you can grab exactly the amount you need without thawing the entire casserole or pot of soup. Plus, it takes less time to defrost and you don't have to pack lunch!

Cooking Terms

Simmer versus Boil: When a liquid simmers, you will see very small bubbles around the edges, but not in the middle. When a liquid boils, you will see large rapidly forming bubbles all over the surface of the liquid.

Mince versus Dice versus Chop: Starting with the smallest, mincing, you will create tiny pieces (about ⅛ inch). Mincing is usually used for garlic, ginger, and jalapeño. Dicing creates ¼-inch pieces. Chopping refers to ½-inch pieces or larger, and sometimes is a more rough chop with pieces that aren't necessarily uniform. If ingredients are to be puréed, they can often be roughly chopped.

Sauté: To sauté food means to cook it in a bit of fat over medium to high heat while stirring.

Deglaze: To deglaze a pan, you add a bit of liquid (often water or stock) to the pan after foods have been sautéed to loosen and scrape up any browned bits of food stuck to the bottom of the pan. This adds flavor and richness to the dish.

Pans, Equipment, and Supplies

Baking Sheet Size: Whenever a recipe includes a baking sheet, you can assume that I am referring to a standard-sized sheet pan that's 12 × 18 × 1 inches. This is also known as a "half sheet pan."

Cast-Iron Skillets: These classic heavy pans are a great investment. They're generally inexpensive and get better with age if properly cared for. Cast-iron takes a little while to preheat, but it gets screaming hot and has excellent heat retention—after it gets hot, you may need to turn down the heat. It's great for dishes you want to ensure get cooked evenly throughout and any time you need a nonstick surface. To clean you skillet, wash it under hot water with a textured (but not metal) sponge and without soap. Be sure to clean it as soon after cooking as possible. If a gentle scrub doesn't do the trick, sprinkle a few tablespoons of coarse salt over the surface and scrub with a dish rag. Rinse and dry thoroughly. You can place it in a warm oven to dry.

Some cast-iron skillets come preseasoned. If you have a new one that isn't, you'll want to season it before use. Preheat oven to 325° F. Wipe the skillet with a wet cloth, and dry thoroughly. Apply a thin coat of oil to the skillet (I use avocado oil). Place skillet upside down on oven rack, and place a sheet of aluminum foil on the bottom rack to catch dripping oil. Turn off the heat after an hour, and allow the skillet to remain in the oven until completely cooled.

Loaf Pan Size: Whenever a recipe includes a loaf pan, you can assume that I am referring to a standard size of 9 × 5 × 3 inches.

Saucepan: A "saucepan" refers to a pot that's deeper and has steeper sides than a frying pan. "Small saucepan" refers a 2-quart pot, "medium saucepan" refers to a 4-quart pot, and "large saucepan" refers to an 8- to 12-quart pot. A "stockpot" can range in size from 8 to 25 quarts.

STOCK UP ON THESE BASICS

- Chef's knife
- Paring knife
- Vegetable peeler
- Kitchen shears
- Garlic press
- Can opener
- Colander
- Salad spinner
- Mesh strainer
- Pastry brush
- Whisk, stainless-steel
- Wooden cutting board
- Plastic cutting board
- Mixing bowl set, stainless-steel

- Cheese grater
- Parchment paper, non-stick
- Saucepans, small (2-quart) and medium (4-quart)
- Sauté pans or skillets, small (8- to 10-inch) and large (4- to 6-quart)
- Stockpot (8- to 12-quart)
- Cast-iron skillet (12- to 13-inch)
- Baking dishes (13 × 9 × 2-inch and 8-inch square)
- Springform pan (9-inch)
- Cupcake tins
- Loaf pan (9 × 5 × 3-inch)

- Baking sheets
- Slotted baking sheets or racks from a broiler pan
- Slotted and solid wooden spoons
- Indoor grill pan
- "Turner" spatula
- Rubber spatulas
- Stiff brush
- Metal tongs
- Soup ladle
- Meat thermometer
- Popsicle molds and sticks

*Also see "Stocking Your Pantry" on page 348.

Tips for Specific Ingredients

Pitting an Avocado: Carefully poke the avocado where it is widest with a sharp knife, until it hits the pit. Drag the tip of the knife down and turn the avocado with your hand so that you are creating one long cut all the way around. Remove the knife and twist the two halves in opposite directions to open the avocado. Hold the half that contains the pit face-up in the palm of your nondominant hand. With your dominant hand, hit the pit with the knife edge, just hard enough to stick. Be very careful. Twist the avocado and knife in opposite directions. The pit should pop out. Hit the knife gently against a cutting board to remove the pit.

Making a Chia Egg: Some recipes note that you can substitute a "chia egg" for a regular egg. To make a chia egg, combine 1 tablespoon chia seeds and 3 tablespoons water in a small mixing bowl. Whisk and allow to sit at room temperature for 12 to 15 minutes. Stir again; it should have formed a gel-like consistency. If not, let it sit for another few minutes. Once it forms a gel, you can use this as a substitute for one egg in designated recipes.

How to Make a Double Boiler: If you don't own a double boiler, I don't see any reason to buy one! A double boiler is a saucepan with a detachable upper compartment. When you boil water in the saucepan, it heats up whatever is in the upper compartment. I mainly use a double boiler for melting chocolate, and this can be done just as easily by stacking a stainless steel or heat-proof glass bowl on top of the saucepan. You want the bowl to be just a few inches wider than the saucepan. With a real-deal or makeshift double boiler, don't let the boiling water touch the bottom of the upper compartment or bowl.

High-Powered Blender: When I reference "high-powered blender," I am referring to a Vitamix, Blendtec, or any blender that can easily blend ice, nuts, or other hard ingredients.

Using Canned Coconut Milk: If you open a can of coconut milk and the water has separated from the cream, add all contents to a blender, and purée until creamy. Then measure as the recipe calls for. Keep leftovers sealed in the fridge up to one week.

Eggs and Egg Shells: I use large eggs in my recipes. And remember: always check for shells, y'all. Always.

Measuring Fat: If a recipe calls for an amount of butter or coconut oil, melted, you will measure the fat when it's solid and then melt it.

Frozen Fruits and Vegetables: You will see a few recipes that use frozen vegetables. That's because frozen vegetables can be fantastic! They're easy to use, less expensive, and certainly less perishable than many vegetables in the produce aisle. In addition, frozen fruits and veggies are often frozen at the peak of production, preserving their nutrient content and ripe flavor. "Fresh" vegetables have often spent long (sometimes hot) hours being shipped into or driven across the country, making them less nutritious and "fresh" tasting than the frozen veggies. My only caveat is to use the Environmental Working Group's "Dirty Dozen" list to select your frozen vegetables. Organic still matters in this case!

Getting the Most from Your Citrus: To get as much juice as possible out of a lemon, lime, or orange, microwave for 6 to 10 seconds (if it's been in the fridge), then use the palm of your hand to apply pressure while rolling the citrus several times over a cutting board. Slice and squeeze. If a recipe calls for both zest and juice, be sure to zest the fruit before squeezing.

Garlic—Minced versus Finely Minced: "Finely minced" is noted for recipes that don't cook for a long time or where the garlic isn't blended into other ingredients. Just give that minced garlic a little extra TLC, so that it is more like a paste in consistency. I'm all about using a garlic press, which is always going to give you finely minced!

When It Comes to Mayo: I love and recommend mayonnaise, but only when it is made with avocado or olive oil, instead of vegetable oils. I prefer avocado oil as the base, but I will take either over anything with sunflower, safflower, corn, canola, or soy oil. Stay away from those!

Miso Type: Whenever I refer to "miso" in the book, I am referring to sweet/mild/white miso paste. Brown or red miso pastes are not interchangeable in the recipes.

Using Raw Nuts: Raw nuts can benefit from soaking in water before adding them to a recipe. I use two different methods in this book:

- Long-Soak Method for Soaking Nuts: Add nuts to a bowl and cover with filtered water by at least 1 inch. Allow to sit in a shaded area at room temperature for anywhere between 8 and 14 hours, before rinsing and draining.
- Short-Soak Method for Soaking Nuts: Add nuts to a saucepan, and cover with 2 inches of water. Bring to a simmer, and simmer two minutes, then drain and rinse with cold water.

Nut and Seed Butters: I use unsweetened, unsalted nut and seed butters in my recipes. I also try to use newer, runnier nut and seed butters, because they add moisture and are easier to blend. If that's not an option, try this trick: Scoop out a few tablespoons less than the recipe calls for and place in a mixing bowl with the missing amount of very hot water. Stir to combine, then allow the mixture to sit for 10 minutes. Stir thoroughly and measure out the amount needed for the recipe.

Salt: When I call for salt throughout the book, I am referring to fine-ground, noniodized sea salt. This is the ideal all-purpose salt for cooking, baking, and seasoning. Sea salt retains beneficial traces of minerals. Do not substitute table salt, which is even more finely ground; using the same amount of table salt will result in a dish that's overly salty. For finishing or garnishing, I recommend sea salt flakes (Maldon sea salt) and pink Himalayan sea salt.

Aged Balsamic Vinegar: I specify "aged," because it is slightly thicker, richer, and sweeter than regular balsamic vinegar, and the two really aren't interchangeable. You can also "age" it yourself by taking regular balsamic vinegar and heating it to a simmer in a small saucepan. Simmer, stirring frequently, until its volume has reduced by about one third. Allow to cool completely before using, and store in the fridge.

Butter: All butter used in recipes is unsalted. If possible, purchase butter from grass-fed cows.

Quinoa: All quinoa cooks the same regardless of color, so just use whatever you can find. Be sure to follow rinsing instructions to avoid a soapy aftertaste.

Scallions or Green Onions: They're the same thing! The recipes refer to them as scallions, but some grocers refer to them only as green onions.

Avocado Ripeness: An avocado is ripe if it gives somewhat easily when you press it with your thumb. If it feels almost hollow and gives very easily, then the avocado has started shrinking away from the skin. It is likely too ripe and may be going bad. If you purchase an underripe avocado, store it in a brown paper bag on the counter with a piece of cut fruit to expedite the ripening process. You can store perfectly ripe avocados in the refrigerator for a couple of days without them ripening further.

Peeling Fruits and Vegetables: If I am using produce that is on the Dirty Dozen list, I always peel as the skin holds a high concentration of pesticides. If it's organic or not one of the Dirty Dozen, I usually don't peel.

Prepping Kale and Collard Greens: To slice the leaves into ribbons, first rinse the leaves and pat dry. Lay a leaf flat on the cutting board. Holding the leaf with your non-dominant hand, use a sharp knife to slice on either side of the thick part of the stem (usually almost to the top of the leaf). Remove stem. Repeat with remaining leaves. Then layer a few leaves on top of each other, and roll into a log shape. Slice crosswise into ribbons.

Chapter 3

BEVERAGES + SMOOTHIES

Perhaps more than any other chapter, this first chapter reflects the growth in my personal wellness journey since my first cookbook. First, you will see some lower-sugar smoothies here. Do I still love fruit and believe that fruit can be a healthy part of your breakfast, lunch, or dinner? Yes, yes, yes! However, I wanted to offer y'all a few sugar-conscious smoothies, which may give you more sustained energy throughout the morning and help minimize sweet cravings in the afternoon. As a result, I recreated my famous LL's Daily Green Smoothie with avocado instead of banana, and I truly find it equally delicious. In addition to smoothies and a smoothie bowl, you'll also see a handful of "fatty" drinks in this chapter. Don't run from the word *fatty*! The healthy fats in these beverages are wonderful for your brain, hormones, and, of course, that crucial satiation factor. My Almond Chai Latte, Creamy Cashew Iced Coffee, and Crash-Free Hot Chocolate can even serve as a meal replacement if you're not super hungry in the morning. I hope this chapter serves as a happy welcome to the second LL Balanced Cookbook.

LL's Daily Morning Elixir

 HANDS-ON TIME: 5 min | **TOTAL TIME:** 5 min to overnight | **YIELD:** 1 serving

I don't remember exactly when I started making my Daily Morning Elixir, but I do know that it has been an absolute game-changer for me. Lemon juice helps move food through your digestive system quickly and efficiently. This flushes out toxins, a process that benefits your whole body and will show up as brighter, healthier skin. Raw apple cider vinegar is rich in gut-friendly probiotics and enzymes, and it helps kill bad bacteria. It has also been shown to improve insulin sensitivity and reduce blood sugar levels. I only recently began adding ginger to my elixir, but it is incredibly anti-inflammatory and anti-oxidative, and it can soothe an upset stomach. In addition to all of these health benefits, I personally love the combination of flavors, particularly with a few drops of liquid stevia added. I feel incredible after drinking my Daily Elixer, and I look forward to it each morning.

Combine all ingredients in a large jar or pitcher, and stir well. Serve immediately, or refrigerate overnight, and enjoy first thing in the morning. (I prefer to make this the night before because 1) I don't have to think about it in the morning, 2) I like that it's chilled, and 3) if using collagen peptides, I find they dissolve better with more time.)

Juice from 1 lemon or lime (2 tablespoons)

1 to 3 teaspoons raw apple cider vinegar (start with 1 and increase gradually)

½-inch piece ginger, peeled and grated

4 cups filtered water

2 to 10 drops liquid stevia

Pinch sea salt (optional)

1 scoop collagen peptides (optional)*

NOTES

If you have any leftover fresh herbs like mint, basil, or even cilantro, throw them into your water as well, mashing them a bit with a straw to release the flavor.

You can split this between two mornings, if 32 ounces feels like too much for you!

* Consuming high-quality collagen peptides made from the collagen of 100 percent pasture-raised, grass-fed cows can noticeably combat the signs of aging, as well as improve joint health. For more information on the health benefits of collagen peptides, see K. L. Clark et al., "24-Week Study on the Use of Collagen Hydrolysate as a Dietary Supplement in Athletes with Activity-Related Joint Pain," *Current Medical Research and Opinion* 24, no. 5 (May 2008): 1485-96, abstract, https://www.ncbi.nlm.nih.gov/pubmed/18416885; and E. Proksch et al., "Oral Supplementation of Specific Collagen Peptides Has Beneficial Effects on Human Skin Physiology: A Double-Blind, Placebo-Controlled Study," *Skin Pharmacology and Physiology* 27, no. 1 (2014): 47-55, abstract, https://www.ncbi.nlm.nih.gov/pubmed/23949208.

Coconut Lime Macadamia Smoothie

 | **HANDS-ON TIME:** 5 min | **TOTAL TIME:** 5 min, plus overnight soaking | **YIELD:** 1 serving

I was a bit nervous when I set about making fruit-free smoothies for this book, but after many unsuccessful attempts, I came up with some great low-sugar creations, starting with this tropical-inspired goodness. Soaking macadamia nuts overnight allows them to blend into a rich, velvety base for the smoothie. Coconut flakes offer a stronger coconut flavor, which is a happy companion to bright lime zest and juice. Frozen zucchini provides bulk, nutrition, and the "chill" you would usually get from frozen fruit in a smoothie. This smoothie is a dreamy way to start a warm summer (or winter with the heat cranked) morning.

The Night Before: Use the long-soak method to soak macadamia nuts overnight (see page 44).

The Next Morning: Drain and rinse. Place nuts and all remaining ingredients in a high-powered blender. Blend until smooth and creamy. Taste for sweetness, and add more liquid stevia if you like. Enjoy immediately.

¼ cup raw macadamia nuts

1 tablespoon unsweetened coconut flakes

½ cup canned coconut milk (full-fat or light)

½ cup filtered water

½ teaspoon firmly packed lime zest (½ lime)

Juice from 1 lime (2 tablespoons)

1½ tablespoons maple syrup or 15 drops liquid stevia, plus more to taste

1 cup frozen zucchini chunks

NOTE

To make frozen zucchini chunks, simply chop however many zucchinis you like into 1-inch pieces, and freeze them in an even layer on a baking sheet lined with parchment paper. Once frozen, transfer to plastic container or sealable plastic bag. You can use this method for frozen fruit as well.

Ideas for
LEFTOVER COCONUT FLAKES

If you have leftover unsweetened coconut flakes, use them in Miso Coconut Roasted Eggplant (page 159) or 5-Layer Magic Bars (page 313) or as a topping for Orange Ginger Tofu (page 243).

Maple Tahini Date Shake

 | **HANDS-ON TIME:** 4 min | **TOTAL TIME:** 4 min | **YIELD:** 1 serving |

For all my babes out there who want something a little more indulgent, but still nutritious, this is the smoothie for you. Actually, I call it a shake because it really tastes and feels like the classic accompaniment to a burger and fries. Well, maybe not 100 percent classic, because I use bananas, rich in potassium and vitamin C, instead of ice cream. I also use dates instead of caramel-from-a-can, and tahini to add a little calcium and a hint of savory flavor. Tiny splashes of maple extract and salt take this recipe to another level, and I am *here* for it. This shake is a perfect pre- or post-workout meal, with its balance of complex carbs, healthy fat, and protein. I love to throw this together when I'm craving something cold and decadent but want to avoid going face-first into a pint of ice cream!

Place all ingredients in the order listed in a high-powered blender, and blend until smooth and creamy. Feel free to add more coconut milk or water (I prefer the former) by the tablespoon as needed to get things moving. Enjoy immediately.

- ½ cup canned coconut milk (full-fat or light)
- ⅓ cup filtered water
- 1 large or 2 small pitted medjool dates
- 1 rounded tablespoon tahini
- 1½ frozen bananas, cut into chunks (1¼ cups)
- Scant ¼ teaspoon ground cinnamon
- ¼ teaspoon maple extract (sub vanilla extract)
- Pinch sea salt

NOTE

Want to make this a green smoothie? Just throw in a few handfuls of fresh organic baby spinach.

LL's Daily Fruit-Free Green Smoothie

 HANDS-ON TIME: 5 min | **TOTAL TIME:** 5 min | **YIELD:** 1 serving

I acknowledge that avocado is technically a fruit, so this smoothie's title is a misnomer. That said, because avocado is so low in carbohydrates and high in fat, we are exempting it from the fruit category for our purposes. One of the most popular recipes from my first book is the LL's Daily Green Smoothie. While I still love that smoothie, I wanted to offer an alternative that's lower in sugar. Using avocado instead of banana maintains the thick, creamy consistency that I adore in smoothies, while taking the sugar count down considerably. A generous dollop of almond butter provides protein and a mild nutty flavor. As with my original green smoothie, you won't taste the spinach at all. You can also try swapping half or all of it for frozen kale.

- 1¼ cups chilled unsweetened almond milk
- ¼ medium avocado, peeled and pitted
- ¾ cup frozen chopped organic spinach
- 2 tablespoons unsweetened, unsalted almond butter (sub peanut butter)
- ¼ teaspoon vanilla extract
- 12 drops liquid stevia, or to taste
- Pinch sea salt (optional)

Place all ingredients in the order listed in a high-powered blender, and blend until smooth and creamy. Feel free to add more almond milk to reach your desired consistency. Enjoy immediately.

Ideas for
LEFTOVER AVOCADO

Store leftover avocado tightly wrapped in plastic wrap with the pit still in to preserve freshness. You can use the leftovers on toast with salt, pepper, onion powder, and a drizzle of lime or lemon juice. Or plan to make LL's Sweetgreen Order Salad (page 275) or Cashew Kimchi Lettuce Cups (page 137). It also makes a great topper for BBQ Sweet Potato Tofu Tacos (page 81). Or simply make this smoothie throughout the week.

Low-Sugar PB&J Smoothie Bowl

 | **HANDS-ON TIME:** 5 min | **TOTAL TIME:** 5 min | **YIELD:** 1 serving |

If you're at all familiar with my recipes, you know that PB&J is a theme throughout! I mean, why reinvent the wheel when something just works so well? Here, that iconic combination shows up in a low-sugar smoothie bowl that is creamy, satisfying, and contains a whole cup of cauliflower rice. That plus organic berries? Hellooo fiber and antioxidants! I swear you can't taste the cauliflower. Whenever I eat this smoothie bowl, I have the most incredible sustained energy throughout the morning. I love to top mine with thawed berries or sliced banana, an extra drizzle of peanut butter, and a handful of granola (not keto-friendly).

¾ cup canned coconut milk (full-fat or light)

¼ cup filtered water

1 cup frozen cauliflower rice

1¼ cups mixed frozen organic berries (can sub 1½ cups of raspberries or blueberries)

2 tablespoons unsweetened, unsalted peanut butter

¼ teaspoon vanilla extract

12 drops liquid stevia, or more to taste

Place all ingredients in the order listed in a high-powered blender, and blend until smooth, using the help of a tamper. Add 1 tablespoon coconut milk at a time if you need help getting the mixture moving. Taste for sweetness, and add more stevia if you like. Enjoy immediately.

NOTE

Feel free to use another sweetener of choice. Even a scoop of vanilla protein powder would be yummy.

Idea for
LEFTOVER CAULIFLOWER RICE

Buy an extra-large bag of cauliflower rice, and use leftovers to make Sour Cream & Onion Cauliflower Risotto (page 152).

Almond Chai Latte

Vg GF DF P | **HANDS-ON TIME:** 15 min | **TOTAL TIME:** 15 min, plus overnight soaking

YIELD: 1 serving | **OPTION:** K

I've been on a "fatty" beverage kick for the last nine months or so because they taste incredible and make me feel relaxed and balanced. What do I mean by "fatty" beverage? Simply, a traditional drink, such as tea, coffee, or hot chocolate, blended with one or more sources of healthy fat. The result? A divine, sippable snack or even breakfast if you're not quite ready for a meal but want to feel sated. This Almond Chai Latte is perfect for someone who wants a touch of caffeine but not as much as in coffee. It might seem odd to include coconut oil in your chai, but trust me—it creates the most wonderful consistency, and you don't taste any coconut. The warming chai spices are bolstered with an extra dose of cinnamon, which can also help slow the absorption of sugar into the bloodstream after a meal. I also love this latte as an afternoon treat, paired with a Grain-Free Gingerbread Streusel Square (page 119) if I'm particularly peckish.

The Night Before: Place almond milk and water in a saucepan, and bring to a to simmer over medium heat. Put tea bag in a heatproof mug or glass, and add simmering milk mixture. Steep for 10 minutes on the counter, then refrigerate overnight (with the bag in).

The Next Morning: Remove tea bag, and pour steeped tea into a saucepan. Bring to a boil over medium heat. While tea is heating, place remaining ingredients in a blender. Once tea is boiling, add it to a blender, and blend until creamy and frothy. Enjoy immediately.

1 cup unsweetened almond milk

¾ cup filtered water

1 chai tea bag

1 tablespoon unsweetened, unsalted almond butter (sub cashew butter)

2 teaspoons coconut oil

2 teaspoons maple syrup (K sub liquid stevia, to taste)

¼ teaspoon almond extract

Pinch ground cinnamon*

Idea for
LEFTOVER CHAI TEA

Try chai tea in Chai-Spiced Cake Donuts (page 303).

---

* Read more about the health benefits of cinnamon in S. Adisakwattana et al., "Inhibitory Activity of Cinnamon Bark Species and Their Combination Effect with Acarbose Against Intestinal A-Glucosidase and Pancreatic A –Amylase," *Plant Foods for Human Nutrition* 66, no. 2 (June 2011): 143–8, abstract, https://www.ncbi.nlm.nih.gov/pubmed/21538147.

Creamy Cashew Iced Coffee

 HANDS-ON TIME: 5 min | **TOTAL TIME:** 5 min, plus overnight soaking

YIELD: 3 to 4 servings | **OPTION:** K

Oh my goodness, *this* iced coffee. I'm all about a steaming cuppa Joe, and typically, iced coffee doesn't really do it for me, unless it's my Creamy Cashew Iced Coffee! Some days (or moods) are just too warm for a hot brew, but I still want my java to taste special and decadent. Blending soaked cashews and a splash of vanilla extract into your almond milk does just that. Cold-brew ice cubes keep your coffee cool while you sip on it throughout the morning, and they also allow you to adjust the caffeine intake to your preference. If you're not an iced coffee person, you can still enjoy the cashew and almond milk mixture as a homemade creamer, or you can add a handful of frozen berries as your "ice cubes" for a beautiful, refreshing alternative.

1½ cups cold-brew coffee

½ cup raw cashews

3½ cups unsweetened almond milk

3 tablespoons maple syrup (K sub stevia drops, to taste—I use 20)

1 teaspoon vanilla extract

Pinch sea salt (optional)

> *Ideas for*
> ### LEFTOVER COLD-BREW COFFEE
>
> Use leftovers to make Chewy Peanut Butter Latte Oats (page 93) or Grain-Free Java Pecan Pie (page 310).

The Night Before: Pour cold-brew coffee into ice cube trays. (I use 1-inch square ice cube molds.) Use the long-soak method to soak cashews overnight (see page 44).

The Next Morning: Drain and rinse cashews, and place in a high-powered blender along with almond milk, maple syrup, vanilla, and salt, if using. Blend until smooth.

Place as many coffee ice cubes as you like in a glass, then top with almond milk mixture, and stir for 30 seconds. (I like to let it sit for 5 minutes or so before enjoying to allow the ice cubes to melt a bit.)

Alternatively, you can combine a few ice cubes and approximately one-third of the almond milk mixture in a blender, and blend until creamy.

Leftovers will keep in the refrigerator for 4 days, but you might need to give it a stir before using.

Crash-Free Hot Chocolate

Vg GF DF P | **HANDS-ON TIME:** 15 min | **TOTAL TIME:** 15 min | **YIELD:** 1 serving | 🕐 | **OPTION:** K

This recipe was inspired by my darling team member, Lelan, who helped me test and edit this book. Lelan was on a hot chocolate kick, and she graciously shared her recipe with me. I made a few tweaks, because I can't leave well enough alone, but I kept her brilliant idea to add arrowroot starch, which makes this hot chocolate exceptionally luscious. I call this hot chocolate "crash-free" because it's low in sugar and contains healthy fat from coconut milk and coconut oil. As a result, this cozy drink will satisfy your sweet tooth while keeping you from experiencing a blood sugar roller coaster. I drink the mocha version a few times per week, because . . . well, chocolate plus coffee!

Pour coconut milk and almond milk into a small saucepan, and bring to a gentle boil (rapid bubbles but not as "noisy" or aggressive as a traditional boil) over medium heat. Place remaining ingredients in a blender. Once milk comes to gentle boil, add it to the blender, and blend until creamy and frothy. Taste for sweetness, and add more syrup or coconut sugar if you like. Enjoy immediately.

- ¼ cup canned full-fat coconut milk
- 1¼ cups unsweetened almond milk (sub ¾ cup strong brewed coffee plus ½ cup unsweetened almond milk for a mocha version)
- 1 tablespoon stevia-sweetened chocolate chips (sub regular chocolate chips)
- 2 teaspoons coconut oil
- 2 tablespoons Dutch-processed cocoa powder (sub cacao but it will have a slightly different flavor)
- ¼ teaspoon arrowroot starch (sub cornstarch)
- ¼ teaspoon vanilla extract
- ⅛ teaspoon sea salt
- 1 tablespoon maple syrup or coconut sugar (K sub 10 to 12 liquid stevia drops, or to taste)

NOTE

If you happen to have maca powder on hand, adding 1 serving adds a wonderful caramel flavor to this hot chocolate. Maca is a vegetable native to Peru, and its root is ground into powder to be used for health purposes. Maca root is an adaptogen, which means that it can help the body adapt to stress and bring bodily processes to homeostasis. I find that including maca somewhere in my day several times per week has a gentle mood- and energy-boosting effect. Follow package instructions for serving size. Look for an organic and reputable brand; I get mine online at Thrive Market (www.thrivemarket.com).

Chamomile Ginger Turmeric Latte

 | **HANDS-ON TIME:** 15 min | **TOTAL TIME:** 30 min | **YIELD:** 1 serving **OPTIONS:**

Here's a caffeine-free option in my creamy beverage arsenal. Turmeric lattes have been on the health and wellness scene for some time now, because turmeric contains a polyphenol called curcumin, which can benefit oxidative and inflammatory conditions. I appreciate the health properties of turmeric, but I don't adore the taste, so I balanced this latte with the gentle floral flavor of chamomile. Including a bit of butter from grass-fed cows provides healthy omega-3 fatty acids, and it acts as an emulsifier, resulting in a heavenly texture. Combining turmeric with a bit of black pepper makes the curcumin more bioavailable, so I don't recommend leaving that out. This latte is one of my favorite ways to end a busy day, as a relaxing post-dinner, pre-bedtime delight. Shout out to my friend Ryan, founder of Placemat, for the inspiration to add a touch of red pepper flakes . . . it just works!

½ cup filtered water

1 cup unsweetened almond milk

1 chamomile tea bag

½ teaspoon ground turmeric

2 teaspoons honey (Vg sub maple syrup or K sub 6 to 8 drops liquid stevia, or to taste)

1 teaspoon butter (Vg DF sub coconut oil)

Scant pinch black pepper

Scant pinch red pepper flakes

½-inch piece ginger, peeled and roughly chopped

¼ teaspoon arrowroot starch (sub cornstarch) (optional)

Place water and almond milk in a small saucepan, and bring to a boil over medium heat. Place tea bag in a large heatproof mug (or glass jar), and add boiling mixture. Steep 5 to 10 minutes (longer for a stronger chamomile flavor), then discard tea bag.

Place steeped tea and remaining ingredients in a blender. Blend until smooth and creamy. If the mixture isn't warm enough for your liking, pour it back into the saucepan, and bring to a simmer. Enjoy immediately.

Chapter 4

BREAKFASTS

*I*f it ain't broke, don't fix it! Many of y'all told me that you liked how I separated sweet and savory breakfast items in my first book, so here we are again! When I'm browsing cookbooks, my eyes are always first drawn to dishes on the sweeter side, and I tend to overlook incredible savory breakfast recipes. I hope that giving each a "spotlight" helps you to take a good, long look at all of your options. Whether you start breakfast at 8 a.m. or 1 p.m., how you break your fast sets the tone for the rest of the day, and I want it to be a good one for you! In both the Sweet and Savory sections, you'll find options for vegan, vegetarian, keto or low-carb, paleo, and omnivorous dietary lifestyles. You'll also see both single-serving and batch-cooking recipes, to suit your preference and schedule. And, if you're anything like me, you might want breakfast for dinner on occasion (read: *often*), so don't be shy about enjoying my breakfast recipes any time of the day.

Savory Breakfasts

One of the changes that came from consciously decreasing my sugar intake is a greater love for savory breakfasts. For most of my life, I would always choose something on the sweeter side to start my day—oatmeal, granola, smoothies, etc. While I still adore those foods (and have them often), I have a newfound love and respect for dishes like my Grain-Free Biscuits with Miso Mushroom Gravy, Sun-Dried Tomato & Broccoli Vegan Frittata, and, of course, eggs in various ways. Plus, my journey with intuitive eating has often led to later breakfasts, and these dishes make for lovely brunch options around 11 a.m.

Speaking of brunch, I'm particularly excited about my Chive & Goat Cheese Fluffy Baked Eggs. They're perfect for a group, require very little prep or cleanup, and absolutely melt in your mouth. I also have an inkling that my Apple Sausage Breakfast Bake will become a go-to for weekends or holiday entertaining. If you're someone who goes for a lil' salt and a lil' heat (spice or temperature) for your first meal, this chapter is dedicated to you. *I get you!*

Apple Sausage Breakfast Bake

(DF) (GF) (P) | **HANDS-ON TIME:** 30 min | **TOTAL TIME:** 1 h, 35 min | **YIELD:** 8 servings

After a memorable brunch that included dipping chicken apple sausages in maple syrup, I knew I had to develop a recipe that combines those flavors. Technically this dish is a mix of sweet and savory, as a hint of maple and the caramelized apples bring out the rich savoriness of ground pork. You'll fall in love with the smell wafting from your oven even before you take your first bite. This freezes beautifully, so I often make a double batch, slice it into pieces, and keep some frozen for busy weekday mornings. You can also try this with ground turkey, but I do recommend getting the 94 percent lean mixture, which includes both dark and white meat. I like to use Honeycrisp or Pink Lady apples, but play around with your favorites.

Preheat oven to 375° F. Line a baking sheet with parchment paper, and grease an 8-inch square baking dish (an 8 × 10-inch pan also works) with avocado oil.

In a large mixing bowl, toss together apples, 1 teaspoon avocado oil, cinnamon, and maple syrup. Spread evenly on baking sheet. Roast for 30 minutes, then allow to cool for at least 5 minutes. Don't clean mixing bowl.

Heat a large sauté pan over medium heat, and add remaining 3 teaspoons avocado oil. When oil moves quickly around the pan and is shimmering, add onions and sausage. Cook, stirring every minute or so to break up chunks of sausage, until the edges are golden brown, approximately 10 minutes. Deglaze with a splash of water (2 tablespoons), scraping up any brown bits from the bottom of the pan. Cook until water evaporates, 1 to 2 minutes. Stir in ½ teaspoon salt and pepper, remove from the heat, then allow to cool for at least 5 minutes.

In the mixing bowl you used for the apples, combine eggs, coconut milk, almond flour, baking soda, vanilla, and remaining 1 teaspoon salt. Whisk to thoroughly incorporate.

Add cooled apples and sausage mixture to egg mixture, and stir well. Scrape into the baking dish in an even layer, and bake for 40 to 45 minutes, until golden brown and puffy around the edges. Allow to cool 20 minutes before slicing and enjoying.

Leftovers will keep tightly sealed in the refrigerator for 4 days or in the freezer for 2 months.

4 teaspoons avocado oil, plus more for greasing, divided

2 medium apples, chopped into ½-inch pieces (a little less than 4 cups—I don't peel but you can)

½ teaspoon ground cinnamon

1 tablespoon maple syrup (sub monkfruit sweetener)

½ medium yellow onion, diced into ¼-inch pieces (¾ to 1 cup)

1 pound ground pork breakfast sausage

1½ teaspoons sea salt, divided

¼ teaspoon black pepper

4 large eggs

½ cup canned full-fat coconut milk (sub heavy cream)

1 cup blanched almond flour

½ teaspoon baking soda

½ teaspoon vanilla extract

NOTE

Omit ½ teaspoon salt from the sausage mixture if you lean toward less seasoning.

SERVING SUGGESTION

Combine 2 tablespoons unsweetened, unsalted almond butter, 3 tablespoons unsweetened almond milk, and a sprinkle of ground cinnamon. Stir until well combined. Drizzle on top of the Apple Sausage Breakfast Bake.

Sun-Dried Tomato & Broccoli Vegan Frittata

Ⓥ ⒹⒻ ⒼⒻ | **HANDS-ON TIME:** 27 min | **TOTAL TIME:** 1 h, 25 min | **YIELD:** 8 servings

I'll never forget the first time I had a slice of "farinata" *(Italian chickpea cake)* from Body & Soul Bakeshop in Union Square Market in New York City. I'd been loving on their muffins and cookies for months, but for some reason I was in a savory mood that day. There was something uniquely satisfying about the dense, creamy texture combined with slightly sweet roasted veggies. Now that I've made chickpea flour a staple in the LL Balanced pantry, I'm thrilled to share a farinata-turned-frittata recipe with you.

Preheat oven to 350° F. Grease a nonstick 9-inch springform pan with olive oil.

Heat a large sauté pan over medium heat, and add olive oil. When oil moves quickly around the pan and is shimmering, add onions, broccoli, and shallots. Cook, stirring every minute or so, until onions and shallots are translucent and broccoli is knife-tender but not mushy, 8 to 10 minutes. You can add splashes of water as needed to prevent sticking and burning. Add salt, basil, pepper, garlic powder, and water. Cook, stirring, until liquid evaporates, 1 to 2 minutes. Set aside to cool.

Place chickpea flour, nutritional yeast, miso paste, and almond milk in a food processor. Process until smooth and creamy (and don't be alarmed when the batter thickens quickly). Add sun-dried tomatoes, and pulse until they are incorporated throughout, but some small bits remain.

Add batter to broccoli mixture, stir to incorporate, then scrape mixture into the springform pan. Use a damp spatula to spread into an even layer. (I know the batter smells a little funky—I promise it goes away after baking.)

Bake for 28 minutes, or until edges are golden brown and pulling away from the sides. The top should be slightly firm to touch, but note that chickpea flour continues to cook more than other flours after it comes out of the oven. Allow to cool for 30 minutes, then run a butter knife around the edge of the pan to make sure nothing is sticking to the sides. Remove the outer ring of the pan. Slice into wedges, and carefully remove from the base of the pan.

Leftover frittata will keep tightly sealed in the refrigerator for 5 days. I don't recommend freezing.

2 tablespoons olive oil, plus more for greasing (use the oil from the sun-dried tomato jar if you like)

½ medium yellow onion, diced into ¼-inch pieces (¾ to 1 cup)

½ medium head broccoli, chopped into ½-inch florets (2½ cups; we want them noticeably smaller than traditional florets)

1 small shallot, diced into ¼-inch pieces (¼ cup)

1½ teaspoons sea salt (feel free to start with less and add to taste)

½ teaspoon dried basil

¼ teaspoon black pepper

¼ teaspoon garlic powder

⅓ cup water

1½ cups chickpea flour

¼ cup nutritional yeast

1 teaspoon mild, white miso paste

1 cup unsweetened almond milk

⅔ cup firmly packed sun-dried tomatoes in olive oil, excess oil shaken off

SERVING SUGGESTION

I like to serve slices of this frittata with an extra drizzle of oil from the jar of sun-dried tomatoes.

B.E.C. Freezeritos

HANDS-ON TIME: 30 min | **TOTAL TIME:** 50 min | **YIELD:** 4 to 6 servings | **OPTION:** GF

"B.E.C." stands for Bacon, Egg, and Cheese, and "freezeritos" stands for freezer burritos . . . what is there not to like? I knew these were a hit when my team member Lelan, recently a first-time mama, began making them regularly for her family. Like Lelan, I think you'll find Freezeritos easy to make, easy to reheat, and easy on the palate (read: *delicious*). Once you've made them a time or two, you can experiment with different fillings. I have made them with roasted red onions and bell peppers, then dipped in salsa for a Southwestern vibe. However you enjoy them, Freezeritos are a fantastic on-the-go breakfast option. Just don't forget to take them out of the freezer the night before, and put a note on your calendar to preheat the oven as soon as you wake up. Then you can bake them while you get ready for the day!

12 ounces bacon (10 to 12 slices)

1 6-ounce bag organic baby spinach

¼ cup water

½ teaspoon garlic powder

2 tablespoons butter (sub avocado oil)

9 large eggs

Salt and black pepper, to taste

6 burrito-sized wraps (I like sprouted whole-grain or brown-rice wraps; GF sub gluten-free wraps)

¼ cup mayonnaise

4 ounces cheddar cheese, shredded (1 cup)

Preheat oven to 375° F. Wrap a baking sheet with aluminum foil, pressing it tightly to the edges. (I like to do one piece lengthwise and two pieces crosswise.)

Cook the Bacon: Place bacon slices on the baking sheet. They might slightly overlap, but they'll shrink as they cook. Bake for 20 minutes, then carefully drain excess grease into a heatproof container to cool. Bake for another 10 to 20 minutes, until the bacon reaches your desired doneness (will depend on the cut and brand of bacon). Allow to cool at least 10 minutes before using in assembly. You can pat off excess grease with a paper towel if you like.

Cook the Spinach and Eggs: While bacon is in the oven, heat a large cast-iron or other nonstick skillet over medium heat. Add spinach and water. Cook, stirring every 45 seconds or so, until spinach has wilted and no excess liquid remains, 3 to 4 minutes. (Placing a lid on the skillet can speed up this process.) Add garlic powder, and stir to incorporate, then cook spinach for another 30 seconds. Transfer to a heatproof bowl, straining off any excess liquid, then set aside to cool.

Place butter in the skillet, and reduce the heat to medium-low. When butter has melted and is slightly bubbling, crack 3 eggs into the pan, trying to keep them separate. If the whites start to bleed into each other, use a spatula to fold the "runaway" egg white back toward the yolk. Add a pinch of salt and pepper to each egg if you like. Grab a baking sheet, and keep it near the stove.

(continued on next page)

Cook until whites are solidified and eggs are flippable, 2 to 3 minutes. Flip, cover the pan, and cook until yolks are mostly set, another 2 minutes or so. (I love a runny yolk, but we don't want soggy Freezeritos.) You want to be patient while cooking the eggs so they don't burn, and you might have to decrease the heat as you go. When yolks are mostly set, transfer eggs to the baking sheet. Repeat process with remaining 6 eggs. You can add more butter as necessary to prevent sticking, but you shouldn't need to with a properly seasoned cast-iron skillet.

Once the spinach is cool enough to handle, squeeze out excess liquid. Don't be shy—you need it pretty dry!

Assemble the Burritos: If the wraps don't feel soft and pliable, place them, one at a time, in the still-warm oven for 30 seconds before you roll each burrito.

Tear off 6 pieces of aluminum foil, approximately 12-inches wide. To the right-hand side of each wrap (leaving at least 1 inch free from the edge), add a smear of mayonnaise, a small handful of sautéed spinach, 1½ fried eggs, 2 slices of bacon, and a sprinkle of cheese (approximately 2 tablespoons). Roll up from right to left, tucking in the sides of the wrap as you go. Squeeze burrito firmly with both hands to press together, then wrap in a piece of aluminum foil. Repeat with remaining wraps and filling. Place in the refrigerator if you plan to serve them all within 4 days or in the freezer for longer storage.

The night before you plan to serve the burritos, remove them from the freezer, and place in the fridge to thaw overnight.

Preheat oven to 350° F. Place wrapped burritos on a baking sheet, and bake for 22 minutes. (I don't line the baking sheet.) If you prefer, you can cook them from frozen by carefully unwrapping them and microwaving them on high for 3 to 4 minutes, flipping the burritos and patting the plate dry halfway. Enjoy immediately.

Burritos will keep tightly sealed in the refrigerator for 4 days or in the freezer for 4 months.

NOTE

Another way to soften wraps is to wrap them in damp paper towels and microwave 15 to 20 seconds.

BREAKFASTS

Grain-Free Biscuits

with MISO MUSHROOM GRAVY

 | **HANDS-ON TIME:** 30 min | **TOTAL TIME:** 1 h, 10 min | **YIELD:** 6 servings |

This recipe sounded fabulous in my head, but I honestly didn't think it would turn out well. Instead, it turned out to be one of my favorite recipes in the book! This dish is packed with umami from mushrooms, tempeh, nutritional yeast, and a generous dollop of miso paste. The key to this dish is taking the time to simmer it from a soupy mixture to a thick, unctuous consistency. This allows the flavors to ripen, overlap, and become delectable best friends. The accompanying biscuits are the perfect vehicle for this rich gravy, and they're a breeze to make. You can totally make a double batch and keep them frozen for other uses. I adore slathering the biscuits with butter and jam, peanut butter and honey, or pesto and a fried egg.

MISO MUSHROOM GRAVY:

2 tablespoons avocado oil, divided

8 or 10 ounces sliced baby bella mushrooms

½ medium yellow onion, diced into ¼-inch pieces (¾ to 1 cup)

1 medium shallot, minced (⅓ cup)

1 teaspoon sea salt, plus more to taste

¾ teaspoon onion powder

½ teaspoon garlic powder

½ teaspoon black pepper

1 tablespoon mild, white miso paste

8 ounces tempeh, crumbled

1 cup low-sodium vegetable stock (sub chicken stock for non-vegetarian)

1 cup canned full-fat coconut milk

2 tablespoons nutritional yeast

GRAIN-FREE BISCUITS:

1¼ cups blanched almond flour

½ cup coconut flour

2 teaspoons baking powder

½ teaspoon sea salt

2 large eggs, room temperature

2 teaspoons apple cider vinegar

⅓ cup coconut oil, melted

6 tablespoons unsweetened almond milk

Make the Miso Mushroom Gravy: Heat a large saucepan over medium heat, and add 1 tablespoon avocado oil and a splash of water (2 tablespoons). When water starts popping, add mushrooms. Cook, stirring every 1 to 2 minutes, until mushrooms are golden brown and reduced in size, approximately 10 minutes. You can add splashes of water as necessary to prevent sticking or burning—just make sure it all evaporates. Transfer mushrooms to a heatproof bowl.

Add remaining 1 tablespoon oil and another splash of water to the pan, reduce heat to medium-low, and add onions and shallots. Cook, stirring every 1 to 2 minutes, until softened and translucent, 8 to 10 minutes. Add a final splash of water, along with salt, onion powder, garlic powder, pepper, and miso. Stir until miso is evenly incorporated throughout, approximately 1 minute.

Add crumbled tempeh, vegetable stock, coconut milk, and nutritional yeast to the pan, and stir to evenly combine. Bring to a simmer, and cook until mixture is thick and creamy, 35 to 40 minutes. You should be able to run a spoon along the bottom of the pan and it will stay separated. Stir in mushrooms. Taste for seasoning, and add more salt if you like. (I add another ½ teaspoon.)

Make the Grain-Free Biscuits: While the gravy is simmering, preheat oven to 350° F. Line a baking sheet with parchment paper.

(continued on next page)

GRAIN-FREE BISCUITS
WITH MISO MUSHROOM GRAVY *(continued)*

In a large mixing bowl, whisk together almond flour, coconut flour, baking powder, and salt. In a separate bowl, whisk eggs. Add vinegar, coconut oil, and almond milk to eggs, and whisk until mostly incorporated. Pour wet ingredients into dry, and fold until the mixture becomes a somewhat dry-looking dough.

Form 6 evenly sized balls of dough (approximately ⅓ cup each), and place on the baking sheet with at least 2 inches between each. Pat each ball into a 1-inch-high disk. You can use lightly dampened fingers to smooth the sides if you like.

Bake for 17 minutes, or until firm but the top still has some give. Allow to cool completely before slicing in half horizontally.

Assemble: Top sliced biscuits with gravy.

Once completely cooled, biscuits and gravy will keep tightly sealed (separately) in the refrigerator for 5 days or in the freezer for 3 months.

BBQ Sweet Potato Tofu Tacos

 | **HANDS-ON TIME:** 25 min | **TOTAL TIME:** 45 min | **YIELD:** 10 to 12 tacos | | **OPTION:** GF

Does this recipe make me super basic? I know, I know—I didn't break the mold with a tofu "hash" recipe. But here's the thing: I've had similar recipes, and I always feel like they don't live up to their potential. So now I'll turn it over to you to let me know if this version does. Taking the time to cook the veggies, then the tofu, then the spice mixture brings out the best in every ingredient. Plus, how can you go wrong with turning anything into a taco? Or if that's not your jam, I love this hash as part of a breakfast plate with fresh fruit and regular or veggie sausage, as well as scooped up with tortilla chips.

Make the BBQ Seasoning: Place seasoning ingredients in a small bowl, and whisk to combine, or place in a sealable jar or container and shake.

Make the Tacos: Drain and rinse tofu, then pat dry. Crumble tofu into a mixing bowl (you want it to look like scrambled eggs in size), and sprinkle with nutritional yeast and turmeric. Gently stir to evenly incorporate, and set aside.

Heat a large sauté pan over medium-high heat, and add avocado oil. When oil moves quickly around the pan and is shimmering, add sweet potatoes. Cook, stirring every 1 to 2 minutes, until edges are golden brown, 5 to 6 minutes. Reduce heat to medium, and add bell peppers, onions, and a splash of water (2 tablespoons). Cook, stirring every 1 to 2 minutes, until sweet potatoes are fork-tender and onions are translucent, 8 to 10 minutes. Add splashes of water as necessary to prevent sticking or burning. Add garlic, and cook, stirring, until garlic is fragrant, approximately 30 seconds.

Add tofu mixture, ¼ cup BBQ Seasoning, and another splash of water to the sweet potato mixture, then gently toss to coat. Cook for another 3 to 4 minutes, stirring a few times. You can add more small splashes of water to prevent sticking, but make sure it cooks off—we don't want soggy filling.

Taste for seasoning, and add more salt if you like, then serve with tortillas and garnishes of your choice.

Leftovers will keep in the refrigerator for 3 days. I don't recommend freezing.

BBQ SEASONING:

¼ cup coconut sugar (sub 3 tablespoons monkfruit sweetener)

2 tablespoons paprika

1 tablespoon sea salt

1 tablespoon chili powder

1 tablespoon garlic powder

4 teaspoons onion powder

1 teaspoon ground cumin

½ teaspoon ground cinnamon

½ teaspoon black pepper

TACOS:

1 pound extra firm tofu

2 tablespoons nutritional yeast

1 teaspoon ground turmeric

2 tablespoons avocado oil

1 large or 2 small sweet potatoes, chopped into ½-inch pieces (2½ to 3 cups)

1 medium red bell pepper, chopped into ½-inch pieces (1½ cups)

½ medium yellow onion, chopped into ½-inch pieces (¾ to 1 cup)

4 cloves garlic, minced

¼ cup BBQ Seasoning

Salt, to taste

10 to 12 6-inch corn or wheat tortillas (GF sub gluten-free tortillas)

Dairy or vegan sour cream, dairy or vegan cheese, sliced scallions, chopped avocado, chopped cilantro, and hot sauce for garnish

Chive & Goat Cheese Fluffy Baked Eggs

V **GF** | **HANDS-ON TIME:** 10 min | **TOTAL TIME:** 30 min | **YIELD:** 4 to 6 servings | | **OPTION:** **DF**

Oh, man, did this take me a few tries, but it was so worth it! As much as I love whipping up a single serving of scrambled eggs, I don't look forward to cleaning the resulting sticky pan. These baked eggs allow you to cook 4 to 6 servings of fluffy, creamy, melt-in-your mouth eggs with only one dish to clean. I've also discovered that bright chives and tangy goat cheese are a match made in heaven with eggs, so don't skip that part of the recipe. That said, if you just can't do dairy, try a few scoops of vegan cream cheese dolloped on top. Next time you're serving breakfast or brunch to a crowd, make your life easier with these fluffy baked "scrambled" eggs.

3 tablespoons butter, melted (**DF** sub olive oil), divided

12 large eggs

¾ cup canned coconut milk (full-fat or light)

4 ounces goat cheese (**DF** sub vegan cream cheese)

1 teaspoon sea salt

1 teaspoon black pepper

2 to 3 tablespoons minced chives

Grated parmesan cheese (optional)

Preheat oven to 350° F. Grease a 9 × 13 × 2-inch baking dish with 1 tablespoon melted butter.

Combine eggs, coconut milk, remaining 2 tablespoons melted butter, one-third of the goat cheese (it doesn't need to be exact), salt, and pepper in a blender, and purée until smooth.

Pour egg mixture into baking dish, and carefully place in the oven. Bake 12 minutes, then remove and stir. Bake another 5 minutes, then check to see if the eggs are mostly set. If not, bake another 2 to 3 minutes, until completely set but still soft and fluffy. Remember that they will continue to cook a bit after you take them out, and the key to this recipe is not overcooking.

Remove from the oven, and top evenly with remaining goat cheese and chives. Sprinkle with a bit of parmesan cheese, if using. Either serve as is or break the eggs up into more of a scramble consistency before serving.

Leftovers will keep tightly sealed in the refrigerator for 4 days or in the freezer for 2 months. Reheat in a 300° F oven until just warmed through; don't cook any longer than necessary. Reheat from the freezer by first thawing them overnight in the fridge before using the same reheating method.

> *Ideas for*
> ## LEFTOVER GOAT CHEESE
>
> Use any leftover goat cheese in Single-Serving French "Toast" Waffles (page 97), Chickpea, Avocado & Goat Cheese Salad (page 286), Carrot & Zucchini Ribbons with Lemony Pistachio Pesto (page 151), or as a topping for Cozy Chunky Minestrone Soup (page 281).

Sweet Breakfasts

While I have a newfound love and respect for savory breakfasts, it's just more fun to develop brekkies on the sweeter side! I mean, who doesn't love the idea of a morning meal that tastes as decadent as dessert? And here, of course, indulgent-tasting recipes are actually packed with nutrition for your body. This chapter runs the gamut from grain-free goodies like my fluffy Chocolate Chip Cookie Dough Pancakes, to vegan delights á la my Chewy Peanut Butter Latte Oats, and even low-carb options such as my French "Toast" Waffles. You'll also see that some are single-serving and some are big-batch. I even include two grab-and-go bar recipes, and everything in this chapter is freezer-friendly, making busy weekday mornings a little easier. Whichever dish(es) you choose, I'm honored to be able to make your mornings feel special, while still being healthy.

Chocolate Chip Banana Bread Steel-Cut Oats

HANDS-ON TIME: 10 min | **TOTAL TIME:** 45 min (Instant Pot); 4h, 10 min to 7 h, 10 min (Crock-Pot)

YIELD: 4 to 6 servings | **OPTION:** DF GF

I absolutely adore the texture of steel-cut oats: they're chewy and dense and slightly nutty. However, I don't adore watching them like a hawk on the stove for 25 minutes. Thus, steel-cut oats are a dreamy candidate for the Instant Pot. Much like with a Crock-Pot, your only job is to throw in everything in, give it a little stir, and relax. As with every Instant Pot recipe in the cookbook, both the Instant Pot method and the Crock-Pot method share a fabulous result; here, that looks like a bowl of creamy, fluffy oats with a pleasant "bite" to them. As if the melty-banana and toasted walnuts weren't inviting enough, adding a handful of chocolate chips to each serving will have you looking forward to breakfast each day of the week.

- ¾ cup raw walnuts (sub pecans)
- 1 cup steel-cut oats (GF sub steel cut oats)
- 1 15-ounce can full-fat coconut milk
- 2 tablespoons coconut sugar (omit for a less sweet version or sub monkfruit sweetener)
- 2 extremely ripe bananas, roughly mashed (1 cup mashed)
- 1 teaspoon vanilla extract (sub ¼ teaspoon maple extract)
- ¼ teaspoon sea salt
- 1½ cups water
- ¾ cup semi-sweet chocolate chips or chopped chocolate (optional but recommended) (DF sub vegan chocolate chips)

Instant Pot Version: Preheat oven to 350° F. Place walnuts on a baking sheet. Roast for 10-12 minutes, until fragrant and slightly darkened in color. Set aside to cool.

Combine all remaining ingredients except chocolate chips in the Instant Pot canister, and stir well. Secure lid, and set Instant Pot to "Manual" 12 minutes. When the Instant Pot beeps to signal the end of the cooking time, allow pressure to release naturally, 18 to 20 minutes. When you open the Instant Pot, the bananas will look really strange; don't worry! Just stir them into the oatmeal.

Crock-Pot Version: Combine oats, coconut milk, coconut sugar, bananas, vanilla, salt, and water in the Crock-Pot, and stir well. Turn Crock-Pot to low, and cook for 4 to 7 hours. The short cooking time will give you a chewier texture (my preference), and the long cooking time will give you a creamier texture.

While oats are cooking, preheat oven to 350° F. Place walnuts on a baking sheet. Roast for 10-12 minutes, until fragrant and slightly darkened in color. Set aside to cool. If the oats won't be ready for a few hours, store cooled walnuts in an airtight container.

(continued on next page)

CHOCOLATE CHIP BANANA BREAD
STEEL-CUT OATS *(continued)*

Both Versions: Once oats are cooked, roughly chop walnuts. Serve oats with a sprinkle of walnuts and chocolate chips, if using. (I suggest letting the oats stand a few minutes after adding the chips, so they get all melty.)

Leftovers will keep tightly sealed in the refrigerator for 5 days or in the freezer for 3 months. Freeze in individual portions. Remove portions from the freezer, and place in the fridge overnight to thaw before reheating the next morning. To reheat, add a serving of oats to a small saucepan along with some water or unsweetened almond milk (approximately ¼ cup per serving). Turn heat to medium-low, and cook, stirring, until creamy and warmed through.

Oil-Free Apple Cinnamon Oatmeal Bars

Vg DF | **HANDS-ON TIME:** 40 min | **TOTAL TIME:** 1 h, 40 min | **YIELD:** 8 to 10 bars | **OPTION:** GF

A few years ago, I made a variation of these bars for a blog post that quickly became one of my all-time most popular. I can't say for sure why, but I'd wager it has to do with their ease and versatility, to say nothing of their flavor, which is something like warm apple pie meets oatmeal in bar form. Deviating from the original recipe, I made these bars vegan, simplified the instructions, and threw in raisins and walnuts for added pops of sweetness and crunch. I love to slightly under-bake these, so the middle has a gooey, almost "overnight oats" texture. Even then, they hold together beautifully, making for a fantastic grab-and-go breakfast on busy mornings.

Preheat oven to 350° F. Place walnuts on a baking sheet. Roast for 10-12 minutes, until fragrant and slightly darkened in color. Allow to cool for 5 minutes, then roughly chop.

Decrease oven to 325° F. Line an 8-inch square baking dish with parchment, allowing at least 1-inch to overhang two opposing sides.

In a small bowl, whisk together chia seeds and water. Set aside to thicken to a gel consistency, approximately 10 minutes. (You may need to stir a few more times so the seeds don't clump.)

Place 2½ cups oats in a food processor or high-powered blender, and blend until it forms a fine flour consistency. Transfer to a large mixing bowl along with remaining 1 cup oats, cinnamon, baking powder, salt, raisins, and walnuts. Whisk to incorporate.

Roughly chop one of the apples to make approximately 2 cups. (I don't peel the apple, but you can if you like.) Place apple pieces in a blender along with maple syrup, almond milk, vanilla extract, and chia seed gel. Purée until smooth (it's okay if there are some small apple bits). Pour into the dry mixture, and stir to form a thick batter.

Spoon approximately half of the batter into the baking dish, and spread into an even layer. Use a dampened spatula to help even out the thickness without sticking.

(continued on next page)

Ingredients

½ cup raw walnuts

1 tablespoon chia seeds

3 tablespoons water

3½ cups rolled oats (GF sub gluten-free oats), divided

2 teaspoons ground cinnamon

1 teaspoon baking powder

¼ teaspoon sea salt

½ cup raisins (optional but recommended) (can sub chopped pitted medjool dates)

2 medium red apples (I like Honeycrisp or Pink Lady)

⅓ cup maple syrup

½ cup unsweetened almond or cashew milk

1 teaspoon vanilla extract

Ideas for
LEFTOVER RAISINS

You can use any leftover raisins in Grain-Free Morning Glory Muffins (page 110) or add them to Gooey Pecan Cinnamon Rolls (page 104) or Pumpkin Spice Cake (page 305).

OIL-FREE APPLE CINNAMON
OATMEAL BARS *(continued)*

Cut the remaining apple into half-moon slices, as thin as you can get them (⅛ to ¼ inch). Place slices in a slightly overlapping layer over the batter, covering the surface and pressing down gently. Save any slices that don't fit to use on top (see photos). Spread remaining batter over the apple layer, again using a dampened spatula to help cover the whole surface. Arrange any leftover apple slices on top, gently pressing them into the oat mixture.

Bake for 22 to 25 minutes, then allow to cool for 15 minutes. Use the overhanging parchment paper to remove from the baking dish. Allow to cool for another 20 minutes before slicing with a sharp knife.

Bars will keep tightly sealed at room temperature for 2 days, in the refrigerator for 6 days, or in the freezer for 3 months.

NOTE

Bake for 22 minutes for a gooey, oatmeal-like texture in the middle or 25 minutes for bars that are more thoroughly set.

Chewy Peanut Butter Latte Oats

  HANDS-ON TIME: 8 min | **TOTAL TIME:** 25 min | **YIELD:** 1 serving | **OPTION:** GF

Here's the deal: as much as I adore a big bowl of creamy oats, I've developed an equal fondness for what I call "chewy oats." Chewy oats maintain their oaty-shape, instead of dissolving through the process of releasing starch. Most of the time, oats and cold water are added to a pot, then brought to temperature and stirred. To create chewy oats, the key is to *first bring the water to boil*, then add the oats and leave them be *without stirring*. This prevents that starch-release, so you get a chewy texture instead of creamy. To make them even more inviting, I combined peanut butter and cold-brew coffee for a flavor combo that will have you jumping out of bed on the coldest days. There's a lot of room for personalization, so have fun tweaking the amount of peanut butter, coffee, salt, and coconut sugar—you get the picture.

Place water in a small saucepan (I use a 1-quart pan), and bring to a boil. Once water is boiling, add oats and salt, then reduce heat to low. Stir only once to distribute salt, then allow to simmer until water has evaporated and oats are plump but not sticking to the bottom of the pan (tilt the pan to check), approximately 15 minutes. Resist the temptation to stir while cooking.

When oats are ready, remove from the heat, and add peanut butter, coffee, vanilla, and coconut sugar, stirring just enough to incorporate. Don't overstir. Taste for sweetness, and add more sweetener if you like. For a thinner consistency add a few tablespoons of almond milk. Serve immediately.

You can make this the night before and reheat the next morning in a small saucepan over low heat, adding a bit of water or almond milk. Stir infrequently, and heat until creamy and warmed through. You can double the recipe and store it in the refrigerator for 4 days or in the freezer for 3 months. If you more than double the recipe, the ingredient ratios start to change, so you'll have to play around with it.

1 cup filtered water

½ cup rolled oats (GF sub gluten-free oats)

Pinch sea salt

1 to 2 tablespoons unsweetened, unsalted peanut butter, to taste (I use 2 tablespoons) (sub almond butter)

2 to 4 tablespoons cold-brew coffee

¼ teaspoon vanilla extract

1 tablespoon coconut sugar, or more to taste (sub maple syrup, honey, or monkfruit sweetener)

2 tablespoons unsweetened almond milk (optional)

NOTE

You can sub 1 to 2 teaspoons instant coffee for the cold-brew coffee, but dissolve it first in 2 tablespoons water. You can also use both for an extra strong coffee flavor.

Chocolate Chip Cookie Dough Pancakes

V GF | **HANDS-ON TIME:** 40 to 50 min | **TOTAL TIME:** 40 to 50 min | **YIELD:** 20 3- to 4-inch pancakes

 | **OPTION:** DF

Since I've never met a pancake I didn't like, I really wanted to take on the challenge of making a grain-free pancake. I prefer ones that are soft and fluffy but still dense enough to keep me going all morning. If you agree, then you will adore these coconut flour-based pancakes. Patience is key in this recipe; if you turn the heat too high in the interest of speed, you'll have a smoky, stack with raw middles instead of one that is golden brown and cooked throughout. I promise it's worth the time, especially when you realize how much they truly taste like Chocolate Chip Cookie Dough.

Combine all dry ingredients except chocolate chips in a large mixing bowl, and whisk to incorporate. Use your fingers to break up any coconut flour clumps.

Combine all wet ingredients in a separate mixing bowl, and whisk to incorporate.

Add wet ingredients to dry, and mix until smooth. Fold chocolate chips into the batter.

Heat a cast-iron skillet or other nonstick pan over medium-low heat. If you don't have a nonstick pan, liberally coat the pan with avocado oil.

Here's the key: these pancakes require patience and paying attention to the heat level. The pan is hot enough when you hover your hand over it a few inches and can feel heat radiating from the surface. When it's ready, stir the batter to evenly distribute the chocolate chips. Add a very scant ¼ cup batter (approximately 3 tablespoons) to pan, forming your first pancake. Repeat with as many pancakes as you can fit, leaving at least 1 inch between. Cook the pancakes for 5 to 6 minutes. This will seem like forever, but if you rush it by cooking over too much heat, they will burn. Flip and cook for another minute (this side is faster!).

For the next round, you will likely need to turn down the heat, and they'll still cook a little faster, so use a spatula to gently slide under the the pancakes to see if they are solid enough to flip. Repeat until all pancake batter is gone, then enjoy immediately.

Once cooled completely, leftover pancakes will keep tightly sealed in the refrigerator for 5 days or in the freezer for 3 months.

DRY INGREDIENTS:

½ cup coconut flour

¼ cup arrowroot starch (sub cornstarch)

1 teaspoon baking powder

½ teaspoon baking soda

¼ teaspoon sea salt

½ cup dark or semi-sweet chocolate chips or chopped chocolate (DF sub vegan chocolate chips)

WET INGREDIENTS:

2 large eggs

1 teaspoon apple cider vinegar

1 scant cup unsweetened almond milk (just a tablespoon or two less than 1 cup)

¼ cup avocado oil, plus more for greasing if not using nonstick pan

¼ cup maple syrup

1 teaspoon vanilla extract

NOTE

Instead of stirring the chocolate chips into the pancake batter, you can opt to place the chips on top of the pancake batter once you've spooned it into the pan. You'll only need about 1 teaspoon chips per pancake, so this method is good if you want to decrease the sugar just a bit.

Single-Serving French "Toast" Waffle

(V) | **HANDS-ON TIME:** 6 min | **TOTAL TIME:** 20 min | **YIELD:** 1 serving | (clock) | **OPTIONS:** (DF) (K)

I developed this recipe when I was focusing on lower-carb recipes to combat my sugar cravings. I named them "French Toast" waffles, because they have the slightly cinnamon-sweet-eggy flavor and consistency of French toast. And I am *here* for it. I love that I can go the single-serving route when I don't want leftovers, but I can also make a few at a time and freeze them. I've now made these waffles countless times with countless toppings, but my favorite toppings are thawed frozen berries and melted coconut butter or chocolate chips and a drizzle of maple syrup.

Thoroughly grease the cooking plates of a waffle maker with avocado oil, even if they are nonstick. (I use a pastry brush to do this.) Plug in waffle maker and preheat.

Combine remaining ingredients in a blender, and purée until smooth. Allow to sit for 10 minutes so it can thicken, then give it a stir. You can also whisk ingredients together in a mixing bowl, then allow to thicken.

Pour batter into waffle maker, close, and cook for approximately 4 minutes (this may vary slightly based on your particular brand). When it's ready, the waffle should come out easily using a fork, and it will be a light golden-brown color.

Serve immediately however you like. If you make more than one waffle, extras will keep tightly sealed in the refrigerator for 5 days or in the freezer for 3 months. Cool completely before storing.

NOTES

If you want to make two waffles, double the batter, and note that each waffle is approximately ¾ cup batter.

Add 2 tablespoons chocolate chips to your batter. Nuff said!

SPECIAL EQUIPMENT:

Waffle iron

INGREDIENTS:

Avocado oil for greasing

2 tablespoons plus 1 teaspoon coconut flour

2 large eggs

3 tablespoons plain goat or cream cheese ((DF) sub canned full-fat coconut milk)

2 teaspoons chia seeds

½ teaspoon baking powder

¼ teaspoon baking soda

⅛ teaspoon sea salt

⅛ teaspoon ground cinnamon

½ teaspoon apple cider vinegar

¼ teaspoon vanilla extract

2 teaspoons coconut sugar ((K) sub monkfruit sweetener) (optional)

Ideas for
LEFTOVER GOAT CHEESE AND CREAM CHEESE

If you have leftover goat cheese, use it in Chive & Goat Cheese Fluffy Baked Eggs (page 82), as a topping for Cozy Chunky Minestrone Soup (page 281), or on Chickpea, Avocado & Goat Cheese Salad (page 286). If you have leftover cream cheese, use it in Smoked Salmon, Olive & Pecan Spread (page 202).

Keto-Friendly No-Bake Breakfast Bars

 | **HANDS-ON TIME:** 10 min | **TOTAL TIME:** 2 h, 30 min | **YIELD:** 9 to 12 bars | | **OPTIONS:**

Oh, the internal debate I had about using the word *keto* in the description of these breakfast bars. But here's the deal: what makes these bars special is their high-fat, low-carbohydrate nutritional profile. As a result, these babies will keep you feeling full, satisfied, and "hanger" free for a long time. That doesn't make them "better" than your favorite oaty or fruity bar, as some people do better with a higher complex-carb lifestyle. But it does make them a fantastic fit for all of my readers who are following a ketogenic diet, and there are a lot of you. That said, anyone will enjoy these breakfast bars, as they are addictively delicious and a breeze to throw together—two main steps, almost zero cleanup, a few hours in the fridge, and you're set for the week. Plus, my mom makes these often, which is pretty much the highest seal of approval for any recipe in this book.

Line an 8-inch square baking dish with parchment paper.

Combine almond flour, sunflower seeds, pumpkin seeds, coconut, chia seeds, and salt in a food processor. Process until it forms a fine crumble, approximately 20 seconds.

Add all remaining ingredients (I use 2 tablespoons monkfruit sweetener, so start with that and add more to taste) to food processor, and process until it forms a cohesive sticky dough. Scoop into the baking dish, and use a dampened spatula to press into an even layer. Garnish with sea salt. Refrigerate until firm to touch, at least 2 hours.

To slice into bars, allow the pan to sit at room temperature for 15 to 20 minutes, until a sharp knife goes through easily (will depend on the temperature of your room). If it's too firm, the pieces will crumble. Slice into whatever shapes or sizes you like. (I usually make 9 if I'm using them just for breakfasts or 12 if I want them to double as snacks.)

Bars will keep tightly sealed in the refrigerator for 1 week or in the freezer for 3 months. If freezing, transfer them to the fridge the night before you want to enjoy them.

½ cup blanched almond flour

½ cup raw sunflower seeds

½ cup raw pumpkin seeds

½ cup unsweetened shredded coconut

¼ cup chia seeds

Pinch sea salt

2 to 4 tablespoons monkfruit sweetener (can sub coconut sugar, but note that it makes them higher-carb)

6 tablespoons melted butter (Vg DF sub coconut oil)

½ cup runny unsweetened, unsalted almond butter (pourable consistency)

1 teaspoon vanilla extract

Coarse sea salt for garnish

SERVING SUGGESTION

To make chocolate-coated bars as pictured, combine ⅓ cup chocolate chips (use stevia-sweetened chips for sugar-free) and 1 tablespoon butter or coconut oil in a microwave-safe bowl. Microwave in 20 second increments, stirring in between, until melted. Place the cooled and cut bars on a baking sheet lined with parchment paper Using a fork, drizzle the chocolate on top. To coat them completely, dip the bars in the chocolate, and use a spoon to thoroughly cover them, then use a fork to lift them out of the chocolate.

Strawberry Almond Cobbler

  HANDS-ON TIME: 15 min | **TOTAL TIME:** 1 h, 10 min | **YIELD:** 6 servings | **OPTION:** DF P

It was a balmy mid-April day in Nashville, and I practically squealed when I saw the first reasonably priced strawberries of the year. After eating several pints unadorned, I found myself craving a berry breakfast cobbler. I had actually "finished" this chapter already, but there was one recipe I didn't completely love. So I threw together the first draft of this cobbler and immediately knew that it would edge out the other recipe. The juicy pop of baked strawberries with slightly sweet, almond-infused cobbler topping is a dream to wake up to. As much as I love this version, I bet this dish would be wonderful with blackberries, fresh peaches, or cherries. If you find yourself with a hankering for a fruity breakfast in the dead of winter, you can sub approximately 24 ounces frozen berries. Just make sure to turn the oven down to 350° F, and bake a bit longer. I've also served this cobbler as dessert with scoops of vanilla ice cream dotted over the top.

2 pints strawberries, leaves and stems removed and chopped into approximately ¾-inch pieces

2 tablespoons arrowroot starch (sub cornstarch)

8 tablespoons coconut sugar, divided (sub 6 tablespoons monkfruit sweetener)

Pinch sea salt

1 cup blanched almond flour

⅔ cup roasted, unsalted almonds, roughly chopped into ¼-inch pieces (sub slivered almonds—no need to chop)

1 teaspoon baking powder

1 large egg, room temperature

6 tablespoons butter, melted (DF P sub coconut oil)

1 teaspoon almond extract

Preheat oven to 375° F. Line a 9 × 13 × 2-inch baking dish with parchment paper.

In a medium mixing bowl, combine strawberries, arrowroot starch, and 3 tablespoons coconut sugar (if subbing monkfruit sweetener, use 2 tablespoons). Toss to coat, then spread evenly in the baking dish.

Rinse mixing bowl, and wipe dry (no need to fully clean). Combine remaining 5 tablespoons coconut sugar (or 4 tablespoons monkfruit sweetener if subbing), salt, almond flour, almonds, and baking powder in the bowl. Stir to incorporate.

In a separate small bowl, crack egg, then add melted butter and almond extract. Whisk until creamy, then pour into dry ingredients. Stir to combine.

Dollop the dough evenly over strawberries. (My dollops are approximately 3 tablespoons each.) Bake cobbler for 40 minutes, or until golden brown and puffy on top. Allow to cool for at least 15 minutes before serving.

Leftovers will keep tightly sealed in the refrigerator for 5 days or in the freezer for 3 months.

Chapter 5

BAKERY

*B*aking is 100 percent my least expensive and most accessible form of therapy. When I'm feeling a little blue or worn out or lazy, baking something scrumptious and nourishing is a surefire way to improve my mood and day. Perhaps it's the precision required—when I'm measuring, timing, cracking, and mixing, my brain cannot wander in a million directions. I am truly living in the moment, instead of worrying about what's happened or what's to come. And more often than not, the actual present moment is just fine! In addition to the baking process, there are few things more lovely than enjoying a freshly baked good. Now that I'm back on the coffee train, I relish alternating bites of a Double Chocolate Avocado Blender Muffin or Spiced Pear Sour Cream Loaf with sips of a hot, creamy coffee. These goodies are also perfect freezer companions, thawing and reheating beautifully for months on end. So if you find yourself on a baking bender with my PB&J Swirl Banana Bread or Lemon "Poppy" Chia Scones, know that they're the gift that keeps on giving, for your mind and your body.

Gooey Pecan Cinnamon Rolls

with CREAM CHEESE FROSTING

(V) | **HANDS-ON TIME:** 45 min | **TOTAL TIME:** 1 h, 5 min | **YIELD:** approximately 10 rolls | (+) | **OPTIONS:** (Vg) (DF)

As soon as I decided to use whole-wheat pizza dough for a few recipes in the book, I knew I needed to make cinnamon rolls. No rising required, no dealing with yeast, just easy-peasy roll-and-bake gooey goodness. Little did I know that I'd be creating a monster *(me)*, because these are almost too alluringly simple to yield something so divine. Nonetheless, these are a much healthier option than traditional cinnamon rolls—swapping white flour for whole-grain flour, refined sugar for coconut sugar, and offering lighter icing alternatives. Feel free to use different nuts or add some chocolate chips, dried cranberries, or raisins. I have an inkling that these will be your new favorite holiday breakfast.

Remove dough from the fridge, and allow it to sit at room temperature for 20 minutes.

Preheat oven to 350° F. Place pecans on a baking sheet. Roast for 10 to 12 minutes, until fragrant and slightly darkened in color. Set aside to cool.

Make the Cream Cheese Frosting: While pecans are roasting, combine cream cheese, maple syrup, and vanilla in the bowl of a stand mixer, and beat on medium speed until smooth and creamy. You can also do this in a mixing bowl with a hand mixer. Add arrowroot starch by the tablespoon to thicken as you like. (I use ¼ cup arrowroot starch.) Set aside until the rolls are baked.

Make the Pecan Cinnamon Rolls: Combine 3 tablespoons melted butter, coconut sugar, cinnamon, salt, and vanilla in a mixing bowl, and stir until it forms a thick paste.

Once the dough has been at room temperature for 20 minutes, grease a large cutting board with a thin layer of avocado oil. Gently spread dough into a rectangle (18 × 9 inches) on the cutting board. If it breaks, pinch the dough back together. (Dough will be quite thin.) If it keeps breaking, allow it to sit for a few more minutes. Eventually it will spread.

Once pecans have cooled, place in a food processor, and pulse until they are finely chopped but not powdery. Alternately, you can finely chop by hand. Using small pieces will ensure they stick to the dough and don't fall out the bottom of the rolls.

(continued on page 106)

SPECIAL EQUIPMENT:

Tape Measure

PECAN CINNAMON ROLLS:

1 pound whole-wheat pizza dough

1¼ cups raw pecans (sub walnuts)

¼ cup melted butter ((Vg) (DF) sub coconut oil), divided

½ cup coconut sugar (sub ⅓ cup monkfruit sweetener)

¾ teaspoon gound cinnamon

¼ teaspoon sea salt

1 teaspoon vanilla extract

Avocado oil for greasing

CREAM CHEESE FROSTING:

8 ounces full-fat cream cheese, softened at room temperature for ½ to 1 hour ((Vg) (DF) sub vegan cream cheese)

¼ cup maple syrup

¼ teaspoon vanilla extract

Arrowroot starch for thickening (sub cornstarch) (optional)

GOOEY PECAN CINNAMON ROLLS WITH CREAM CHEESE FROSTING *(continued)*

Evenly dollop cinnamon-sugar paste over the dough, and spread in an even layer, leaving approximately ½ inch free around the edges. It's okay if it's not perfect; it will melt together as it bakes. Top with pecan pieces in an even layer, and gently press them into the dough. (It might look like a lot of pecans, but trust me.)

Starting from one long side, gently roll into a log-shape, pinching the dough together at the end to seal. Squeeze the log to make it a little more compact and shorter, ensuring everything stays together.

Using a very sharp knife, slice the log into approximately 10 even disks, and place them in an 8- to 10-inch cast-iron skillet or round nonstick pan. Leave at least ¾ inch between each. Gently press down on each roll to flatten by about ¼ inch—you want them to be a little squattier. Some pecans will fall out; just throw them in the skillet as well.

Brush rolls with remaining 1 tablespoon melted butter, then bake for 18 minutes. For a golden-brown top, place under the broiler for 2 to 3 minutes. Watch closely.

Remove the rolls from the oven, and immediately cover them with a generous layer of frosting.

Leftovers will keep tightly sealed in the refrigerator for 4 days or in the freezer for 3 months. I reheat them in the microwave for 20 to 25 seconds for best results, but you can also reheat in the oven at 300° F until warmed through.

Double Chocolate Avocado Blender Muffins

  | **HANDS-ON TIME:** 15 min | **TOTAL TIME:** 1 h, 10 min | **YIELD:** 6 servings | **OPTIONS:** DF K

Easily one of my all-time favorite recipes, these muffins were created on a skeptical whim to use up some leftover avocado. From the Chocolate Chia Pudding in my first book, I knew that the flavor combo could work, but I wasn't sure if they'd rise like traditional muffins. I was also determined to make them one-step-simple in the blender. Well, somehow they turned out on round one, and it took everything in my power not to eat the entire batch in a day. If you are a devoted chocolate lover like me, these rich, ultra-fudgy muffins are calling your name. You could also play with adding ⅓ cup chopped roasted walnuts, and I've even gone so far as to melt together equal parts peanut butter, chocolate chips, and coconut oil in the microwave and use it as a glaze or frosting.

Preheat oven to 350° F. Line a 12-cup cupcake tin (or two 6-cup tins) with liners.

Combine all ingredients except chocolate chips, in the order listed, in a high-powered blender or food processor. Purée until smooth. If using a blender, you may need to use the tamper to help blend. You can also stop a few times to scrape down with a spatula, which can help ensure everything is blended evenly.

Remove food processor or blender container from the base (carefully remove food processor blade as well), then stir in ¾ cup chocolate chips (or 1 cup chocolate chunks). Distribute batter evenly among the cupcake liners, filling approximately three-quarters of the way. Shake tins gently to even out batter. Sprinkle batter with remaining ⅓ cup chocolate chips (or ¼ cup chocolate chunks).

Bake for 17 minutes, until muffins are firm to touch but "jiggle" a little. Resist the urge to open the oven! Allow to cool in the tin for 10 minutes. The muffins will deflate just a bit but should not cave in. After 10 minutes, use a fork to gently remove muffins from tins. They will still be pretty soft at this point, but they will continue to firm as they cool. Place on a cooling rack, and allow to cool for another 15 minutes. Sprinkle coarse sea salt on top of muffins.

Leftover muffins will keep tightly sealed at room temperature for 2 days, in the refrigerator for 5 days, or in the freezer for 3 months. (I keep my muffins in the refrigerator.) To reheat, microwave them for 13 seconds.

(continued on page 109)

1 cup unsweetened almond milk

2 large eggs, room temperature

1 medium ripe avocado, mashed (½ cup)

½ cup maple syrup

2 teaspoons vanilla extract

1 teaspoon apple cider vinegar or white vinegar

½ cup Dutch-processed cocoa powder (you can use cacao, but it will be a little lighter in color, and the flavor isn't quite as rich)

1½ teaspoons baking powder

1 teaspoon baking soda

⅛ teaspoon sea salt

1 cup chickpea flour

¾ cup plus ⅓ cup dark or semi-sweet chocolate chips (sub 1¼ cups dark chocolate chunks) (DF sub vegan chocolate chips)

Coarse sea salt for garnish

NOTE

Chickpea flour is not interchangeable with other flours. If you want to sub another flour, you will have to play with the ratios. See "Low-sugar version" (page 109) for almond flour substitution.

DOUBLE CHOCOLATE AVOCADO BLENDER MUFFINS *(continued)*

🇰 LOW-SUGAR VERSION

Reduce the almond milk to ½ cup, sub ½ cup monkfruit sweetener for maple syrup, sub 1 cup blanched almond flour for chickpea flour, and sub stevia-sweetened chocolate chips for regular chips. You'll have enough batter to fill tins approximately two-thirds of the way full instead of three-quarters. Bake for 22 minutes, or until a toothpick inserted into the center comes out mostly clean with just a bit of batter and the muffins feel firm to touch. Cooling instructions are the same.

Grain-Free Morning Glory Muffins

Ⓥ ⒼⒻ ⒹⒻ Ⓟ | **HANDS-ON TIME:** 35 min | **TOTAL TIME:** 1 h, 35 min | **YIELD:** 12 muffins

This is another blog-to-book recipe, because it was such a hit! Actually, the original recipe made jumbo-sized muffins and used buckwheat flour, but most of my readers don't have a jumbo muffin tin or buckwheat lying around. Thus, this 2.0 version uses staple LL Balanced ingredients and is even more delicious, in my opinion. These low-sugar, grain-free muffins are portable, freezable, and chock-full of fiber and micronutrients. They make you feel like you've treated yourself to something really special. You can also customize them to your taste: use pecans instead of walnuts or pear instead of apple, or sub ½ cup chocolate chips for the raisins or currants.

Preheat oven to 350° F. Line a 12-cup cupcake tin (or two 6-cup tins) with liners.

Place walnuts on a baking sheet. Roast for 10-12 minutes, until fragrant and slightly darkened in color. Set aside to cool for at least 5 minutes.

Combine almond flour, coconut flour, monkfruit, cinnamon, baking soda, and salt in a large mixing bowl, and whisk to incorporate.

Crack eggs into a separate mixing bowl. Stir in avocado oil, coconut milk, and vanilla.

Place chopped apples and carrots in a food processor or high-powered blender, and pulse until a chunky crumble forms. Stir into wet ingredients.

Add wet ingredients to dry, and stir until evenly incorporated. Roughly chop walnuts, and fold into the batter along with raisins, if using.

Evenly scoop batter into cupcake liners, using approximately 6 tablespoons per muffin. Use lightly dampened fingers or spatula to gently press the batter into an even layer. It should be even with the top of the liners.

Bake muffins for 27 minutes, or until tops are golden brown and firm to touch. Allow to cool in the tins for 15 minutes before removing them and placing on a cooling rack. Allow to cool for another 15 minutes before enjoying.

Leftover muffins will keep tightly sealed at room temperature for 2 days, in the refrigerator for 4 days, or in the freezer for 3 months.

½ cup raw walnuts

1½ cups blanched almond flour

⅓ cup coconut flour

½ cup monkfruit sweetener (sub ⅔ cup coconut sugar)

2 teaspoons ground cinnamon

2 teaspoons baking soda

½ teaspoon sea salt

4 large eggs, room temperature

⅓ cup avocado oil

¾ cup canned full-fat coconut milk

2 teaspoons vanilla extract

1 medium red apple, cored and chopped into 1-inch chunks (1¼ cups)

2 medium carrots, peeled and chopped into 1-inch chunks (1 cup)

⅓ cup raisins or dried currants (my preference) (optional)

NOTE

I use Pink Lady or Honeycrisp apples. I keep the skin on, but you can peel them if you prefer.

Lemon "Poppy" Chia Scones

 | **HANDS-ON TIME:** 15 min | **TOTAL TIME:** 45 min | **YIELD:** 6 scones | | **OPTION:** DF

I cannot tell y'all how many grain-free scone recipes I've tested over the years. Actually, I can: a heckuva lot. I've desperately wanted to offer y'all a healthier version of this classic baked good, but my attempts always resulted in a muffin in scone form. I kept at it until I created this Lemon "Poppy" Chia version. Finally! The key was using less coconut flour than I use in loaves or muffins, only one egg, and just enough liquid to hold the dough together. The zip from lemon zest and juice is an ideal contrast to the hearty scone texture, and my simple glaze makes enjoying them even more decadent.

Preheat oven to 350° F. Line a baking sheet with parchment paper.

Make the Scones: Combine all dry ingredients in a large mixing bowl, and whisk to incorporate. Combine all wet ingredients in a mixing bowl, and whisk to incorporate.

Add wet ingredients to dry, and fold until a dry dough forms (it shouldn't completely crumble, but it shouldn't be sticky). If it seems too dry, you can add almond milk, 1 teaspoon at a time, until it holds together. Form dough into a ball, place on the baking sheet, and flatten into a 6-inch circle, approximately 1 inch high. Use lightly dampened fingers to smooth any cracked sides.

Using a sharp knife, slice dough into 6 triangles. Gently separate them, and spread at least 1 inch apart on the baking sheet.

Bake for 20 to 22 minutes, until the edges and bottoms are golden brown. Allow to cool for 10 minutes on the baking sheet, then carefully transfer to a cooling rack. Place a piece of parchment under the rack to capture drippings from the glaze.

Make the Glaze: Whisk all glaze ingredients together in a microwave-safe bowl. If it's not mixing well, microwave in 10-second intervals, stirring between, until smooth and creamy. Add more almond milk as needed to reach a pourable consistency. Pour glaze over scones while they are still somewhat warm. Enjoy immediately.

Scones will keep tightly sealed at room temperature for 3 days or in the freezer for 3 months.

DRY INGREDIENTS:

1 cup blanched almond flour

½ cup coconut flour

6 tablespoons monkfruit sweetener (sub coconut sugar; note that the result will be a touch darker in color)

½ teaspoon baking powder

¼ teaspoon baking soda

¼ teaspoon sea salt

2 tablespoons chia seeds

Zest from 2 lemons (2 tablespoons loosely packed)

WET INGREDIENTS:

1 large egg, room temperature

3 tablespoons butter, melted (DF sub melted coconut oil)

3 tablespoons unsweetened almond milk

Juice from ½ lemon (1 tablespoon)

¾ teaspoon almond extract

GLAZE:

2 tablespoons melted coconut butter (sub creamy almond butter, but note that it will look different than in the photo)

Juice from ½ lemon (1 tablespoon)

1 to 3 tablespoons unsweetened almond milk, room temperature

2 drops liquid stevia, or to taste

PB&J Swirl Banana Bread

(V) (GF) (DF) | **HANDS-ON TIME:** 20 min | **TOTAL TIME:** 1 h, 50 min | **YIELD:** 1 loaf (8 to 10 servings) | **OPTION:** (P)

For the last two years, this PB&J Swirl Banana Bread has stayed at the top of my list of hit recipes. I get it; peanut butter and jelly is probably the best food duo of all time, and who doesn't love a thick slice of banana bread? If you're not a fan of peanut butter (?!?) or you can't use it for some reason, almond butter is fantastic in this recipe as well. I have used strawberry, blackberry, blueberry, and raspberry jams, and the last is my favorite. While strawberry jam tastes fabulous, it doesn't show up very well in the swirl. So if you're looking for some serious "swirlage," I suggest using one of the others.

Preheat oven to 350° F. Line a nonstick 9 × 5 × 3-inch loaf pan with parchment paper. Make sure at least 1 inch overhangs the sides.

Combine almond flour, arrowroot starch, baking powder, and salt in a large mixing bowl, and whisk carefully (to avoid a starch cloud) to blend.

Combine bananas, eggs, coconut sugar, ⅓ cup peanut butter, and vanilla in a high-powered blender or food processor, and blend or process until smooth. You can also mash bananas well in a mixing bowl, then stir in the eggs, coconut sugar, peanut butter, and vanilla. Scrape banana mixture into the dry ingredients, and stir to evenly blend.

Scrape half of the batter into the loaf pan, and spread in an even layer. Dollop small spoonfuls of the remaining ⅓ cup peanut butter and ¼ cup jam over batter. Try to keep the dollops away from the sides of the tin; this will ensure that your slices hold together. Use a toothpick or butter knife to swirl peanut butter and jam together. Top with remaining batter, then dollop on the remaining ¼ cup jam. Swirl jam over the top.

Bake for 35 minutes, then carefully cover with tented aluminum foil to prevent further browning. Bake for another 17 to 20 minutes, until a toothpick inserted in the center comes out clean and the edges are golden brown.

Allow to cool for 15 minutes. Use the sides of the parchment paper to remove bread, and place it on a cooling rack. Allow to cool for another 20 minutes before slicing.

Bread will keep tightly sealed at room temperature for 2 days, in the refrigerator for 5 days, or in the freezer for 3 months.

3 cups blanched almond flour

½ cup arrowroot starch (sub cornstarch)

2 teaspoons baking powder

½ teaspoon sea salt

3 very ripe bananas, well-mashed (1½ cups)

3 large eggs, room temperature

¼ cup coconut sugar

⅔ cup unsweetened, unsalted runny peanut butter (smooth or crunchy; (P) sub almond butter), divided

1 teaspoon vanilla extract

½ cup jam or jelly of choice (I recommend a no-sugar added brand), divided

NOTE

You want the peanut butter to be runny and drippy, so you'll get the best results by using a new jar and mixing in any separated oil.

BAKERY

Raspberry "Pop" Pies

Ⓥ ⒼⒻ Ⓟ | **HANDS-ON TIME:** 35 min | **TOTAL TIME:** 1 h, 30 min | **YIELD:** 5 to 6 pies | ❄ | **OPTION:** Ⓚ

I don't give caveats with the vast majority of my recipes, but I have to shoot y'all straight. These Raspberry "Pop" Pies are not difficult to make, but they *are* a little tedious. Specifically, creating the rectangles of dough requires some patience and care. That said, your reward far outweighs a few cumbersome steps, because you will have created your very own version of a childhood favorite. The thinner you can roll out your dough, the better filling-to-crust ratio you'll get, and isn't it all about that ratio? This is such a fun recipe to tackle on a lazy weekend, and there's something incredibly satisfying about seeing beautiful golden-brown hand pies hot out of the oven. Feel free to try different berries or other fillings . . . chocolate chips and almond butter, banana and peanut butter, sautéed apples from my Apple Sausage Breakfast Bake (page 71), or even my Condensed Coconut Milk (page 345).

Make the Pastry Crust: Combine all ingredients except water in a food processor. Pulse until it forms pieces the size of small peas. (Alternately, combine almond flour, coconut flour, arrowrood starch, coconut sugar, and salt in a large mixing bowl. Whisk to incorporate, then add butter. Use fingers to rub butter into the flour until it forms pieces the size of small peas.) Add ice water, 1 tablespoon at a time, and either pulse or mix with your fingers just until it forms a shaggy dough. The amount of water will depend on the day's humidity. You want it to hold together but not feel sticky. Form dough into a disk approximately 2 inches high, then wrap with plastic wrap, and refrigerate 20 minutes.

After 20 minutes, remove dough from the fridge. Place an 18-inch piece of parchment paper on the counter, and sprinkle with a thin layer of arrowroot starch. Place dough on parchment, and sprinkle more starch on top. If your parchment is sliding, you can lightly grease the countertop to stabilize.

Using a rolling pin, roll dough into a 10 × 13-inch rectangle (as close as you can get), less than ¼-inch thick. Dust with starch as necessary to prevent sticking. Using a tape measure and a knife, cut a 4 × 3-inch rectangle. Use a spatula to gently lift the rectangle, and use it as a template to cut out as many pieces as you can (carefully place

(continued on next page)

SPECIAL EQUIPMENT:

Rolling pin

Tape measure

PASTRY CRUST:

1 cup blanched almond flour

½ cup coconut flour

½ cup arrowroot starch, plus more for dusting (sub cornstarch)

2 tablespoons coconut sugar (Ⓚ sub monkfruit sweetener)

¼ teaspoon sea salt

½ cup (1 stick) cold butter, cut into ½-inch cubes

2 to 6 tablespoons ice water

FILLING:

1¼ cups frozen raspberries (ideally organic)

3 tablespoons coconut sugar (Ⓚ sub monkfruit sweetener)

1 tablespoon arrowroot starch (sub cornstarch)

¼ teaspoon vanilla extract

Ideas for
LEFTOVER FROZEN RASPBERRIES

Use leftover frozen raspberries to make my Low-Sugar PB&J Smoothie Bowl (page 57).

---

the template piece on top of the dough, and cut around it to create another). I can usually make four rectangles with my first roll of dough. If you prefer, you can cut out a 4 × 3-inch piece of paper, and use that as your measuring template instead. Place rectangles on the baking sheet.

Gather dough scraps, sprinkle with arrowroot starch, and roll out again to ¼ inch thick. Dust with more starch as necessary. Use the template rectangle to create more pieces. Continue this process until you don't have enough dough left to make a rectangle. I can get usually get 10 to 12 rectangles total. You want an even number of rectangles.

Make the Filling: Combine all filling ingredients in a microwave-safe bowl. Microwave 15 to 25 seconds, until raspberries are soft enough to stir everything into a sticky mixture.

Assemble the Pies: Scoop approximately 2 tablespoons raspberry mixture onto the center of one of the dough rectangles. Repeat until half of the rectangles are topped with filling. If there's any filling leftover, distribute it evenly over the rectangles. Carefully top the filling with another rectangle of dough, and gently press around the edges to seal. You can use a water-dampened fork to create little tine marks around the edges. You can also use any leftover scraps to fill in cracks or breaks. Use a skewer, fork, or chopsticks to poke holes across the top for an "authentic" look. Repeat with remaining rectangles, making 5 to 6 hand pies. (Note: this process can get a little messy, and that's okay. I think they're the most beautiful when a little juice is spilling out.)

Bake pies for 22 to 25 minutes, until light golden brown around the edges. Allow to cool for 10 minutes, then gently transfer pies to a cooling rack. Allow to cool for another 10 to 15 minutes before enjoying.

Leftover pies will keep tightly sealed at room temperature for 3 days, in the refrigerator for 5 days, or in the freezer for 3 months.

NOTE

To glaze the pies as I did for the picture: Microwave ¼ cup ½-inch pieces red beet (peeled) with ¼ cup water for 30 seconds. Set aside to cool completely. Drain, saving the bright pink liquid. Combine 2 tablespoons beet water with 3 tablespoons melted coconut butter, and whisk until creamy. Then add more beet water as you like to darken color, and add more coconut butter as needed to maintain consistency. I also topped each glazed pop-pie with India Tree naturally dyed sprinkles.

Ideas for
LEFTOVER PASTRY CRUST

If you have any pastry scraps left over, gather them together, and flatten into a circle. Put a blob of peanut or almond butter in the middle, and sprinkle with some ground cinnamon and coconut sugar or monkfruit sweetener. Seal by bringing edges together to form a little pocket. Place on baking sheet, and bake as you would the raspberry-filled pies. This is just a fun little treat and a way to use all your dough.

BAKERY

Grain-Free Gingerbread Streusel Squares

 GF DF P | **HANDS-ON TIME:** 30 min | **TOTAL TIME:** 1 h, 50 min | **YIELD:** 12 squares

There are few things that make me look forward to winter, but gingerbread-flavored goodies are one. These grain-free squares are full of warm, toasty spices, and they're happiest alongside a cup of hot tea or coffee in the morning. Because of their admirable fiber, fat, and protein quotient, they are a much healthier alternative to anything in your local Starbucks pastry case.

Preheat oven to 350° F. Line an 8-inch square glass baking dish with parchment paper, allowing approximately 1 inch to overhang two opposing sides.

Place pecans on a baking sheet. Roast for 10 to 12 minutes, until fragrant and slightly darkened in color. Set aside to cool.

Place dates in a high-powered blender or food processor, and top with hot tap water. Allow to sit for 10 minutes.

In a large mixing bowl, combine 2 cups almond flour, 2 teaspoons cinnamon, 1 teaspoon ground ginger, ½ teaspoon nutmeg, and salt. Whisk to thoroughly blend.

Add molasses and vanilla to the blender or food processor with the date mixture (once it has been sitting for 10 minutes), and blend until smooth; it's okay if there are still some tiny date pieces, but you want it mostly homogeneous. Particularly with a blender, this might require a few rounds of scraping down the sides.

Pour an even amount of date mixture into two medium-sized bowls; this will be approximately ½ cup plus 1 to 2 tablespoons in each bowl (I know this is a pain but it's worth it). Add ¼ cup melted coconut oil to one bowl and stir. To the other bowl, add arrowroot starch and stir.

Add the date and coconut oil mixture to the almond flour mixture, and stir to evenly combine. It will seem quite dry, but it will all incorporate if you keep stirring (it's still a dry, crumbly dough though). Scrape this dough into the baking dish, and smooth into an even layer using a dampened spatula or dampened fingers.

Spread date and arrowroot starch mixture evenly over this base layer.

(continued on next page)

1 cup raw pecans

12 to 13 dates pitted medjool dates, room temperature (1¼ cups firmly packed)

½ cup hot water (can be from the tap, not boiling)

2¼ cups blanched almond flour, divided

2½ teaspoons ground cinnamon, divided

1½ teaspoons ground ginger, divided

¾ teaspoon ground nutmeg, divided

½ teaspoon sea salt

2 tablespoons molasses

1 teaspoon vanilla extract

6 tablespoons melted coconut oil, divided

1 tablespoon arrowroot starch (sub cornstarch)

2 tablespoons coconut sugar

BAKERY

GRAIN-FREE GINGERBREAD
STREUSEL SQUARES *(continued)*

Finely chop roasted pecans. In a small mixing bowl, combine pecans, remaining ¼ cup almond flour, remaining spices (½ teaspoon cinnamon, ½ teaspoon ginger, and ¼ teaspoon nutmeg) remaining 2 tablespoons coconut oil, and coconut sugar. Use clean fingers to mix ingredients together to form a crumble consistency. Spread crumble evenly over top of date layer, and gently press to help it stick.

Bake for 35 minutes. The bars might bubble up in the center while they bake, but they'll go down as they cool. Allow to cool for 25 minutes before using the overhanging parchment to lift out of the pan onto a cooling rack. Allow to cool for another 20 minutes before slicing.

Bars will keep tightly sealed at room temperature for 2 days, in the refrigerator for 5 days, or in the freezer for 3 months.

Ideas for
LEFTOVER DATES

If you have extra dates, you can make a sauce by placing ½ cup pitted dates, 1 cup water, and a splash of vanilla extract in a high-powered blender, and blending until creamy. Use as a topping for oatmeal or toast or as a dip for fruit. Or make my Maple Tahini Date Shake (page 53).

Blueberry Peanut Butter Crumble Bars

(V) | **HANDS-ON TIME:** 20 min | **TOTAL TIME:** 1 h, 45 min | **YIELD:** 9 bars | **OPTIONS:** (DF) (GF)

What is it about peanut butter and berries that is so universally appealing? Dense and buttery on the bottom, gooey and sweet in the middle, and doused with a generous layer of crumble topping, what's not to adore? These bars are surprisingly filling and hold together quite well (especially out of the fridge), making them a great grab-and-go breakfast option on busy mornings. That said, nothing replaces heating one up in the oven and adding an extra schmear of peanut butter and a drizzle of maple syrup for a divine indulgence.

Preheat oven to 375° F. Line an 8-inch square baking pan with parchment paper, allowing at least 1 inch to overhang two opposing sides.

Make the Base and Crumble: Place 2 cups oats in a food processor or high-powered blender, and process or blend until you reach a flour consistency (powdery with no oat chunks, approximately 30 seconds). Place oat flour in a large mixing bowl, along with remaining 1¾ cup oats, coconut sugar, salt, and cinnamon. Whisk to evenly incorporate. No need to clean the processor or blender.

In another bowl, whisk together melted butter, egg, peanut butter, and vanilla. Add to dry ingredients, and stir until evenly incorporated. (I like to do this with lightly dampened hands.) The mixture should be a semi-sticky crumble that holds together when pressed. Scrape approximately two-thirds of the crumble (approximately 3 cups, loosely packed) into the baking dish, use lightly dampened fingers to pat firmly into an even layer.

Make the Blueberry Filling: In a food processor or blender, combine all filling ingredients. Pulse or blend just until it forms an icy crumble—you shouldn't see blueberry chunks anymore, but you don't want it to turn into a liquid. Scrape blueberry filling on top of the base, and spread in an even layer. Top with remaining crumble, and press it down gently into the blueberry filling.

Bake for 40 to 45 minutes, until edges are golden brown. Allow to cool for 30 minutes in the baking dish, then use the parchment to lift from the pan. Transfer to a cooling rack, and allow to cool for another 20 minutes. Slice using a very sharp knife, wiping the knife between cuts with a damp dish towel.

Once completely cooled, bars will keep tightly sealed at room temperature for 2 days, in the refrigerator for 5 days, or in the freezer for 3 months.

BASE AND CRUMBLE:

3¾ cups instant or quick 1-minute oats, divided ((GF) sub gluten-free oats)

½ cup coconut sugar (sub 6 tablespoons monkfruit sweetener)

½ teaspoon sea salt

½ teaspoon ground cinnamon

½ cup (1 stick) butter, melted ((DF) sub melted coconut oil)

1 large egg, room temperature (sub 1 chia egg, see page 43)

⅓ cup unsweetened, unsalted runny peanut butter (sub almond or sunflower seed butter)

2 teaspoons vanilla extract

BLUEBERRY FILLING:

2½ cups frozen blueberries

2 tablespoons arrowroot starch (sub cornstarch)

3 tablespoons coconut sugar (sub monkfruit sweetener)

NOTE

You want the peanut butter to be runny and drippy, so you'll get the best results by using a new jar and mixing in any separated oil.

BAKERY

Spiced Pear Sour Cream Loaf

V GF | **HANDS-ON TIME:** 35 min | **TOTAL TIME:** 2 h, 25 min | **YIELD:** 1 loaf (8 to 10 servings)

Never added sour cream to your baked goods? Well, you are in for a treat! It might sound odd, but sour cream adds richness, moisture, and the perfect tangy "foil" to caramelized pears in this recipe. It also helps the leavening agents do their job, making the loaf rise and turn golden brown around the edges. This quick bread is my absolute favorite breakfast or snack on a crisp winter day. Broil slices for a few minutes, top them with grass-fed butter and a sprinkle of sea salt, and enjoy with a hot cup of tea. If you prefer, you can use apples instead of pears; I recommend Honeycrisp or Pink Lady. I include this loaf in my Holiday Desserts Cooking class because it presents beautifully.

Preheat oven to 375° F. Line a 9 × 5 × 3-inch loaf pan with parchment paper. Make sure at least 1 inch overhangs the sides.

Heat a sauté pan over medium heat, and add butter. When butter has melted and is slightly bubbling, add pears. Cook, stirring every 1 to 2 minutes, until soft and golden brown around the edges, approximately 10 minutes. You can add a splash of water (2 tablespoons) to prevent burning. After 10 minutes, add 1 tablespoon coconut sugar and ¼ teaspoon cinnamon, and cook, stirring, for another minute. Remove pears from the heat, and set aside to cool for 10 minutes.

In a large mixing bowl, whisk together almond flour, coconut flour, baking powder, baking soda, nutmeg, ginger, salt, and remaining 1¼ teaspoons cinnamon.

In a blender, place half of the sautéed pears (approximately 1 cup), remaining ½ cup coconut sugar, sour cream, eggs, and vanilla. Purée until smooth and creamy.

Add wet ingredients to dry, and stir to evenly blend. Fold in remaining sautéed pears, including any pan juices. Scrape batter into the loaf pan, and use a dampened spatula or fingers to smooth the top.

Bake for 50 to 55 minutes, until golden brown, somewhat crusty to touch on top, and a toothpick inserted in the center comes out clean. Allow to cool for 20 minutes in the pan. Using the parchment paper, lift the bread from the pan, and transfer to a cooling rack. Allow to cool for another 40 minutes before slicing (or it will fall apart).

Once completely cool, loaf will keep tightly sealed at room temperature for 2 days, in the refrigerator for 5 days, or in the freezer for 3 months.

Ingredients

- 2 tablespoons butter
- 2 medium semi-ripe pears, chopped into ¾-inch pieces (a little less than 3 cups)
- ½ cup plus 1 tablespoon coconut sugar, divided (sub monkfruit sweetener)
- 1½ teaspoons ground cinnamon, divided
- 1½ cups blanched almond flour
- ¾ cup coconut flour
- 1½ teaspoons baking powder
- ½ teaspoon baking soda
- ½ teaspoon ground nutmeg
- ½ teaspoon ground ginger
- ¼ teaspoon sea salt
- ½ cup full-fat sour cream
- 3 large eggs, room temperature
- 1 teaspoon vanilla extract

NOTE

Use pears that are just a little tender to touch, not those that can be easily bruised. Use whichever variety you like; I use comice or red pears. Feel free to peel, but I like to keep the skin on.

Ideas for
LEFTOVER SOUR CREAM

Use up any leftover sour cream in Artichoke Leek & White Bean Gratin (page 251), Sour Cream & Onion Cauliflower Risotto (page 152), and Best Potato Salad (page 167).

BAKERY

Chapter 6

SNACK-ITIZERS

*H*ere we are with another Snack-itizer section! I decided to keep the silly name from my first cookbook because, well, it gives me lots of wiggle room. Snack-itizers can be something you formally serve to a group of people, or they can be whipped up, thrown in the fridge, and nibbled on throughout the week. The dishes in this chapter are at home in either setting. Pro tip: throw some herbs and flaky Maldon sea salt on top of your finished product, wipe the edges clean, and *voila!* Casual to fancy in less than a minute.

I have a particularly grand time bringing Snack-itizer recipes to life, because it's where I try things that may sound a little . . . unfamiliar? For example, my Sun-Dried Tomato & Walnut Paté and Cashew Kimchi Lettuce Cups might have your head tilting a bit, but I promise they're uniquely delicious! I also have a blast creating healthier versions of your favorite game-day, potluck, or BBQ finger foods, such as my Pigs in a Blanket, Sticky Cajun-Spiced Chicken Wings, and loaded "Hot" Honey Cheddar-Stuffed Sweet Potato Skins. And if you're like me and sometimes make meals out of chips and dip, I've got you covered as well. Siete Foods nacho chips plus my Buffalo Cauliflower Hummus was lunch for a week straight, and I'm not mad about it.

Sticky Cajun-Spiced Chicken Wings

 HANDS-ON TIME: 30 min | **TOTAL TIME:** 1 h, 45 min, plus 4 hours marinating

YIELD: 3 to 4 servings **OPTIONS:**

I don't know why, but wings were always incredibly intimidating to me. Perhaps because they're usually found at bars and restaurants or stadiums, as opposed to the average dinner table (at least, in my experience). But I love them, and I know most people do as well, so I overcame this fear to bring y'all baked wings that are tender, flavorful, and healthier than the usual fried suspects. Turns out, the key to baking chicken wings is time and patience. They need more than an hour in the oven to get a rich, caramelized exterior and fall-apart interior. I use my Cajun Seasoning for this recipe because it packs a punch with little work, but feel free to play with different seasonings, using the same cooking technique. You could also try them with my BBQ Seasoning (page 334) or serve them with my Buffalo Avocado Ranch Dressing (page 339).

CAJUN SEASONING:

1 tablespoon paprika

2 teaspoons garlic powder

2 teaspoons onion powder

1½ teaspoons sea salt (feel free to start with 1 teaspoon if you're salt-sensitive)

1 teaspoon black pepper

1 teaspoon dried oregano

1 teaspoon red pepper flakes (use ½ teaspoon if you're heat-sensitive)

1 tablespoon coconut sugar (K sub monkfruit sweetener)

WINGS:

2 pounds chicken wings

¾ cup plain, full-fat yogurt (DF P sub ¾ cup unsweetened almond milk or canned full-fat coconut milk plus 2 tablespoons lemon juice or apple cider vinegar)

1 batch Cajun Seasoning

3 tablespoons maple syrup

1 tablespoon avocado oil

Buffalo Avocado Ranch Dressing for dipping (optional, page 339)

Make the Cajun Seasoning: Place seasoning ingredients in a small bowl, and whisk to combine, or place in a sealable jar or container and shake.

Make the Wings: Place wings and yogurt in a sealable plastic bag or marinating container, and shake to evenly coat. Marinate for at least 4 hours and up to overnight.

Preheat oven to 375° F. Line a baking sheet with parchment paper.

Lay a kitchen towel or double layer of paper towels on the countertop, and remove wings from the bag or marinating container, shaking off excess yogurt. Place wings side-by-side, but not overlapping, on the towels. Use another kitchen towel or layer of paper towel to press down on wings, soaking up as much yogurt as possible.

In a large mixing bowl, combine Cajun Seasoning, maple syrup, and avocado oil, and stir to form a paste. Add wings (make sure no paper towel is sticking to them), and rub with paste to evenly coat. Place wings on baking sheet, leaving at least 1 inch between each.

Bake wings for 1 hour and 15 minutes, or until golden brown and sticky. (Use this time to make and refrigerate the Buffalo Avocado Ranch Dressing, if using.) Don't worry if the bottoms look burned—that's what we want. Just peel off any burned pieces sticking to the sides. If you like, broil for 3 to 4 minutes to caramelized the skin even more. Watch closely. Enjoy immediately.

Leftover wings will keep tightly sealed in the refrigerator for 4 days. I don't recommend freezing.

> **NOTE**
>
> You can easily make a double batch of chicken wings. Use two baking sheets, and place both in the oven at the same time. Swap their positions halfway through baking. You might need a slightly longer cook time.

"Hot" Honey Cheddar-Stuffed Sweet Potato Skins

(V) (GF) **HANDS-ON TIME:** 45 min | **TOTAL TIME:** 1 h, 35 min | **YIELD:** 12 servings

The description of this recipe says it all, except they're not actually "hot" with spices. There's a little kick from red pepper flakes and chili powder. That said, feel free to adjust the spice level on this favorite game-day app.

Preheat oven to 400° F. Line a baking sheet with parchment paper. Trim off ends from sweet potatoes. Place on the baking sheet, and use a knife to prick 3 to 4 holes in each. Roast sweet potatoes for 1 hour, or until tender and easily pierced with a fork. Allow to cool 15 minutes.

While potatoes roast, heat a small sauté pan over medium heat, and add 1 tablespoon avocado oil. When the oil moves quickly around the pan and is shimmering, add shallots and sauté until soft and translucent, 4 to 5 minutes. Set aside to cool.

In a small bowl, whisk together remaining 1 tablespoon avocado oil, ¼ teaspoon chili powder, pinch red pepper flakes, ¼ teaspoon salt, and honey. You can microwave for 8 seconds or so to help combine.

Combine 1 cup cheese, remaining 1 teaspoon salt, black pepper, and ½ cup yogurt in a large mixing bowl. Discard parchment from baking sheet, and grease pan with avocado oil (this helps crisp the potato edges).

Once the potatoes have cooled for 15 minutes, carefully slice them in half lengthwise. Use a spoon to scoop out the inside of each half, keeping the skin intact as much as possible. Add potato pulp to the cheese mixture.

Place potato skins on the greased baking sheet. Brush half of the honey–chili mixture in a thin layer on the skins.

Add remaining honey–chili mixture to the sweet potato mixture, and mash together until incorporated. Taste for seasoning, and add more salt if you like. Set oven to broil. Spoon filling into the skins, then top with remaining 1 cup cheese. Sprinkle with remaining ½ teaspoon chili powder and a pinch of red pepper flakes.

Broil potato skins for 3 to 4 minutes, until cheese is bubbling and light golden brown. Watch closely. Serve hot, topped with a spoonful of remaining yogurt and scallions.

Once cooled, leftovers will keep tightly sealed in the refrigerator for 4 days or in the freezer for 2 months. I reheat on a lined baking sheet at 300° F until cheese is melted and insides are warmed through.

6 medium orange sweet potatoes, rinsed and patted dry (4½ inches long)

2 tablespoons avocado oil, plus more for greasing, divided

1 large or 2 small shallots, minced (½ cup)

¾ teaspoon chili powder, divided

2 pinches red pepper flakes, divided

1¼ teaspoons sea salt, plus more to taste, divided

1 tablespoon honey

8 ounces sharp cheddar cheese, shredded (2 cups), divided

¼ teaspoon black pepper

1 cup plain, full-fat Greek yogurt, divided (sub sour cream)

4 scallions, base and dark green tops removed and sliced into ¼-inch rounds (½ cup)

Ideas for
LEFTOVER SCALLIONS

Use leftover scallions (chopped) in scrambled eggs, over salads, on roasted sweet potatoes, or on avocado toast.

SNACK-ITIZERS

Tahini Brussels Sprouts

with PISTACHIOS & DATES

 | HANDS-ON TIME: 15 min | TOTAL TIME: 45 min | YIELD: 6 servings |

I knew Nashville was movin' on up when we got a True Food Kitchen right smack in the middle of where fast-food restaurants used to exist. Founded by Dr. Andrew Weil, True Food Kitchen is a healthy, chef-driven, seasonally focused chain that offers delicious anti-inflammatory meals and beverages. One of my favorite True Food Kitchen dishes is a cauliflower appetizer that includes harissa spice, dates, and pistachios. As much as I adore cauliflower, I had an inkling that I'd prefer the flavor combination with Brussels sprouts. I love to serve it in mini compostable bamboo cups as a cooking class starter, but this dish also makes for a great side dish. Note that traditional harissa spice includes ingredients I don't often use, so I made something similar with what I keep in my pantry.

Preheat oven to 400° F. Line a baking sheet with parchment paper. Depending on the size of your Brussels sprouts, you may want to use two baking sheets. If you crowd them on the baking sheet, they won't crisp.

In a large heatproof bowl, combine Brussels sprouts pieces, avocado oil, and ½ teaspoon salt. Toss to coat, then spread evenly onto baking sheet(s). No need to clean the mixing bowl.

Roast Brussels sprouts for 35 minutes, or until tender and crispy at the edges. If using 2 baking sheets, swap their positions halfway through.

In the same mixing bowl, combine remaining ¼ teaspoon salt, lemon juice, tahini, maple syrup, miso, paprika, garlic powder, onion powder, black pepper, cumin, turmeric, and 2 tablespoons water. Whisk until it forms a sauce. If it isn't a pourable consistency, add 1 to 2 more tablespoons of water. (I usually add 1 tablespoon.)

Once Brussels sprouts have finished roasting, add them to the sauce, and toss to evenly coat. Fold in pistachios and dates. Serve however you like, adding fresh mint and chopped pistachios for garnish.

Leftovers will keep for 3 days in the refrigerator. I don't recommend freezing.

Ingredients

2 pounds Brussels sprouts, base and any brown or holey leaves removed, sliced in half vertically (if they are particularly large, slice into thirds or quarters—we want 1-inch pieces)

2 teaspoons avocado oil

¾ teaspoon sea salt, plus more to taste, divided

Juice from 1 lemon (2 tablespoons)

1½ tablespoons runny tahini

2 teaspoons maple syrup

1 teaspoon mild, white miso paste

1 teaspoon paprika

1 teaspoon garlic powder

½ teaspoon onion powder

½ teaspoon black pepper

¼ teaspoon ground cumin

¼ teaspoon ground turmeric

2 to 4 tablespoons filtered water

⅓ cup roasted, salted pistachios, roughly chopped, plus more for garnish

4 to 6 pitted medjool dates, roughly chopped (½ cup)

⅓ ounce fresh mint, thinly sliced, for garnish (⅓ cup loosely packed)

SNACK-ITIZERS

NOTE

I find it easier to chop dates that are chilled. Even then, the pieces will stick together a little when sliced, so just pull them apart.

> *Ideas for*
> **LEFTOVER PISTACHIOS**
>
> Use any pistachios you have leftover to make Pistachio Pesto (page 336).

Buffalo Cauliflower Hummus

Vg DF GF K P | **HANDS-ON TIME:** 20 min | **TOTAL TIME:** 50 min, plus 1 h chilling | **YIELD:** 8 to 10 servings ❄

As a long-time lover of traditional chickpea-based hummus, I was incredibly skeptical about a hummus made from cauliflower. I mean, really? Well . . . yeah, really! It actually works, when you make sure to keep tahini and olive oil in the mix for that signature creaminess. In fact, cauliflower provides the ideal neutral backdrop for almost any flavor profile you like. I use a little Frank's RedHot and sriracha for a sweet and spicy kick, but you can certainly play around with this whole "cauli-hummus" thing once you're comfortable with the recipe. This is an awesome game-day crowd-pleaser with some chopped veggies or your favorite tortilla chips.

Preheat oven to 415° F. Line a baking sheet with parchment paper.

Place cauliflower florets and shallot rings on the baking sheet, and toss with avocado oil and ¼ teaspoon salt. Spread in an even layer. Roast for 30 minutes, until cauliflower has some golden-brown bits around the edges and shallots are softened and translucent. Allow to cool for 10 minutes.

Once cooled, place in a food processor along with remaining ¼ teaspoon salt, olive oil, tahini, Frank's RedHot, lemon juice, miso, sriracha, garlic, and pepper. Purée until mostly smooth, 3 to 5 minutes. Taste for more seasoning, and add more salt if you like. (I add another pinch.) Refrigerate hummus at least 1 hour before serving.

Hummus will keep tightly sealed in the refrigerator for 5 days. I don't recommend freezing.

1 medium head cauliflower, chopped into 1½-inch florets (6 to 7 cups)

1 medium shallot, sliced into ¼-inch rings (⅓ cup)

2 teaspoons avocado oil

½ teaspoon sea salt, plus more to taste, divided

⅓ cup olive oil

¼ cup tahini

2 tablespoons original Frank's RedHot

Juice from 1 lemon (2 tablespoons)

2 teaspoons mild, white miso paste

2 teaspoons sriracha

1 clove garlic, roughly chopped

¼ teaspoon black pepper

Ideas for
LEFTOVER SRIRACHA

Use leftover sriracha in Honey Walnut Shrimp (page 212), Vegan Tomato-y Collard Greens (page 155), and Sheet Pan Sesame Tofu & Bok Choy (page 244).

Cashew Kimchi Lettuce Cups

Jess Rice is a plant-based chef in Nashville, and I owe her for creating the Kimchi Spring Rolls at Avo Restaurant. Jess has been featured on Trisha Yearwood's Food Network cooking show and has cooked for other celebrities such as Miley Cyrus and Kelly Clarkson. In my eyes, though, Jess's greatest accomplishment is the heavenly balance of textures and sweet-savory flavor in her Kimchi Spring Rolls. Creating my own version was an absolute no-brainer for this book, but the spring-roll wrapping process evades me. So I kept it simple and turned them into lettuce cups. Your guests will be delighted by this nutrient-rich appetizer!

Make the Filling: Place all filling ingredients in the order listed in a food processor or high-powered blender. Process or blend until a chunky paste forms. (A blender creates a creamier consistency with less "bite" and texture, so I prefer using the processor.) Scrape mixture into a bowl, and set aside.

Make the Peanut Sauce: Place all sauce ingredients in a glass jar with a lid or other sealable container. Shake vigorously to evenly incorporate. You may need to break up the miso a bit with a fork before shaking. You can also whisk in a bowl or purée in a blender if you prefer. Refrigerate for at least 15 minutes before serving to allow it to thicken. (For leftovers add water one tablespoon at a time to thin.)

Assemble the Lettuce Cups: Scoop 2 or 3 tablespoons of filling (depending on whether you use bibb or romaine) on as many leaves as you want to enjoy immediately. (I use more filling on romaine because it's sturdier). Sprinkle with sesame seeds, and add a few cucumber sticks and onion, if using.

If not eating immediately, keep ingredients stored separately, as lettuce cups get soggy quickly if made in advance, especially with bibb. Also note that the filling will firm up a bit in the fridge. If you want to thin it, stir in water or kimchi juice, 1 tablespoon at a time, until it reaches your desired consistency. Filling and sauce will keep tightly sealed in the refrigerator for 5 days. I don't recommend freezing.

Ideas for
LEFTOVER KIMCHI

Don't want to eat the rest of your kimchi straight-up? Use leftovers in my 5-Ingredient Kimchi Coleslaw (page 163).

FILLING:

- ¾ cup Korean kimchi, drained of excess liquid
- ¼ cup runny tahini (pourable consistency)
- 2 tablespoons plus 1 teaspoon low-sodium tamari
- 2 cups raw cashews
- 2 tablespoons coconut sugar (K sub monkfruit sweetener)
- 1 tablespoon plus 1 teaspoon toasted sesame oil

PEANUT SAUCE:

- ½ cup unsweetened, unsalted runny peanut butter (creamy or crunchy; sub almond butter or tahini)
- 1 clove garlic, finely minced (sub 2 tablespoons finely minced shallot)
- 2 tablespoons plus 1 teaspoon coconut sugar (K sub monkfruit sweetener)
- 2 tablespoons low-sodium tamari
- 1 tablespoon lime juice, apple cider vinegar, or kimchi juice
- 1 teaspoon mild, white miso paste
- ½-inch piece ginger, peeled and grated (sub scant ¼ teaspoon ground ginger)
- ½ cup filtered water, plus more as needed

ASSEMBLY:

- 1 head bibb or romaine lettuce, base trimmed and leaves rinsed and patted dry
- 1 tablespoon sesame seeds
- 1 small cucumber, sliced into matchsticks, ¼-inch thick
- Finely minced red onion (optional)

Caramelized Onion & Chive Dip

Vg DF GF | **HANDS-ON TIME:** 1 h, 10 min | **TOTAL TIME:** 1 h, 10 min, plus 1 h chilling | **YIELD:** 8 to 10 servings ❄

I never want my plant-based or dairy-free darlings to miss their snacking favorites, and I know I'm not alone in placing old school French onion dip near the top of the list. My version of this dip satisfies sweet and savory cravings, with the combination of candy-like caramelized onions and umami-rich tofu, nutritional yeast, and miso paste. If you really want to recreate the classic experience, treat yourself to some avocado oil–fried potato chips (there are several brands out there), and scoop away.

Make the Caramelized Onions: Turn on exhaust fan. Heat a large saucepan over medium-high heat, and add avocado oil. When oil moves quickly around the pan and is shimmering, add onions. Allow to cook without stirring until it looks like the onions are burning, 4 to 6 minutes. Add ½ cup water to deglaze, scraping up any brown bits from the bottom of the pan. (Be careful as this will cause steam.) Stir onions briefly, reduce heat slightly, and repeat burning and deglazing process once more, using the remaining ½ cup water (another 4 to 6 minutes).

Reduce heat to medium-low (you can turn off exhaust fan), and cook onions, stirring every 5 minutes or so, until they are a dark, jammy consistency, approximately 35 minutes. Feel free to add splashes of water to prevent sticking or burning as they cook. Stir in balsamic vinegar, and set aside to cool.

Make the Dip: While onions are cooling, place avocado oil, almond milk, tofu, nutritional yeast, lemon juice, salt, pepper, garlic powder, and miso in a food processor, and purée until smooth and creamy. Add more almond milk, 1 tablespoon at a time, as necessary to blend.

Once onions have cooled 10 minutes, add approximately one-third of the onions (a rounded ½ cup) to the food processor with tofu mixture, and purée until smooth. Transfer mixture to a large bowl, and stir in remaining caramelized onions. Taste for seasoning, and add more salt if you like. Refrigerate, uncovered, at least 1 hour and up to 24 hours before serving.

If serving cold, stir chives into the chilled dip just before serving.

If serving warm, place dip in a medium saucepan, and heat over low heat, stirring constantly, until warmed through. Stir in chives and serve.

Leftover dip will keep tightly sealed in the refrigerator for 4 days. I don't recommend freezing.

CARAMELIZED ONIONS:

1 tablespoon avocado oil

2 medium yellow onions, sliced into ¼-inch half-moons (6 cups)

1 cup water

2 teaspoons aged balsamic vinegar

DIP:

2 tablespoons avocado oil

¼ cup unsweetened almond milk, plus more as necessary

15 ounces firm organic tofu, drained and patted dry

¼ cup nutritional yeast

Juice from 1 lemon (2 tablespoons)

1 teaspoon sea salt, plus more to taste (feel free to start with less and add to taste)

¼ teaspoon black pepper

¼ teaspoon garlic powder

1 teaspoon mild, white miso paste

½ ounce freshly minced chives (½ cup)

NOTE

It's important to cut the onion into slices that are the same size to make sure they all cook at the same rate.

Pigs in a Blanket

with GRAINY HONEY MUSTARD

HANDS-ON TIME: 40 min | **TOTAL TIME:** 1 h | **YIELD:** 18 piglets | **OPTION:** ⓥ

When I started to play around with whole-wheat pizza dough for this book, a healthier "pigs-in-a-blanket" recipe immediately came to mind. Is it the most nutritious, whole-food recipe around? Certainly not! But the LL Balanced space is about progress, not perfection. Finding high-quality hot dogs is nonnegotiable in my book, but Trader Joe's and Applegate Farms make some. Plus, you could totally use veggie dogs in this recipe instead.

Make the Pigs in a Blanket: Remove dough from the fridge, and allow to sit at room temperature for 20 minutes. Slice hot dogs crosswise into 3 pieces each (this makes 18 pieces, each a little shorter than 2 inches). Once dough has been at room temperature for 20 minutes, preheat oven to 400° F. Line a baking sheet with parchment paper.

Grease a large cutting board with a thin layer of avocado oil. Gently spread dough into a rectangle (approximately 18 × 9 inches) on the cutting board. If it breaks, just pinch the dough back together. Dough will be quite thin. If it keeps breaking, allow it to sit for a few more minutes. Eventually it will spread. Coat with 2 tablespoons melted butter in an even layer. Using a sharp knife or pizza cutter, slice dough into 2-inch strips (you'll need 9 strips). I suggest using a measuring tape. Then slice each strip diagonally, making very long, thin triangles. It's okay if they're not perfect.

Wrap the Piggies: Grab one piece of hot dog, and place it on the wide end of one dough triangle. Roll tightly all the way up, then pinch the tip into the dough. Place on the baking sheet with the dough–tip side facing up. Repeat with remaining hot dog pieces and dough, leaving at least ½ inch between them on the baking sheet. Bake for 18 minutes, or until the bottoms and edges of the wrap are golden brown.

Make the Grainy Honey Mustard: Whisk all the mustard ingredients together in a small bowl.

When the pigs come out of the oven, brush them with remaining 1 tablespoon melted butter and sprinkle with salt, if using. Allow to cool 10 minutes before serving with Grainy Honey Mustard.

Leftovers will keep tightly sealed in the refrigerator for 4 days or in the freezer for 4 months. I reheat them in the microwave, as the oven can dry them out.

SPECIAL EQUIPMENT:

Tape measure

PIGS IN A BLANKET:

1 pound whole-wheat pizza dough

12 ounces grass-fed uncured hot dogs (ⓥ sub veggie dogs)

Avocado oil for greasing

2 tablespoons butter, melted, plus 1 tablespoon, melted, for garnish

Coarse sea salt for garnish

GRAINY HONEY MUSTARD:

½ cup whole-grain mustard (sub 6 tablespoons Dijon mustard)

3 tablespoons honey

3 tablespoons ketchup

¼ teaspoon onion powder

Sun-Dried Tomato & Walnut Paté

Ⓥ DF GF K | **HANDS-ON TIME:** 35 min | **TOTAL TIME:** 35 min, plus 4 to 8 h chilling | **YIELD:** 6 to 8 servings ❄

Six years have passed since my time at the Natural Gourmet Institute in New York City, but my tastebuds still remember some experiences poignantly. One such dish was a paté that we made out of lentils and walnuts. I love traditional chicken liver paté, and I was struck by how similar the lentil version was to the original. I decided to use tempeh in my version of vegan paté, because I think the nutty flavors contribute a convincing richness, as does the inclusion of sun-dried tomatoes. Now it's up to y'all to call my bluff or agree that plants can satisfy a desire for this classic French appetizer!

1 cup raw walnuts

1 tablespoon avocado oil

½ medium yellow onion, diced into ¼-inch pieces (¾ to 1 cup)

8 ounces tempeh (1 block), cut into 1-inch cubes

4 cloves garlic, minced

½ cup sun-dried tomatoes in olive oil, drained

1 teaspoon mild, white miso paste

1½ tablespoons low-sodium tamari

Preheat oven to 350° F. Place walnuts on a baking sheet. Roast for 10-12 minutes, until fragrant and slightly darkened. Set aside to cool.

Heat a large sauté pan over medium-high heat, and add avocado oil. When oil moves quickly around the pan and is shimmering, add onions and tempeh along with a splash of water (2 tablespoons). Cook, stirring every few minutes, until tempeh and onions have golden-brown edges, approximately 10 minutes. To make sure you get a little caramelization, allow the mixture to almost start to burn every few minutes. Deglaze with a splash of water, scraping up any brown bits from the bottom of the pan. Reduce heat to low, and add garlic. Cook for another 30 to 45 seconds, stirring, then set pan aside to cool for 10 minutes.

Place cooled walnuts and tempeh mixture in a food processor. Pulse until mixture forms a chunky crumble, 10 to 15 seconds. Scrape down the sides, and add sun-dried tomatoes, miso, and tamari. Pulse until mixture is mostly smooth, approximately 1 minute.

Line a 9 × 5 × 3-inch loaf pan with parchment paper. Scrape paté into pan. Spread into a compact, even layer. (I find it helpful to use a lightly dampened spatula to spread it.)

Refrigerate for at least 4 hours, ideally 8, before carefully removing from the pan and slicing.

Leftover paté will keep tightly sealed in the refrigerator for 5 days. I don't recommend freezing.

Chapter 7

SIDES

Y'all, I'm going to put something out there. If you like it, you can take it. If you don't, send it right back! I think side dishes are just as, if not more, important, than the entrée of a meal. This is partly because sides are often the primary source of micronutrients: vitamins and minerals that are crucial to a properly functioning ecosystem. Perhaps more importantly, though, choosing the right side dish can take your meal from good to spectacular. Anyone who has ever eaten steak and potatoes, curry and rice, or grilled chicken with perfectly roasted broccoli knows what I mean. My hope and dream for these side dishes is that they will contribute to and enhance your dining experience through their flavors, textures, and temperatures. Some of my favorite pairings are Best Potato Salad with Steak Bites, Creamy Corn & Chive Farro with BBQ "Baked" Lentils, Miso Coconut Roasted Eggplant with Macadamia Sesame Crusted Tuna, and Broccoli Gorgonzola Salad with Chicken Parmesan (trust me!). Plus, the coolest thing about side dishes is that they can be entrées as well. Double your portion, add a little protein and fat, and you've just added to your dinner recipe repertoire.

Broccoli Gorgonzola Salad

with MISO MAPLE DRESSING

V GF | **HANDS-ON TIME:** 20 min | **TOTAL TIME:** 50 min, plus 1 h chilling | **YIELD:** 4 to 6 servings ⊕ ❄ | **OPTION:** K

This dish was inspired by a salad at Emmy's Squared, a boutique pizza chain offering unique flavors of Sicilian-style pie. I was utterly blown away by the combination of ingredients—pickled onion, blue cheese, cashews, and broccoli—and I knew I wanted you to be able to experience this happy umami-rich surprise. I don't know their recipe, but I think I got pretty close, and I love being able to whip this up in my own kitchen. That said, I still adore ordering this salad, a glass of wine, and a Colony pizza at Emmy's Squared.

Make the Miso Maple Dressing: Place miso and vinegar in a small bowl. Use a fork to break up the miso, and whisk until smooth. Whisk in maple syrup, salt, pepper, and onion powder. While whisking continuously, slowly pour in avocado oil until dressing is a uniform consistency. Alternately, double the batch, and purée all ingredients in a blender (one batch is usually too small for most blenders). Leftovers will keep tightly sealed in the refrigerator for 5 days.

Make the Broccoli Gorgonzola Salad: Preheat oven to 350° F, and add cashews to a baking sheet. Roast for 12 to 14 minutes, until fragrant and slightly golden. Allow to cool for 10 minutes. While cashews roast, in a small bowl, combine onions, vinegar, and maple syrup. Stir well and set aside.

Place broccoli and salt in a medium saucepan, and cover with at least 1 inch cold water. Bring to a boil, and boil for 1 minute, then drain and rinse with cold water until broccoli reaches room temperature. Place broccoli on a clean dish towel, wrap, and squeeze out excess liquid over the sink. Place in a large mixing bowl.

Drain onions, shaking off excess liquid, and add to the broccoli. Once cashews have cooled, roughly chop them, and add to the broccoli, along with gorgonzola (I use ¾ cup, but you can start with ½ cup and see if you want more). Toss to evenly incorporate.

Add enough dressing to coat. Taste and add more as desired. Chill salad for at least 1 hour before serving.

Leftover salad will keep tightly sealed in the refrigerator for 3 days. I don't recommend freezing.

MISO MAPLE DRESSING:

1 tablespoon mild, white miso paste

2 tablespoons apple cider vinegar

2 teaspoons maple syrup (K sub 2 drops liquid stevia, or to taste)

¼ teaspoon sea salt

¼ teaspoon black pepper

¼ teaspoon onion powder

6 tablespoons avocado oil

BROCCOLI GORGONZOLA SALAD:

¼ medium red onion, thinly sliced into half moons (1 cup loosely packed)

⅓ cup apple cider vinegar

1 tablespoon maple syrup (K sub 3 drops liquid stevia)

½ cup raw cashews

1 medium crown broccoli, chopped into 1-inch florets (smaller than I usually do for roasting; 4½ to 6 cups)

¼ teaspoon sea salt

2 to 3 ounces crumbled gorgonzola cheese (½ to ¾ cup)

NOTE

Emmy's Squared uses raw broccoli, which isn't my personal jam, but if you enjoy broccoli raw, you can omit the steps for boiling it and squeezing out liquid.

Buttery Lemon Pepper Leeks

Ⓥ ⒼⒻ Ⓚ Ⓟ | **HANDS-ON TIME:** 20 min | **TOTAL TIME:** 25 min | **YIELD:** 3 to 4 servings |

Leeks are one of my absolute favorite veggies, and I feel like they're totally underrated. These gargantuan "green onions" with their countless, dirt-filled layers can seem a bit intimidating. But let me tell you, a little TLC goes a long way here! Once cooked (the right way), leeks become a lusciously tender, mildly sweet accompaniment to countless meals. I think leeks and butter are one of the great food combinations, so perhaps try a vegan butter if you can't do dairy.

Remove and discard ½ inch from the base of each leek, as well as almost all of the dark leafy top (I leave approximately 1 inch on). Slice leeks in half lengthwise, and remove the outer layer of each half. (If all of this seems confusing, the point is: we want to keep the light-colored parts of the leeks because they're tender.)

Place leeks in a large mixing bowl full of room temperature water. Gently rinse and separate the leaves, then allow to sit 5 minutes. Skim the leeks off the top of the water, making sure not to stir up any dirt that has fallen to the bottom of the bowl. Pat leeks mostly dry.

Heat a large saucepan over medium-low heat, and add butter and a splash of water (2 tablespoons). When butter has melted, add leeks. Stir to coat with butter, then cover and allow to cook until leeks are softened and "melty" looking, 10 to 12 minutes.

Once leeks are softened, uncover and reduce heat to low. Add garlic, lemon zest, lemon juice, salt, and pepper, and cook another minute, stirring. Taste for seasoning, and add more salt if you like. (I add another ¼ teaspoon.) Don't be alarmed if some of the garlic looks blue in color; this is just a fun little reaction that it has from the leeks. Top with parmesan cheese, if using. Serve immediately.

Leeks will keep tightly sealed in the refrigerator for 4 days. I reheat them by adding them to a saucepan with a splash of water and heating until warmed through. I don't recommend freezing.

3 small or 2 large leeks

2 tablespoons butter

3 cloves garlic, minced

Zest from 1 lemon (2 teaspoons)

Juice from 1 lemon (2 tablespoons)

¼ teaspoon sea salt, plus more to taste

½ teaspoon black pepper

Freshly grated parmesan cheese for garnish

NOTES

If you want to use up the tougher parts of the leeks that you removed, you can toss them with a little avocado oil, salt, and pepper, and roast at 400° F until tender.

The size of the leeks relates to how wide the leeks are, not how tall.

SIDES

Carrot & Zucchini Ribbons

with LEMONY PISTACHIO PESTO

GF **P** | **HANDS-ON TIME:** 45 min | **TOTAL TIME:** 45 min | **YIELD:** 4 to 6 servings | **OPTIONS:** **DF** **Vg** **K**

Can someone please explain why it is more fun and satisfying to eat food in noodle shape? Regardless, I'm happy to submit to the phenomenon, especially with recipes such as this! Starting with crisp veggie "ribbons," I took my Pistachio Pesto recipe and added a generous scoop of lemon zest. The result is a side that is bright, refreshing, and surprisingly filling. You could even serve this as a main dish, topped with grilled shrimp, and it would be beautiful on a picnic or potluck table. If you want a lower-carb option, feel free to sub another four zucchinis for the carrots.

Make the Lemony Pistachio Pesto: Place all pesto ingredients in a food processor, and pulse until it reaches your desired consistency. (I like it pretty finely chopped.) You may need to stop and scrape the sides down a time or two.

Make the Carrot & Zucchini Salad: Peel carrots, and remove tips and bottoms; discard. Use a vegetable peeler to make carrot "ribbons," shaving them directly into a large mixing bowl. Eventually they'll get flimsy and difficult to peel. (I find that holding the carrot against a flat surface instead of over the bowl allows me to get more ribbons.)

Remove tops and bottoms of zucchini, and use a vegetable peeler to make zucchini "ribbons" of the outer layers, placing them in the same bowl. Stop as soon as you get to the seeds. (I use the same trick as above to get as many ribbons as possible.)

Add ½ cup pesto to the carrots and zucchini, tossing to coat the vegetables. Add more pesto as desired. (I find if I use more than ½ cup, it gets a little soggy.) Roughly chop pistachios, and add to vegetables along with goat cheese, if using. Gently toss to coat. Taste for seasoning, and add more salt if you like. If you don't think you'll eat the whole dish in one meal, you can hold off on tossing veggies with pesto and goat cheese, and add them just before serving time.

Leftovers, if components are stored separately in the fridge, with keep up to 3 days. I don't recommend freezing.

LEMONY PISTACHIO PESTO:

½ cup roasted, salted pistachios

2 ounces fresh basil, stems removed (2 cups, packed)

2 tablespoons nutritional yeast

Zest from 1 lemon (2 teaspoons)

Juice from 1 lemon (2 tablespoons)

1 teaspoon mild, white miso paste

¼ teaspoon black pepper

1 to 2 cloves garlic, roughly chopped

½ cup olive oil

CARROT ZUCCHINI SALAD:

4 medium carrots (**K** sub zucchini)

4 medium zucchinis

⅓ cup roasted, salted pistachios

4 ounces crumbled goat cheese (½ cup) (**DF** **Vg** sub vegan cream cheese) (optional)

Salt, to taste

> *Ideas for*
> ### LEFTOVER CARROT AND ZUCCHINI
>
> Roughly chop leftover bits of vegetables, and use in LL's Daily Fruit-Free Green Smoothie (page 54).

SIDES

Sour Cream & Onion Cauliflower Risotto

Ⓥ ⒼⒻ Ⓚ | **HANDS-ON TIME:** 25 min | **TOTAL TIME:** 25 min | **YIELD:** 4 servings |

I concocted this delightful dish when I was eyeball-deep in experimenting with lower-carbohydrate, higher-fat meals to kick sugar cravings. While I've introduced more carbs back into my diet, I still love making this on the regular! This "risotto" offers a classic sour cream and onion flavor without any weird additives or oils, and you also get serious nutrition to boot. You could try substituting full-fat plain yogurt or cream cheese for the sour cream, if you happen to have some on hand. I have a feeling this crazy-easy and satisfying side is going to be a favorite of y'alls!

- 2 tablespoons butter
- 24 ounces frozen cauliflower rice (2 12-ounce packages)
- ¾ teaspoon sea salt, plus more to taste (I use 1¼ teaspoons total)
- ¾ teaspoon onion powder
- ½ teaspoon black pepper, plus more to taste
- ¾ cup full-fat sour cream (sub full-fat plain yogurt)
- ½ cup unsweetened almond milk, plus more as desired
- ¾ cup freshly grated parmesan cheese, plus more for garnish
- 1 bunch scallions, 1 inch removed from top and ¼ inch removed from base, then sliced into ¼-inch-thick rounds (1 cup)

Place butter in a large saucepan over medium heat. When butter has melted and is lightly bubbling, add cauliflower, and cook, stirring every minute or so to break up chunks, until cauliflower is softened and tender, 10 to 12 minutes. Add salt, onion powder, pepper, sour cream, almond milk, and cheese, and stir to incorporate. Cook, stirring, until slightly thickened and any liquid in the bottom of the pan has evaporated, another 3 to 5 minutes.

Turn off heat, and fold in scallions. Taste for seasoning, and add salt and pepper if you like. Top with parmesan cheese, if using. Serve immediately.

Leftovers will keep tightly sealed in the refrigerator for 4 days. Risotto will thicken as it cools, especially in the fridge, so use 2 tablespoons almond milk or water to thin when reheating. I don't recommend freezing.

Ideas for
LEFTOVER PARMESAN CHEESE

Make parmesan crisps with leftover grated parmesan cheese: preheat oven to 400° F. Line a baking sheet with parchment paper. Make 1 tablespoon mounds of grated parmesan on the baking sheet, leaving approximately 2 inches between each. Flatten each mound into an even layer, then bake for 6 to 8 minutes, until darkened in color and crispy around the edges. Allow to cool completely before using a spatula to remove crisps from the baking sheet. Keep tightly sealed at room temperature for up to 4 days.

SIDES

Vegan Tomato-y Collard Greens

Vg GF DF K P | **HANDS-ON TIME:** 15 min | **TOTAL TIME:** 1 h, 15 min (Instant Pot); 6 h, 15 min to 8 h, 15 min (Crock-Pot)

YIELD: 4 to 6 servings

If you've ever eaten at a southern "meat 'n' three," you've likely seen (and hopefully tried) collard greens. Nestled in a rich, savory broth and dappled with chunks of country ham, this dish is a delectable way to eat your leafies! When some plant-based friends came to visit Nashville, I was bummed that they couldn't enjoy traditional collards, so I made it my mission to create a vegan version. Using reliable "chameleon" ingredients such as coconut milk, molasses, tamari, and nutritional yeast, I recreated the experience of classic collard broth, sans ham! Because I'm not vegan, I love these greens served with white rice and my Sticky Cajun-Spiced Chicken Wings (page 129) and an extra splash of hot sauce.

Instant Pot Version: Place all ingredients in the canister of an Instant Pot, and stir to combine. Set to "Manual" 35 minutes. When the Instant Pot beeps to signal the end of cooking time, allow pressure to release naturally. Press "Cancel," then "Sauté," and cook, stirring every few minutes until the liquid has reduced to a thicker consistency, 10 to 15 minutes.

Crock-Pot Version: Place all ingredients in a Crock-Pot, and stir to combine. Cook for 6 to 8 hours on low, until collards are broken down and tender.

Collards will keep tightly sealed in the refrigerator for 5 days or in the freezer for 3 months.

2 bunches collard greens, rinsed, drained, stems removed, and sliced into 1-inch ribbons (see page 45)

2 cups low-sodium vegetable stock

1 cup canned full-fat coconut milk

1 15-ounce can no-salt-added diced tomatoes

½ medium yellow onion, diced into ¼-inch pieces

5 cloves garlic, finely minced

2 tablespoons nutritional yeast

1 teaspoon onion powder

½ teaspoon paprika

3 tablespoons low-sodium tamari

1½ tablespoons molasses

SIDES

SERVING SUGGESTION

I like to make a little sauce to go on top of these greens (pictured). Mix 3 tablespoons sriracha, ¼ cup unsweetened, unsalted peanut butter, and ¼ cup water. Add more water as needed to reach desired consistency.

Creamy Corn & Chive Farro

 | **HANDS-ON TIME:** 10 min | **TOTAL TIME:** 55 min | **YIELD:** 6 servings |

As my darling team member Lelan noted, this recipe is "me" in a dish! Farro is my favorite grain, and nutritional yeast, coconut milk, and tahini show up in many of my recipes. I also find myself particularly enamored with chives these days. To me, they're similar to shallots in their usage, providing a milder and slightly sweeter "bite" than onions or garlic (which, obviously, I love as well). I've started keeping a bunch of chives in my fridge to snip over just about every savory dish you can imagine, including this one. I love serving my Creamy Corn & Chive Farro with thick broiled slices of halloumi cheese. To me, it's true comfort food, because it sticks to your ribs, tastes incredible, and provides nourishment to your body. Keep chives wrapped in a damp paper towel in the fridge to presere freshness longer.

- 2 cups low-sodium vegetable stock (sub chicken stock for non-vegan version)
- 1 cup canned full-fat coconut milk
- 3 tablespoons tahini
- ½ teaspoon sea salt, plus more to taste
- 1 cup uncooked farro, rinsed and drained
- ½ ounce fresh chives, minced (½ cup) (yes, this will look like a lot!)
- 1½ cups frozen organic corn
- ¼ cup nutritional yeast
- ¼ teaspoon black pepper

In a blender, place stock, coconut milk, tahini, and salt. Purée until smooth. Pour into a medium saucepan, and stir in farro.

Bring to a boil over medium-high heat, then reduce to the lowest possible setting, and simmer, covered, until most of the liquid is absorbed and the farro is tender but not mushy (try not to check more than once or twice), approximately 45 minutes.

Remove from the heat, stir in remaining ingredients, and taste for seasoning, adding more salt and pepper if you like. It continues to thicken a bit, so feel free to thin it with splashes of water or stock. Serve immediately.

Leftovers will keep tightly sealed in the refrigerator for 5 days or in the freezer for 3 months. I reheat in a small saucepan with ⅓ cup water or stock stirred in.

> *Ideas for*
> **LEFTOVER FROZEN CORN**
>
> If you have leftover corn, plan to make my Sweet Potato, Peanut Black & Bean Burgers (page 262) or throw it into my One-Pot Pineapple Paprika Fajitas (page 227)

SIDES

Miso Coconut Roasted Eggplant

Ⓥ Ⓖ Ⓕ Ⓟ | **HANDS-ON TIME:** 25 min | **TOTAL TIME:** 55 min | **YIELD:** 6 servings ⏱ | **OPTION:** Ⓚ

There's something about the delicate balance of sweet, savory, and umami that has me coming up with countless ways to use Asian condiments. In particular, miso plays a starring role in elevating the modest eggplant to something truly spectacular. By cross-hatching the eggplant and filling each nook and cranny with sauce, every bite is packed with flavor and melts in your mouth; no spongy texture here! In addition to coconut flakes as a garnish, this eggplant is wonderful topped with sesame seeds, slivered almonds, sliced scallions, Thai basil, and red pepper flakes.

Preheat oven to 400° F, and line two baking sheets with parchment paper.

Holding each eggplant upright, slice vertically into 4 slabs. (I leave the leafy tops on, but you can cut them off.) Each slice should be approximately ¾- to 1-inch thick. Trim a little disk off the rounded edge of the two side pieces, so that they can lie flat.

Place eggplant slabs on the baking sheets, flesh side up. Using a sharp knife, make checkerboard slices almost all the way to the bottom, but not completely, by slicing vertical lines then horizontal lines (see photo). Each "checker" square should be approximately ¾-inch wide.

In a blender, combine tamari, miso, sesame oil, tahini, maple syrup, and garlic. Blend until smooth, at least 1 minute, to ensure garlic cloves are broken down. (You can also just whisk everything together in a bowl, but you'll need to finely mince the garlic and spend a little extra time making sure that the miso is mixed in. I like to use a fork to press the miso against the side of the bowl to thin it out.)

Pour approximately 1 tablespoon tamari mixture over each eggplant slab, then rub it over the top to evenly coat. Save leftover sauce. Roast eggplant for 30 minutes, until golden brown and caramelized on top.

While eggplant is roasting, place coconut flakes in a small saucepan, and heat over medium heat. Stir constantly, and as soon as the flakes start to turn golden brown around the edges, remove the pan from the heat. Keep stirring another 30 seconds. They will continue to darken in color. Transfer coconut to a small heatproof bowl (don't let it sit in saucepan or it will burn).

Once eggplant is finished roasting, serve with a sprinkle of toasted coconut and an extra drizzle of sauce.

Eggplant will keep tightly sealed in the refrigerator for 3 days. I don't recommend freezing.

2 medium globe eggplants

⅓ cup low-sodium tamari

2 tablespoons mild, white miso paste

2 tablespoons toasted sesame oil

2 tablespoons tahini

2 tablespoons maple syrup (Ⓚ sub monkfruit sweetener)

2 cloves garlic, roughly chopped

¼ cup unsweetened coconut flakes

Ideas for
LEFTOVER COCONUT FLAKES

Other recipes that use unsweetened coconut flakes are Coconut Lime Macadamia Smoothie (page 50) and 5-Layer Magic Bars (page 313). Or try them as a topping for my Orange Ginger Tofu (page 243).

SIDES

Italian Green Bean & Toasted Quinoa Salad

GF **V** | **HANDS-ON TIME:** 30 min | **TOTAL TIME:** 50 min, plus 10 min chilling | **YIELD:** 6 to 8 servings

🕐 ❄ ⊕ | **OPTIONS:** **Vg** **DF**

This side dish makes almost everyone happy. Kiddos and adults alike enjoy the flavor of Italian dressing, and you can customize the "add-ins" to your liking. It also seems to taste better with each passing day (until its "expiration" date, of course). I love having this in the fridge as a quick work-lunch, as it can double as a main dish. I just throw some greens in the bottom of a bowl, add a generous heap of this salad and an extra sprinkle of salt and pepper, and it's good to go. If you want to amp up the protein, toss half a can of chickpeas (drained) or some chopped grilled chicken into the mix.

Make the Italian Dressing: Place all dressing ingredients in a blender, and purée until smooth and creamy.

Make the Quinoa Salad: Place quinoa in a fine-mesh seive, and rinse under running water until there are no small foamy bubbles and the water runs clear, approximately 1 minute. Drain well. Place quinoa in a 2-quart saucepan. Cook over medium heat, stirring, until quinoa has a nutty fragrance and starts to stick to the pan, 4 to 5 minutes. Stir in shallots and 2 cups water. Bring to a boil, then reduce heat to the lowest setting. Cover saucepan and simmer until the liquid has evaporated (you can peek quickly), 15 to 20 minutes. Remove from the heat, but keep covered. Allow to sit 5 minutes, then uncover, and fluff with a fork.

While quinoa is cooking, bring 6 cups water to a boil in a 4- to 6-quart saucepan, then add green beans. Boil 30 seconds, then drain beans in a colander, and rinse with cold water for 30 seconds. Pat dry with a dish towel. Chop into 1-inch pieces, and set aside. If you want to use a microwave to warm your green beans, nuke them for 2 to 4 minutes, drain excess water, allow to cool for 1 or 2 minutes, then chop.

Place quinoa in a large heatproof bowl, and refrigerate 10 minutes. Remove from the fridge, and stir in green beans, bell peppers, cucumbers, and sun-dried tomatoes. Add half of the dressing, then taste and add more as desired. (I start with half then add a drizzle of dressing on each serving.) Top with parmesan, pistachios, and bacon, if using. Serve immediately as a warm salad or eat cold after refrigerating.

Leftovers will keep tightly sealed in the refrigerator for 4 days. If you want to freeze the salad, omit the cucumbers, which can get mushy, and substitute 1½ cups steamed broccoli or more green beans. Freeze up to 2 months.

ITALIAN DRESSING:

½ cup extra virgin olive oil

⅓ cup white balsamic vinegar (sub apple cider vinegar and add an extra ½ teaspoon maple syrup or honey)

2 cloves garlic, minced

¾ teaspoon sea salt (feel free to start with ½ teaspoon and add to taste)

½ teaspoon black pepper

1 teaspoon dried oregano

½ teaspoon onion powder

2 tablespoons freshly grated parmesan cheese (**Vg** **DF** sub nutritional yeast)

2 teaspoons maple syrup or honey

QUINOA SALAD:

1 cup dried quinoa

1 small shallot, minced (¼ cup)

8 cups water, divided

8 ounces frozen green beans

1 medium red bell pepper, diced into ¼-inch pieces (1¼ cups)

1 medium cucumber, sliced in half horizontally, seeds removed, and sliced into ½-inch half moons (1½ cups)

½ cup sun-dried tomatoes in olive oil, excess oil shaken off, chopped into ¼-inch pieces

Grated parmesan cheese, to taste (**Vg** **DF** sub nutritional yeast)

½ cup roasted, salted pistachios or crumbled bacon (optional)

SIDES

5-Ingredient Kimchi Coleslaw

 HANDS-ON TIME: 15 min | **TOTAL TIME:** 15 min, plus 1 h chilling | **YIELD:** 6 to 8 servings

 | **OPTIONS:**

I *love* me some coleslaw! Coleslaw reminds me of lazy summer BBQs, ladies' lunches, and my favorite "mom and pop" restaurants . . . hallmarks of my beloved southern culture. So it makes perfect sense to add kimchi to the mix, right? Well, it does to me, and I'm not sure I'll ever make coleslaw without it! Coleslaw can lean toward the sweeter side, so kimchi provides the heat and acid that's often missing from traditional recipes (in my opinion). Plus, this recipe couldn't be easier to throw together, especially because I'm all about that pre-shredded coleslaw mix! Feel free to shred your own, of course, but I take the shortcut here.

In a large mixing bowl, combine mayonnaise, honey, and mustard, and whisk until smooth. Add kimchi and coleslaw mix, and use clean hands to mix together. Apply a good amount of pressure to the slaw mix to help soften and break it down; it will noticeably reduce in volume. Feel free to add more kimchi. (Sometimes I stir in another ¼ to ½ cup.) Add any other optional ingredients to taste. Refrigerate at least 1 hour before serving.

Leftover slaw will keep tightly sealed in the refrigerator for 4 days. You might need to drain off excess liquid before serving. I don't recommend freezing.

Ideas for
LEFTOVER KIMCHI

If you don't like to eat kimchi straight-up, you can make this recipe and my Cashew Kimchi Lettuce Cups (page 137) the same week so you won't have much leftover. Kimchi is also amazing on scrambled eggs.

¼ cup mayonnaise (sub vegan mayonnaise)

2 tablespoons honey or maple syrup (sub liquid stevia drops or monkfruit sweetener, to taste)

2 tablespoons Dijon mustard

½ cup firmly packed kimchi, plus more to taste (shake off excess liquid)

12 ounces pre-shredded coleslaw mix

Salt and pepper, sliced scallions, several spoonfuls of sweet pickle relish or a few chopped dill pickles (optional)

SIDES

NOTE

Depending on the brand or style of kimchi, you might want to roughly chop it before adding it to the slaw. I use a traditional Korean kimchi.

Bacon-y Cabbage & Onions

GF DF K P | **HANDS-ON TIME:** 30 min | **TOTAL TIME:** 35 min | **YIELD:** 6 servings

This recipe came to life simply because I had half a head of green cabbage and half a package of bacon left over. Cabbage and bacon are an absolute match made in heaven, bringing out the best in one another like any healthy relationship! Vidalia onions add a hint of sweetness, which helps cut the richness in each mouthful. I've made this recipe so many times, I could practically do it with my eyes closed (not recommended, people). This dish also offers a more traditional way of cooking bacon, so you can decide which is your preferred method.

Turn on exhaust fan, and place a dish towel or several layers of paper towels near your stove. Heat a large cast-iron or other nonstick skillet over medium-high heat. Test heat by touching a piece of bacon to the pan. When it sizzles on impact, the pan is ready. Add bacon slices, making sure they don't overlap. If you're cooking a whole package, add only half of the slices (6 to 7 pieces). Cook without moving the pieces until they have noticeably shrunk in size and edges are curling, 3 to 4 minutes. Use tongs to flip, and repeat cooking and flipping until bacon is done to your liking. (I like crispy bacon, so my total cook time is approximately 10 minutes.) Be careful about popping grease; you may need to turn the heat down.

Transfer cooked bacon to the dish towel or paper towels. If making the whole package of bacon, repeat cooking process with remaining slices. When all bacon is cooked, carefully drain grease from the pan into a heatproof bowl or jar.

Reduce heat to medium-low (it may already be there), and add back 2 tablespoons of bacon grease. When the grease moves quickly around the pan and is very lightly "popping," add onions and cabbage. It might look like it won't all fit, but place a lid on top anyway. Let it cook down until the lid settles onto the pan, 4 to 5 minutes. At this point, remove the lid, and give the mixture a good stir. Increase the heat to medium. Cook until veggies are softened and translucent, another 6 to 8 minutes. Turn off heat, and add garlic, salt, and pepper, stirring constantly. Cook another minute, stirring, until garlic is softened and fragrant.

(continued on page 166)

6 ounces bacon (6 to 7 strips)

2 tablespoons bacon grease

1 small Vidalia onion or other sweet onion, sliced into ¼-inch half moons (2 cups)

½ medium head green cabbage, tough core removed, sliced into ½-inch thick ribbons (6½ to 8 cups)

6 cloves garlic, minced

½ teaspoon sea salt, plus more to taste

¼ teaspoon black pepper, plus more to taste

Ideas for
LEFTOVER COOKED BACON

I suggest cooking a 12-ounce package and freezing leftovers. If you don't want to freeze it, you can use it in my Best Potato Salad (page 167) or as a topping for my Sweet Potato, Peanut & Black Bean Burgers (page 262) or my Macadamia & Roasted Grapefruit Salad (page 295).

SIDES

BACON-Y CABBAGE & ONIONS *(continued)*

Crumble or chop 6 or 7 slices of bacon, and fold it into cabbage. Taste for seasoning, and add more salt and pepper if you like. You can also add a bit more bacon grease to taste. Serve immediately.

If you plan to have leftovers, don't add the bacon to the pan. Instead crumble 1 bacon strip over each serving.

Leftovers will keep tightly sealed in the refrigerator for 4 days. Store bacon separately in the fridge, and reheat in the microwave for 10 to 15 seconds; I find this is best for crispiness. I don't recommend freezing.

NOTE

Cooking the bacon in the skillet instead of on a baking sheet in the oven adds a deep bacon flavor in the pan before we add the remaining ingredients. For an oven method, see Best Potato Salad on the next page.

Ideas for
LEFTOVER BACON GREASE

Allow leftover bacon grease to cool completely, then store in the fridge, tightly sealed, up to a week. Use it instead of butter to make grilled cheese in a pan, or slather it on veggies before roasting them in the oven (I particularly like this with Brussels sprouts and potatoes). You can also use it as the oil for popping popcorn (top with grated parmesan cheese), sautéing dark leafy greens like kale, collards, or chard, and frying or scrambling eggs (top with a dollop of pesto).

SIDES

Best Potato Salad

Close to my apartment is a rotisserie-chicken joint called Smokin' Thighs. On a hot summer day, I love slurping on iced tea and enjoying BBQ chicken tacos with their life-changing potato salad. You heard me. The Smokin' Thighs potato salad is not only the best I've ever had, it's quite possibly my favorite potato side dish ever! I asked for the details, but all I got was "sour cream" (which I totally respect), so I had my work cut out for me to recreate the recipe. Turns out, according to my taste buds at least, the keys are: slightly mashed taters, hints of sweet and acid in addition to creaminess, and a gratuitous amount of chives. Oh, and bacon doesn't hurt either. I honestly think I could eat this potato salad every day without getting sick of it, and I tip my hat to Smokin' Thighs for bringing the Best Potato Salad into my life!

Preheat oven to 375° F. Wrap a baking sheet with aluminum foil, pressing it tightly to the edges. I like to do one piece lengthwise and two pieces crosswise.

Place bacon slices on the baking sheet. They might slightly overlap, but they'll shrink as they cook. Bake for 20 minutes, then carefully drain excess grease into a heatproof (glass or metal) container to cool. Bake another 10 to 20 minutes, until the bacon reaches your desired doneness (will depend in part on the cut or brand of bacon). You can pat off excess grease with a paper towel if you like. Allow to cool at least 10 minutes before crumbling and using in the salad.

Place potatoes in a large pot, and cover with at least 2 inches of cold water. Stir in ½ teaspoon salt. Bring to a boil (be patient!), and boil until knife-tender but not falling apart, 8 to 10 minutes. Drain potatoes in a colander, and rinse with cold water for 1 minute.

In a large mixing bowl, combine remaining 1 teaspoon salt (feel free to use less and add to taste), sour cream, mayonnaise, black pepper, onion powder, garlic powder, honey, and vinegar. Whisk to blend. Stir in shallots and chives, then add potatoes (make sure all water has drained

(continued on page 169)

6 ounces bacon (6 to 7 strips) (V optional, but recommended)

2 pounds red potatoes, rinsed and patted dry, then sliced into ½-inch rounds, trimmed of any funky-looking bits or ends

1½ teaspoons sea salt, plus more to taste, divided

1 cup sour cream

½ cup mayonnaise

1 teaspoon black pepper

1 teaspoon onion powder

¼ teaspoon garlic powder

2 tablespoons honey

1 tablespoon apple cider vinegar

1 large or 2 small shallots, minced (½ cup)

½ ounce chives, minced (½ cup) (sub 1 bunch scallions, sliced into ¼-inch rounds)

SIDES

BEST POTATO SALAD *(continued)*

from them). Use a fork to partially mash potatoes into the sauce, evenly incorporating. You want the potatoes to be broken down, but not fully mashed—you should see chunks. Fold in crumbled bacon, if using.

Refrigerate at least 1 hour before serving, ideally 3 to 4. Leftovers will keep tightly sealed in the refrigerator for 5 days or in the freezer for 2 to 4 months, but note that bacon will be soft.

Ideas for
LEFTOVER SOUR CREAM

Use any leftover sour cream in Spiced Pear Sour Cream Loaf (page 124), Artichoke Leek & White Bean Gratin (page 251), or Sour Cream & Onion Cauliflower Risotto (page 152). Or just use it as a topping for BBQ Sweet Potato Tofu Tacos (page 81), Cauliflower Walnut Tacos (page 257), or One-Pot Pineapple Paprika Fajitas (page 227).

NOTES

I don't peel potatoes if they're organic.

If you plan to have leftovers, add bacon to individual servings to prevent it from getting soggy. (I microwave leftover bacon for 10 to 15 seconds to crisp it again before adding to servings.) If you prefer to cook bacon on the stovetop, see the Bacon-y Cabbage & Onion recipe (page 164).

Bourbon Balsamic Skillet Mushrooms

Vg GF K P | **HANDS-ON TIME:** 20 min | **TOTAL TIME:** 20 min | **YIELD:** 4 servings |

This is your ace-up-the-sleeve dish when you need something quick, easy, and crowd-pleasing for the holiday table. Despite the simple ingredient list, these skillet mushrooms taste fancy, if you know what I mean. When bourbon hits your hot pan, the alcohol evaporates, and you're left with malty, piquant undertones. Aged balsamic adds a candied sharpness to round out this simple and simply lovely side. The mushrooms make an enviable couple with most perennial herbs, such as rosemary, thyme, oregano, or sage. Feel free to double the recipe. Serve these mushrooms with a burger or steak with caramelized onions, use them in place of meat in my French Dip Calzone (page 183), add them to a breakfast plate of fried eggs and bacon, or use them as a topper for pesto and avocado toast.

2 tablespoons butter or olive oil (butter is my strong preference)

16 ounces sliced white button or baby bella mushrooms

2 tablespoons aged balsamic vinegar

2 tablespoons bourbon

¼ teaspoon sea salt, plus more to taste

¼ teaspoon black pepper

If mushrooms have dirt on them, wipe with a damp dish towel.

Heat a large cast-iron skillet or nonstick sauté pan over medium heat, and add butter. When butter has melted and is lightly bubbling, add mushrooms. Cook, stirring every few minutes, until liquid has evaporated and they have some golden-brown edges, approximately 12 minutes.

Reduce heat to low, and add vinegar, bourbon, salt, and pepper. Stir to incorporate, and cook, stirring, until liquid has evaporated and mushrooms have a nice glossy coating, another 1 to 2 minutes. Taste for seasoning, and add more salt if you like. (I add another ¼ teaspoon.) Enjoy immediately.

Mushrooms will keep tightly sealed in the refrigerator for 6 days or in the freezer for 6 months.

> *Ideas for*
> **LEFTOVER BOURBON**
>
> If you don't usually keep bourbon around, buy a small bottle for this recipe, and make my Maple Bourbon Baked Pears (page 321) the same week.

SIDES

Mediterranean Spaghetti Squash Bake

(V) (GF) (K) | **HANDS-ON TIME:** 55 min | **TOTAL TIME:** 1 h, 55 min | **YIELD:** 8 servings

Spaghetti squash is rich in antioxidants and fiber, and it's a pretty solid low-carb substitute for pasta. Plus, it has a mild taste that works with almost any flavor profile. Here, it provides an ideal backdrop for strong flavors such as briny olives, chewy-sweet sun-dried tomatoes, and a pop of Greek-inspired spices. If you're a pasta lover looking for a nutrient-dense, cozy alternative, this is the dish for you.

Preheat oven to 400° F. Line a baking sheet with parchment paper.

Trim off the base and top of spaghetti squash, and slice in half lengthwise. Place cut-side down on baking sheet, and roast 25 to 40 minutes (this will depend on the size and ripeness of the squash), until a toothpick can easily pierce the flesh. Allow to cool 15 or 20 minutes before handling. Keep oven at 400° F.

Dice the sun-dried tomatoes into ¼-inch pieces. Drain artichoke hearts, squeeze out excess liquid, then roughly chop. Drain olives, and dice into ¼-inch pieces. Tip: Use kitchen shears to cut the tomatoes, artichoke hearts, and olives if you prefer.

Grease a 9 × 13 × 2-inch baking dish with avocado oil.

Heat a large sauté pan over medium-low heat, and add 2 tablespoons avocado oil. When oil moves quickly around the pan and is shimmering, add onions. Cook, stirring every minute or so, until softened and translucent, 5 to 6 minutes. Feel free to add splashes of water (2 tablespoons at a time) to prevent sticking or burning. Add garlic, salt, oregano, basil, onion powder, and cumin, and cook another minute, stirring constantly. Add sun-dried tomatoes, artichoke hearts, diced tomatoes, olives, and 1 cup cheese. Cook, stirring, until cheese is melted, about 5 minutes. Transfer mixture to a large heatproof mixing bowl.

Once the squash is cool enough to touch, use a fork to scrape out the seeds and "goo" in the middle of each half. Discard. Then scrape the "noodles" into the same large mixing bowl as the veggies. Toss to mix well. (I use tongs to then toss everything together.) Scrape squash mixture into the baking dish, and spread in an even layer. Top with remaining 1 cup cheese. Bake for 40 minutes, until the top is golden brown with slightly crispy edges.

Leftovers keep in the refrigerator for 4 days. I don't recommend freezing.

1 medium spaghetti squash

½ cup sun-dried tomatoes in olive oil, excess oil shaken off

1 14-ounce can whole artichoke hearts

⅔ cup pitted kalamata olives

2 tablespoons avocado oil, plus more for greasing

½ medium red onion, chopped into ½-inch pieces (¾ cup)

5 cloves garlic, finely minced

2 teaspoons sea salt (feel free to start with less and add to taste)

1 teaspoon dried oregano

1 teaspoon dried basil

½ teaspoon onion powder

¼ teaspoon ground cumin

1 14½-ounce can no-salt-added diced tomatoes

8 ounces mild white cheddar cheese, shredded (2 cups), divided

Ideas for
LEFTOVER KALAMATA OLIVES

Use leftover olives in my Picnic Macaroni Salad (page 189) or use them instead of green olives in my Smoked Salmon, Olive & Pecan Spread (page 202).

LUNCH + DINNER ENTRÉES

Welcome to the "meat" of the cookbook! An entrée often provides the majority of the fat and protein in your meal, helping you stay full and satiated for hours on end. In these sections, I'm thrilled to offer you a little bit of everything—red meat, seafood, poultry, and plant-based goodness! Within each section, you will find a range of recipes for a range of lifestyles, time-constraints, and taste buds. As you make your way through these recipes, do the best you can to source the highest quality proteins available to you. Keep in mind that if a recipe requires a bit more labor or steps, it will yield a lot of food and will almost always be freezer-friendly. I am enamored with every single recipe here, and I was not shy about cutting out dishes that I didn't find amazing. So with fervent prayer, I hope that these recipes make your life easier, healthier, and more delicious, as well as allow you more time for eating at your family table.

Red Meat Entrées

I would argue that quality is most important when it comes to the red meat we purchase. Red meat tends to be higher in fat than other types of animal protein, and toxins are stored in fat. Known as Persistent Organic Pollutants (POPS), these toxins can consist of the chemicals, pesticides, and added hormones used in large-scale Concentrated Animal Feeding Organizations, *aka* industrial meat production. I don't say this to be a Debbie-downer, but instead to remind y'all to do the best you can when it comes to the meat you choose. If there's a place to splurge in your grocery list, I think it should be on 100 percent grass-fed, pasture-raised meat. That way, you can enjoy delectable, rich red meats that contain healing, bioavailable omega-3 fatty acids, instead of harmful, inflammatory POPS.*

That being said, I think you will love the recipes in this chapter! I'm all about taking advantage of ground meat—beef, turkey, and chicken make regular rotations in my kitchen. It's easy to freeze, affordable, and so versatile, forming the base of my Cheddar-Stuffed Buffalo Meatballs, "Big Mac" Meatza, Chili Black Bean Burgers, and more. I also love purchasing the less-popular, tougher cuts, like round roasts and shoulders, and cooking them down until they're fall-apart tender, as with my French Dip Calzone and Mongolian Molasses Pork. Though you won't find fancy cuts or techniques around here when it comes to red meat, I do hope you find these recipes not only easy, but family- and wallet-friendly.

* For more information on toxins stored in fat, see Michele La Merrill et al., "Toxicological Function of Adipose Tissue: Focus on Persistent Organic Pollutants," *Environmental Health Perspectives* 121, no. 2 (February 2013): 162–69, https://www.ncbi.nlm.nih.gov/pmc/articles/PMC3569688/.

Cheddar-Stuffed Buffalo Meatballs

GF K | **HANDS-ON TIME:** 35 min | **TOTAL TIME:** 55 min | **YIELD:** Approximately 17 meatballs

After years of making a variety of meatballs and meatloaves, I've realized that the best result comes from a combination of beef and turkey. This pairing, combined with a few tablespoons of mayo (yep!), makes for the most tender texture. My love for Frank's RedHot continues on in this recipe, pairing gloriously with an oozy cheddar cheese filling. For a dairy-free version, feel free to sub a vegan cheese of your choice, but I don't suggest leaving it out altogether. These meatballs are divine on their own, but you can also throw them into a roll with an extra smear of mayo, some finely diced white onion, shredded lettuce, and another sprinkle of cheddar.

Preheat oven to 375° F. Line a baking sheet with parchment paper, and place a slotted baking sheet or ovenproof cooling rack on top. Make sure parchment overhangs the edges by at least an inch. Grease the baking sheet with 2 teaspoons avocado oil. (I suggest using a pastry brush.)

Heat a small sauté pan over medium heat, and add remaining 2 teaspoons avocado oil. When oil moves quickly around the pan and is shimmering, add shallots, and cook, stirring, until softened, 3 to 4 minutes. Reduce heat to low, and add garlic and onion powder. Stir continuously for another 30 seconds. Remove from the heat, and allow to cool for 5 minutes.

While veggies are cooling, place all remaining ingredients except cheese in a large mixing bowl. Once veggies have cooled for 5 minutes, add to the bowl. Use clean hands to thoroughly incorporate ingredients.

Scoop up approximately ¼ cup meatball mixture, and form a rough ball shape. (I like to use a dampened 2-inch retractable ice cream scoop or dampened ¼ cup measure.) Place on the baking sheet, then repeat with remaining mixture. Use your thumb or a tablespoon measure to make a well in each meatball, approximately 1 inch wide. Fill each hole with a cheese cube. Pinch the meatballs closed, and roll into a round shape. (I find it helpful to rinse my hands a few times while doing this to prevent sticking.) Space meatballs approximately 1 inch apart.

Bake meatballs for 21 minutes, then test to see if ready by slicing one in half. It's completely cooked if no pink remains. If you see any pink, bake for another 2 to 3 minutes. Allow to cool for 10 minutes before using a spatula to remove the meatballs from the broiler rack.

Leftover meatballs will keep tightly sealed in the refrigerator for 5 days or in the freezer for 2 months.

4 teaspoons avocado oil, divided

1 medium shallot, diced into ¼-inch pieces (⅓ cup)

5 cloves garlic, minced

½ teaspoon onion powder

2 large eggs

2 tablespoons mayonaise

2 tablespoons original Frank's RedHot

1½ tablespoons low-sodium tamari

½ cup blanched almond flour

¼ teaspoon black pepper

1 pound ground beef, 85/15 blend recommended

1 pound dark meat ground turkey

6 ounces cheddar cheese, cut into ¾-inch cubes (make at least 17, can make a few extra)

SUGGESTED SIDES

Creamy Corn & Chive Farro
(page 156)

Buttery Lemon Pepper Leeks
(page 148)

Chili Black Bean Burgers

with QUICK BBQ SAUCE

  GF DF | **HANDS-ON TIME:** 30 min | **TOTAL TIME:** 50 min | **YIELD:** 8 burgers

It turns out that puréeing black beans and adding them to ground beef creates a dreamy burger patty texture. Don't ask me about the science behind it (or do let me know if you know)! Instead, ask me how something as simple as a burger can feel completely special with the right addition of spices and condiments. Actually, I don't know the answer to that either; I just know that it works! These burgers are officially one of my all-time favorites, and you don't even need access to a grill to bring them to life. I absolutely love making these on a hot summer night and enjoying them with a chilled kombucha (or beer) paired with my Best Potato Salad (page 167).

Preheat oven to 400° F. Line a baking sheet with parchment paper. Make sure parchment overhangs the edges by at least an inch. Top with a slotted baking sheet or ovenproof cooling rack, and grease well with oil or melted butter.

Make the Chili Black Bean Burgers: Place beef and almond flour in a large mixing bowl, and set aside. No need to mix yet.

Place all remaining burger ingredients in a food processor or high-powered blender. Process or blend until a mostly smooth paste forms.

Add bean mixture to the beef and almond flour, and use clean hands to evenly incorporate. This is a fairly wet mixture, but you should be able to form shapes with it.

Fill a bowl with lukewarm water, and grab a ½ cup measure. Dip the measuring cup into the water, shaking off excess, then scoop up ½ cup packed burger mixture. (I like to hold the measuring cup with one hand and shake it with the other hand to loosen mixture, but you can also scrape it out with a spoon.) Place on the slotted baking sheet, then repeat with the rest of the mixture until you have 8 patties. Be sure to wet the cup after each scoop. Evenly distribute any leftover mixture among the patties.

Rinse and lightly dampen hands. Smooth each burger into a ball, then flatten into an approximately 4-inch diameter patty. Leave at least ½ inch between each. Bake burgers for 20 minutes.

(continued on page 182)

CHILI BLACK BEAN BURGERS:

Avocado oil or melted butter for greasing

2 pounds ground beef, recommend 85/15 blend

1 cup blanched almond flour

1 15-ounce can no-salt-added black beans, drained and rinsed

2 large eggs

2 tablespoons mayonnaise

1½ teaspoons sea salt (feel free to use less if you're salt-sensitive)

2 tablespoons ketchup

2 teaspoons chili powder

1 teaspoon onion powder

½ teaspoon garlic powder

½ teaspoon red pepper flakes

¼ teaspoon black pepper

¼ teaspoon ground cumin

QUICK BBQ SAUCE:

6 tablespoons ketchup

1½ teaspoons molasses

1 tablespoon maple syrup or honey (sub monkfruit sweetener)

1 tablespoon low-sodium tamari

1 tablespoon apple cider vinegar

CHILI BLACK BEAN BURGERS
WITH QUICK BBQ SAUCE *(continued)*

Make the Quick BBQ Sauce: While burgers are baking, whisk the sauce. Whisk all sauce ingredients together in a small bowl.

Once the burgers have baked 20 minutes, set the oven to broil. Broil for 2 to 4 minutes, until slightly charred on top. Watch closely. Serve burgers with sauce and buns of your choice, if you like.

Burgers will keep tightly sealed in the refrigerator for 5 days or in the freezer for 2 months. Leftover sauce will keep tightly sealed in the refrigerator for 5 days.

NOTE

Use soft buns for these burgers. The patties hold together well, but they're tender; don't use ciabatta or an overly toasted English muffins because the burger will squeeze out of the sides of the bread pieces.

SERVING SUGGESTION

Make it a cheeseburger! After the burgers have baked 20 minutes, remove them from the oven, and top with cheese. Set the oven to broil, and return the burgers to the oven. Broil 2 to 4 minutes, until cheese is melted and bubbling.

SUGGESTED SIDES

Caramelized Onion & Chive Dip (use as a burger topping) (page 138)

Chickpea, Avocado & Goat Cheese Salad with Grainy Mustard Dressing (page 286)

Charred Green Bean & Farro Salad with Avocado Ranch Dressing (page 293)

"Hot" Honey Cheddar Stuffed Sweet Potato Skins (page 130)

Best Potato Salad (page 167)

5-Ingredient Kimchi Coleslaw (page 163)

LUNCH + DINNER ENTRÉES

French Dip Calzone

with SUN-DRIED TOMATO MARINARA

HANDS-ON TIME: 1 h, 10 min | **TOTAL TIME:** 2 h, 55 min (Instant Pot); 7 h, 35 min (Crock-Pot)

YIELD: 8 servings

Mercy, is this calzone good! I've had such a blast playing with whole-wheat pizza dough, and this calzone iteration might be my favorite. The combination of tender, savory beef, melty cheese, and tangy marinara is all of my Saturday night dreams come true! (I'm such a dork.) Is this the world's healthiest recipe? Not necessarily. But it is a much healthier alternative to most take-out options, which use refined flour, excess sodium, and harmful vegetable oils. If you don't want to deal with dough, you can toss some of the meat and marinara together to make a bolognese for pasta. Or just make the meat, and enjoy it over salads or stuffed into baked potatoes or as a side to roasted veggies.

Meat Filling—Instant Pot Version: To make the meat filling in an Instant Pot, place onions, beef broth, onion powder, garlic powder, tamari, honey, mustard, and molasses in the canister. Stir to evenly incorporate. Add meat, and stir to coat well. Secure lid, and set to "Manual" 45 minutes. When the Instant Pot beeps to signal the end of cooking time, allow pressure to release naturally, or at least for 20 minutes. Turn to "Venting," and release any remaining pressure, then open.

Meat Filling—Crock-Pot Version: In a Crock-Pot, place the onions, beef broth, onion powder, garlic powder, tamari, honey, mustard, and molasses. Stir to evenly incorporate. Add meat, and stir to coat well. Set temperature to low. Cook approximately 7 hours, until meat is fall-apart tender.

Sun-Dried Tomato Marinara—Both Versions: While the meat is cooking, make the Sun-Dried Tomato Marina. Place all ingredients in the order listed in a food processor, and purée until smooth. Transfer to a saucepan, and bring to a simmer over medium heat. Cook for 10 minutes, stirring every minute or so. If it's splashing, reduce the heat. Set aside to cool for at least 20 minutes before using in recipe. Rinse food processor, but no need to fully clean.

When the meat is done, use a mesh strainer or slotted spoon to remove the meat and onions from the broth, and place them in a heatproof bowl. Allow to cool for 5 minutes. Taste the broth for seasoning, and add salt if you like. Set aside.

(continued on page 185)

SPECIAL EQUIPMENT:

Tape Measure

MEAT FILLING:

1 yellow onion, diced into ¼-inch pieces (1¾ cups)

3 cups low-sodium beef broth (can sub chicken broth; I recommend beef)

1 teaspoon onion powder

½ teaspoon garlic powder

2 tablespoons low-sodium tamari

2 tablespoons honey (sub monkfruit sweetener)

1½ tablespoons Dijon mustard

1 tablespoon molasses

2 pounds boneless round roast, sliced in 1-inch-thick slabs (I leave excess fat on, but if you want to trim some, that's fine)

Salt, to taste

SUN-DRIED TOMATO MARINARA:

1 15-ounce can no-salt-added diced tomatoes

½ cup firmly packed sun-dried tomatoes in olive oil, plus 1 tablespoon of the oil

½ ounce fresh basil (½ cup, packed)

5 cloves garlic, roughly chopped

½ teaspoon sea salt

½ teaspoon dried oregano

¼ cup tomato paste (sub ketchup)

(continued on page 185)

Remove dough from the refrigerator and allow to rest for 20 minutes.

Place the meat and onions in a food processor along with ½ cup broth. Pulse until finely shredded. If you don't have a food processor or don't want to use one, you can add ½ cup broth to the bowl, and shred the meat with two forks.

Assemble the Calzone: Preheat oven to 375° F. Once the dough has been at room temperature for 20 minutes, grease a baking sheet thoroughly with 1 tablespoon melted butter. Gently spread dough into a rectangle. It should cover almost the entire pan. If it keeps breaking, allow it to sit for a few more minutes. Eventually it will spread.

Brush 1 tablespoon melted butter on dough in an even layer. If you used the food processor to shred your meat, carefully remove blade, and use tongs to take the beef out (shake off any excess liquid to prevent sogginess), spreading it over half of the dough, lengthwise. Leave approximately 1 inch free around the edges. Evenly dollop on ¾ cup Sun-Dried Tomato Marinara, then top with cheese. Fold other half of dough over the filling, pinching the edges together to seal. Brush top with the remaining 1 tablespoon melted butter, then make four to five 3-inch slits along the top of the dough to allow steam to escape.

Bake the calzone for 20 minutes, then allow it to rest for 5 minutes before slicing.

While the calzone is baking, make a dipping sauce with broth. If using an Instant Pot, press the "Sauté" function, and cook until broth has reduced by approximately one-third, 10 to 12 minutes. If using a Crock-Pot, transfer the broth to a saucepan, and heat over medium heat. Simmer until the calzone is done.

Leftover calzone will keep tightly sealed in the refrigerator for 3 days or in the freezer for 3 months.

CALZONE:

1 pound whole-wheat pizza dough

3 tablespoons melted butter (sub olive oil), divided

6 ounces cheddar cheese, shredded (1½ cups)

SUGGESTED SIDES

Roasted Romaine with Basil Caesar Hummus Dressing (page 298)

Sour Cream & Onion Cauliflower Risotto (page 152)

Italian Green Bean & Toasted Quinoa Salad (page 160)

"Big Mac" Meatza

with SPECIAL SAUCE

 HANDS-ON TIME: 20 min | **TOTAL TIME:** 55 min | **YIELD:** 6 servings

Confession: when I was in college, Big Macs were 100 percent my guilty pleasure and late-night treat of choice. I found them utterly irresistible, and I have not-so-secretly wanted to recreate the experience in LL Balanced style. For me, the key is the balance of creamy sauce with a soft beef patty and crunchy lettuce. The bun is really superfluous (which is not always the case). Hence, this "Big Mac" Meatza, the ideal recipe to satisfy both myself and my low-carb friends. Bonus: You can use leftover Special Sauce as a dip for roasted veggies.

Preheat oven to 415° F. Line a baking sheet with parchment paper.

Make the Special Sauce: In a medium mixing bowl, combine mayonnaise, mustard, tomato paste, honey, ½ teaspoon salt, ½ teaspoon pepper, and lemon juice. Whisk to incorporate. Refrigerate.

Make the Meatza: In a large mixing bowl, combine ground beef, eggs, onion powder, almond flour, and 2 tablespoons of the sauce. Use clean hands to mix everything together.

Stir ¼ cup each of the onions and pickles into the remaining sauce.

Spread meat mixture in an even layer on the baking sheet, covering it completely. Bake for 12 minutes. Carefully pour any excess fat off the baking sheet into heatproof bowl (not in the sink) and discard once cooled. Pat the surface of the meat with paper towels or dish towels to remove excess liquid.

Spread approximately three-quarters of the spread onto meat in an even layer. Evenly sprinkle on cheese. Bake for another 12 minutes.

Allow to cool for 10 minutes, then top the meatza with extra sauce, remaining onions and pickles, and shredded romaine. Slice into portions.

Leftover meatza will keep in the refrigerator for 4 days or in the freezer for 2 months. Reheat in a 350° F oven until the cheese is melty again.

SPECIAL SAUCE:

¾ cup mayonnaise

2 tablespoons Dijon mustard

¼ cup tomato paste (sub ketchup and decrease honey to 2 teaspoons)

2 tablespoons honey

1½ teaspoons sea salt, divided (feel free to start with less and add to taste)

1 teaspoon black pepper, divided

Juice from 1 lemon (2 tablespoons)

MEATZA:

2 pounds ground beef (85/15 blend recommended)

2 large eggs

½ teaspoon onion powder

½ cup blanched almond flour

½ cup finely diced white onion, divided

½ cup finely diced dill pickle, divided

6 ounces sharp cheddar cheese, shredded (1½ cups)

1 cup shredded romaine lettuce

SUGGESTED SIDES

Vegan Tomato-y Collard Greens (page 155)

Creamy Corn & Chive Farro (page 156)

Best Potato Salad (page 167)

NOTE

If you're planning to have leftovers, add the romaine on individual servings instead of on the whole meatza.

Picnic Macaroni Salad

with ITALIAN DRESSING

HANDS-ON TIME: 55 min | **TOTAL TIME:** 55 min, plus 4 to 8 h chilling | **YIELD:** 8 servings

❄ ⊕ | **OPTION:** GF

I'll never forget a warm spring day, years ago now, when a close friend and I took a train to Boston for a work event, and we were left with the entire afternoon free. We went to a spectacular Italian deli and stocked up on charcuterie, cheese, bread, wine, and, my favorite of all, the most delicious cold pasta salad. We took it all to a sunny park in the middle of the city and happily ate and drank the afternoon away. While this memory can only live in the past, I can at least bring that pasta salad to the present. And here it is! This recipe is all about the quality of the add-ins, so choose top-quality salami and mozzarella, candy-sweet cherry tomatoes, bright basil, and the saltiest, richest olives you can find.

Make the Italian Dressing: Place all dressing ingredients in a blender, and purée until smooth. Refrigerate while you prepare the salad.

Make the Macaroni Salad: In a large mixing bowl, combine cooked noodles and all the remaining ingredients, except basil. Add dressing to taste. (I use the entire batch, but you can start with half and go from there.) Refrigerate at least 4 hours, ideally 8 hours or overnight, before serving. Garnish with fresh basil and extra grated parmesan cheese before serving.

Salad will keep tightly sealed in the refrigerator for 4 days. Note that chickpea- and veggie-based pastas do not keep well. I don't recommend freezing regardless of the type of pasta.

NOTE

To keep pasta from sticking together, toss it with a bit of avocado oil after draining.

SUGGESTED SIDES

Carrot & Zucchini Ribbons with Lemony Pistachio Pesto (page 151)

Macadamia & Roasted Grapefruit Salad with Lemony Vinaigrette (page 295)

ITALIAN DRESSING:

½ cup extra virgin olive oil

⅓ cup white balsamic vinegar (sub apple cider vinegar and increase syrup or honey by ½ teaspoon)

2 cloves garlic, minced

¾ teaspoon sea salt (start with ½ teaspoon and add to taste)

½ teaspoon black pepper

1 teaspoon dried oregano

½ teaspoon onion powder

2 tablespoons freshly grated parmesan cheese (sub nutritional yeast)

2 teaspoons maple syrup or honey (sub liquid stevia, to taste)

MACARONI SALAD:

16 ounces pasta of choice, cooked al dente, rinsed, and cooled (GF sub gluten-free pasta)

½ yellow bell pepper, diced into ¼-inch pieces (¾ cup)

1 pint cherry tomatoes, halved

⅔ cup sliced black olives

¼ medium red onion, finely minced (⅓ cup)

6 ounces uncured nitrate-free salami (I like Applegate Farms brand)

8 ounces fresh mini-mozzarella balls, sliced in half

¼ cup freshly grated parmesan cheese, plus more for garnish

½ ounce fresh basil (½ cup finely chopped)

Steak Bites

with BALSAMIC CREAM SAUCE & ROASTED ASPARAGUS

GF DF K P | **HANDS-ON TIME:** 40 min | **TOTAL TIME:** 1 h, plus 8 to 24 h marinating | **YIELD:** 4 servings

Who needs to deal with cooking a big ole' steak when you can have these juicy steak bites in a fraction of the time? Seriously, these melt-in-your-mouth morsels are so satisfying, and I am officially hooked! The key to this recipe is not overcooking the meat. All these little pieces need is a quick sear to caramelize the edges and take the center from red to pale pink. Once you have the cooking method down, the sky's the limit for ways you can doctor up these bites. I happen to be fond of this one, which uses goodness from the bottom of the pan to make a balsamic cream sauce and presents the whole lot over tender roasted asparagus. However, I think my steak bites would be right at home in a stir-fry, tossed in pesto pasta, or simply dipped in BBQ sauce.

The Night Before: Combine sirloin pieces, vinegar, honey, mustard, garlic powder, ¼ teaspoon salt, and ¼ teaspoon pepper in a sealable plastic bag or marinating container. Shake and squeeze to make sure ingredients are evenly incorporated. Marinate in the refrigerator at least 8 hours and up to 24 hours.

The Next Day: Remove the meat from the refrigerator, and allow it to sit at room temperature for 30 minutes.

Preheat oven to 375° F. Line a baking sheet with parchment paper.

Place asparagus on baking sheet. Drizzle 2 teaspoons avocado oil over asparagus, and sprinkle with remaining ¼ teaspoon salt and remaining ¼ teaspoon pepper. Toss to coat, then spread stalks in an even a layer; it's okay if some are overlapping. Roast asparagus for 30 minutes, stirring halfway to expose any that might be overlapping, until knife-tender and golden brown around the edges.

While asparagus is roasting, use tongs to remove meat from marinade, and place in a bowl, shaking off excess liquid. Pat meat dry with a dish towel or paper towels.

Place a heatproof bowl near your stove, and turn on the exhaust fan. Heat a large cast-iron or other nonstick skillet over medium-high heat, and add remaining 2 tablespoons avocado oil. When oil moves quickly around the pan and is shimmering, add half the meat. Sear meat without stirring for approximately 30 seconds to 1 minute. Then use a

(continued on page 192)

Ingredients

- 1 pound lean sirloin or top round London broil, trimmed of excess fat and cut into 1-inch pieces
- ¼ cup apple cider vinegar
- 1 tablespoon honey or maple syrup (sub monkfruit sweetener)
- 2 teaspoons Dijon mustard
- ¼ teaspoon garlic powder
- ½ teaspoon sea salt, plus more to taste, divided
- ½ teaspoon black pepper, plus more to taste, divided
- 2 pounds asparagus, woody ends removed, cut into 2-inch pieces
- 2 tablespoons plus 2 teaspoons avocado oil, divided
- 1 small shallot, diced into ¼-inch pieces (¼ cup)
- ⅓ cup water
- 1 cup canned full-fat coconut milk, plus more for thinning
- 1½ tablespoons aged balsamic vinegar

STEAK BITES WITH BALSAMIC CREAM & ROASTED ASPARAGUS *(continued)*

spatula or tongs to flip, and repeat searing for another 30 seconds to 1 minute. Immediately transfer to the bowl, leaving juices in the pan. You want to still see some pink in the meat. Repeat with remaining meat.

Reduce heat to low, and add shallots and water. Cook, stirring constantly, until shallots are softened and translucent, 2 to 3 minutes. Add coconut milk and vinegar, then use a spatula to scrape any brown bits off the bottom of the pan. Bring to a simmer, and cook until noticeably reduced and very light brown (like gravy) in color, stirring every minute or so, 8 to 10 minutes. If it seems more like a jam consistency, add more coconut milk as needed to thin.

Add steak back to the pan, and cook, stirring, another minute. Taste for seasoning, and add more salt and pepper if you like. Remove from the heat, and serve steak and sauce over asparagus.

Leftovers will keep tightly sealed in the refrigerator up to 3 days. Because these are such small lean pieces of meat, they won't be as tender when you reheat them. I don't recommend freezing.

SUGGESTED SIDES

Bourbon Balsamic Skillet Mushrooms (page 170)

Buttery Lemon Pepper Leeks (page 148)

Sour Cream & Onion Cauliflower Risotto (page 152)

Miso Coconut Roasted Eggplant (page 159)

Bacon-y Cabbage & Onions (page 164)

NOTES

The longer you marinate the meat, the less time it needs to cook, as the acid in your marinade "cooks" it a bit. Take that into consideration when searing.

To remove the woody end from an asparagus stalk, hold the stalk gently, and bend it until it snaps. Wherever it snaps is where it begins to get tough. Save the tender part, and discard the end.

Perfect Pork Chops

with PEACH HONEY JAM

GF | **HANDS-ON TIME:** 45 min | **TOTAL TIME:** 1 h, 15 min | **YIELD:** 3 to 4 servings |

A pork chop recipe was always on this book outline, but after no less than ten cooking attempts, I had all but given up. Pork chops (especially boneless ones) are lean, and despite pulling out every trick I knew, they kept turning out dry and chewy. So I did something I try rarely to do: I reached out to Chef Sean Brock and pleaded for his help. Sean is the authority on cooking meat in the Southeast, if not the entire country, and I was overwhelmingly grateful when he agreed. I left our chop tutorial with a belly full of tender pork and in awe of the nuanced tips and techniques that he so graciously shared. While mine will always be a cut below Sean's (see what I did there?), I learned enough to teach you how to make a delicious, juicy pork chop. You must read these instructions in advance and follow them, because the magic is in the details. In particular, the resting times: before the chops cook, after they come out of the pan, and after they come out of the oven. If you use a thermometer and "respect the resting," you can make some fabulous chops too!

Make the Pork Chops: Remove chops from the refrigerator, pat dry with a dish towel, then place on a plate or baking sheet. Sprinkle each chop with a pinch of salt (⅛ teaspoon) and a scant pinch of pepper, then flip and repeat on the other side (this should be approximately ¾ teaspoon salt and ½ teaspoon pepper total). Allow chops to rest at room temperature for 25 minutes.

After 25 minutes, preheat oven to 300° F.

Turn on your exhaust fan, and place a baking sheet near the stove. Heat a cast-iron or other nonstick skillet over medium-high heat, and add avocado oil. It's very important that you are patient and allow the skillet to heat properly. It's equally important that you stay on medium-high and not high heat.

Use tongs to grab one of the chops, and touch a side of it to the pan. If the chop sizzles on impact, the pan is ready to go. Add chops to the pan, leaving at least 1 inch between each, and sear for 6 to 8 minutes. Every minute or so, apply gentle pressure to chops with a flat spatula, to make sure they are getting evenly seared. Check around 6 minutes, and

(continued on page 195)

SPECIAL EQUIPMENT:

Meat thermometer

PORK CHOPS:

1½ pounds boneless center-cut pork chops (ideally three 8-ounce chops)

¾ teaspoon salt, plus more to taste

½ teaspoon black pepper

2 tablespoons avocado oil

PEACH JAM:

2 tablespoons butter

3 medium peaches, pitted and sliced into ¼-inch-thick wedges (3 cups; I keep the skin on but you can peel if you prefer.)

1 tablespoon honey (sub monkfruit sweetener)

Juice from ½ lemon (1 tablespoon)

4 ounces brie cheese, sliced into ½-inch thick rounds or rectangles (will depend on the shape of the brie)

Fresh basil or thyme for garnish

flip once the bottom is golden brown. Turn the heat down just a bit, and repeat searing and gentle pressing on the other side, 3 to 4 minutes.

Place chops on the baking sheet, and reduce heat to medium-low. Use a meat thermometer to test the temperature in the thickest part of each chop. If any are 145° F or higher, transfer from the baking sheet to a heatproof plate, as they will not need time in the oven.

Make the Peach Jam: Allow chops to rest while you make the peach jam. Place butter in the skillet. Once butter is melted, add peaches, honey, and lemon juice. Cook, stirring and gently mashing every minute or so, until the peaches are broken down and thickened into a jammy consistency, 10 to 12 minutes. Reduce heat to the lowest setting. (I like to add a pinch of salt to the jam, but that's totally optional.)

Place chops that need more cooking in the oven. Bake until the chops reach 145° F, testing with a meat thermometer every 3 minutes. Baking should take 6 to 15 minutes. Remove from the oven.

Turn the oven to broil. Place brie slices on top of the peach jam in the skillet. Place the skillet under the broiler, and broil until brie starts to melt and has golden-brown edges, 2 to 4 minutes. Watch closely. Remove the skillet from the oven.

Make sure all chops have had at least 5 minutes to rest after coming out of the oven, then nestle them into the skillet. Cover each with some jam and melted brie. Garnish with fresh herbs, and serve immediately.

Leftovers will keep tightly sealed in the refrigerator for 3 days or in the freezer for 3 months. I do not suggest reheating pork; I just let it sit at room temperature for 20 minutes before serving. You can reheat the peach and brie mixture in the microwave or on the stove with a splash of water (2 tablespoons).

SUGGESTED SIDES

Tahini Brussels Sprouts with Pistachios & Dates (page 133)

"Hot" Honey Cheddar-Stuffed Sweet Potato Skins (page 130)

Charred Green Bean & Farro Salad with Avocado Ranch Dressing (page 293)

NOTE

If one of your chops is noticeably thinner than the other, wrap a piece of twine around the circumference, and tighten until it thickens to match the other chops.

Mongolian Molasses Pork

GF DF P | **HANDS-ON TIME:** 15 min | **TOTAL TIME:** 1 h, 30 min (Instant Pot); 5 h (Crock-Pot)

YIELD: 6 servings | **OPTION:**

Why is fall-apart-tender meat so dang good? I'm thinking it has something to do with how the fat renders into every crack and crevice, making each bite simply unctuous. Is this making your mouth water (like mine)? If so, you will adore this Mongolian Molasses Pork! Adding LL Balanced flair with a hearty dollop of molasses offers a rich, caramel undertone to wonderful Asian flavors. Whether you go the Instant Pot or Crock-Pot route, this is a simple "dump and stir" recipe that requires only a few minutes of actual work. You can serve it in tacos or even as a stuffing for whole roasted sweet potatoes. I also love to serve it with white rice, avocado, and roasted cashews.

Instant Pot Version: Place pork slices in the canister of an Instant Pot. Sprinkle with arrowroot starch, and toss to evenly coat. Add ginger, onions, garlic, tamari, stock, molasses, and coconut sugar. Stir to incorporate, then seal and set to "Manual" 35 minutes. When the Instant Pot beeps to signal the end of cooking time, allow pressure to release naturally, approximately 15 minutes. Remove lid.

Press "Cancel" then "Sauté," then immediately press "Adjust" until it is set to "Normal" heat if it isn't already. Once mixture is simmering, stir in carrots and scallions. Sauté until liquid is noticeably thickened and carrots are tender but not mushy, stirring every minute, 6 to 8 minutes. Taste for seasoning, and add salt and pepper if you like. Press "Cancel" to turn off heat.

Crock-Pot Version: Place pork slices in a Crock-Pot. Sprinkle with arrowroot starch, and toss to evenly coat. Add ginger, onions, garlic, tamari, stock, molasses, and coconut sugar. Stir to incorporate, then cook on low heat for 4 to 4 ½ hours, until meat is fall-apart tender. Stir in carrots and scallions, and cook another 25 minutes, until tender but not mushy. Taste for seasoning, and add salt and pepper if you like.

Serve over cooked rice, and top with cashews and lime wedges.

Leftovers will keep tightly sealed in the refrigerator for 4 days or in the freezer for 3 months.

2 pounds pork shoulder or Boston butt, excess fat removed, sliced against the grain into ¼-inch-thick slices

1 tablespoon arrowroot starch (sub cornstarch)

1-inch piece ginger, peeled and grated

½ medium red onion, chopped into ½-inch pieces (¾ to 1 cup)

5 cloves garlic, minced

⅓ cup low-sodium tamari

½ cup low-sodium chicken or beef stock

3 tablespoons molasses (K sub monkfruit sweetener)

3 tablespoons coconut sugar (K sub monkfruit sweetener)

2 medium carrots, peeled and sliced on the diagonal into ¼-inch-thick rounds (1¼ cups) (K sub turnips)

1 bunch scallions, 1 inch of top and ¼ inch of base removed, sliced on the diagonal into 1-inch pieces (1¼ cups)

Salt and pepper, to taste

Toasted cashews and lime wedges for garnish

SUGGESTED SIDES

Tahini Brussels Sprouts with Pistachios & Dates (page 133)

"Hot" Honey Cheddar-Stuffed Sweet Potato Skins (page 130)

Vegan Tomato-y Collard Greens (page 155)

LUNCH + DINNER ENTRÉES

Seafood Entrées

*I*n the three years since I wrote my first cookbook, wild seafood has become far more available and noticeably more affordable. Most grocery stories, not just the "healthy" ones, carry frozen wild fillets and shellfish, and they're usually fresh and delicious. This made creating a new seafood section so much easier and more fun. I love picturing y'all across the country, excited to try my BBQ Blackened Salmon or Honey Walnut Shrimp or Thai Coconut Poached Cod, finding exactly what you need at your local store. That said, I know this won't be the case for everyone, so don't forget about amazing companies like Thrive Market and Vital Choice, which offer incredible high-quality seafood that you can order straight to your door. In this chapter, you'll see creative twists on familiar flavors like pesto, Italian dressing, and sesame ginger, so that even seafood newbies can find something they love. Don't forget to take advantage of canned wild seafood when you need a quick meal. I love using canned wild tuna or salmon instead of eggs in my Classic Egg Salad recipe (page 289).

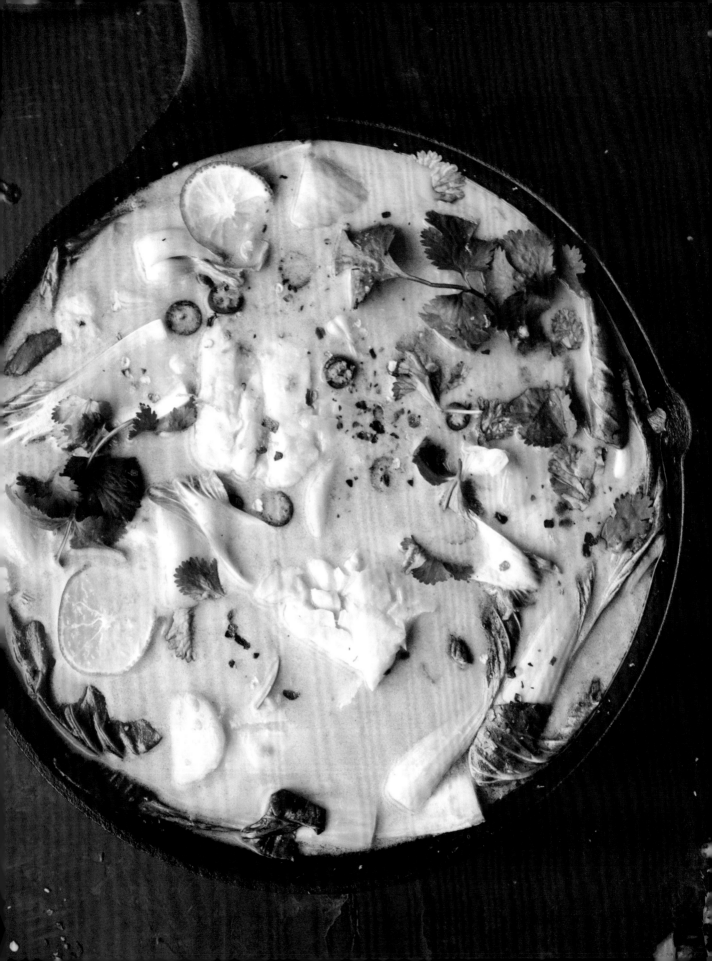

Thai Coconut Poached Cod

GF DF P | **HANDS-ON TIME:** 30 min | **TOTAL TIME:** 35 min | **YIELD:** 4 servings | ⏱ | **OPTION:**

Poaching is such an underrated cooking technique. It requires a bit of finesse, because the key is keeping the liquid at a low temperature, just below a simmer. But this attention to detail is well worth the result: buttery, melt-in-your-mouth cod steeped in a rich, bright broth, full of healing, anti-inflammatory foods like turmeric, red pepper, and ginger. Once you get the hang of the recipe, you can be creative with the veggies and add-ins. You could also try it with salmon, halibut, shrimp, or chicken. You'll just want to watch the poaching time, and adjust accordingly.

Place garlic and ginger in a small bowl. Stir in turmeric, paprika, pepper, red pepper flakes, and salt until it forms a paste.

Remove the base of the bok choy, and separate individual stalks. Rinse and pat dry. If using regular-sized bok choy, slice stalks in half crosswise.

Heat a cast-iron skillet (at least 15-inch) or sauté pan over medium heat, and add coconut oil. When oil moves quickly around the pan and is shimmering, add onions, shallots, and a splash of water (2 tablespoons). Cook, stirring every few minutes, until soft and translucent, 8 to 10 minutes. Add garlic mixture and a splash of water, and cook, stirring constantly, for another minute. Add coconut milk, stock, lime juice, and syrup, then stir until incorporated.

Adjust heat until the liquid reaches 140° to 160° F on your thermometer. You want it to be warm, but there shouldn't be any bubbles around the edges. Add cod fillets and bok choy, stirring gently to cover as much as possible with liquid. It's okay if some pieces stick out. Cook for 5 minutes, then flip fillets, and cook for another 2 to 3 minutes. Test with the thermometer; fillets are ready when they reach 140° F, are opaque, and start to fall apart. If they are not ready, cook another 3 to 4 minutes, then test again.

Stir in water chestnuts, then taste liquid for seasoning, and add more salt if you like. Top with garnishes of your choice.

Leftovers will keep in the refrigerator for up to 3 days. I don't recommend freezing.

SUGGESTED SIDE

Macadamia & Roasted Grapefruit Salad with Lemony Vinaigrette (page 295)

SPECIAL EQUIPMENT:

Meat thermometer

INGREDIENTS:

6 cloves garlic, minced

1½-inch piece ginger, peeled and grated

½ teaspoon ground turmeric

½ teaspoon paprika

¼ teaspoon black pepper

Pinch red pepper flakes

¾ teaspoon sea salt, plus more to taste

1 bunch baby bok choy (4 ounces) (sub ½ bunch regular-sized bok choy)

2 tablespoons coconut oil (sub avocado oil)

½ medium yellow onion, diced into ¼-inch pieces (¾ to 1 cup)

1 large or 2 small shallots, minced (½ cup)

1 15-ounce can full-fat coconut milk

2 cups low-sodium chicken or vegetable stock

Juice from 1 lime (2 tablespoons)

1 tablespoon maple syrup (K sub monkfruit sweetener)

1 pound cod fillets, fresh or thawed-from-frozen

1 8-ounce can water chestnuts, drained

Fresh cilantro leaves, finely sliced Serrano peppers, red pepper flakes, and lime juice for garnish

LUNCH + DINNER ENTRÉES

Smoked Salmon, Olive & Pecan Spread

GF K | **HANDS-ON TIME:** 5 min | **TOTAL TIME:** 25 min, plus 1 h chilling | **YIELD:** 6 to 10 servings |

My mom served me cream cheese and olive sandwiches after school as a kiddo, and I'm thankful she introduced me to this combination while my palate was still "open-minded," because now I can share it with you! There is something "moreish" about salty smoked salmon and olives, unctuous cream cheese, and pecans. My favorite way to enjoy this spread is generously layered between two pieces of untoasted sourdough sandwich bread. It also makes a wonderful dip for crackers or veggies.

Preheat oven to 350° F. Place pecans on a baking sheet. Roast for 10 to 12 minutes, until fragrant and slightly darkened in color. Set aside to cool.

In the bowl of a stand mixer, combine cream cheese, yogurt, lemon juice, and black pepper. (You can also do this in a mixing bowl if you have a hand-mixer.) Turn to medium speed, and mix until creamy and fluffy, 1 ½ to 2 minutes. You may need to stop and scrape down the sides once or twice.

Roughly chop cooled pecans, and add to the cream cheese mixture along with the olives and dill. Mix again on low speed just until everything is evenly incorporated, about 20 seconds. Scrape and remove paddle, then add salmon, and fold in with a spatula. (I hand-fold the salmon because I like to be able to bite into some pieces; if I mix it in with the mixer, even on low, it blends the salmon more than I'd like. But feel free to!) Transfer spread to a sealable container, and refrigerate for at least 1 hour before serving.

Leftover spread will keep tightly sealed in the refrigerator for 3 days. I don't recommend freezing.

Ideas for
LEFTOVER SMOKED SALMON

Most grocery stores sell 4-ounce packages of smoked salmon, but if you happen to have leftovers, I love using it as a topping for avocado toast, or even just buttered toast, or served with my Chive & Goat Cheese Fluffy Baked Eggs (page 82).

SPECIAL EQUIPMENT:

Stand or hand mixer

INGREDIENTS:

⅓ cup raw pecans

8 ounces plain cream cheese, room temperature

½ cup plain full-fat Greek yogurt (sub sour cream)

Juice from ½ lemon (1 tablespoon)

¼ teaspoon black pepper

Scant ⅓ cup pitted green olives, finely chopped (ideally pimento-stuffed)

4 ounces cold-smoked salmon, finely chopped

1 tablespoon minced dill, plus more for garnish

SUGGESTED SIDES

Picnic Macaroni Salad with Italian Dressing (page 189)

Charred Green Bean & Farro Salad with Avocado Ranch Dressing (page 293)

SERVING SUGGESTION

Spread on crisp bread crackers or dark toasted rye or pumpernickel bread and top with thinly sliced cucumbers. Garnish with minced dill.

Macadamia & Sesame Crusted Tuna

GF DF P | **HANDS-ON TIME:** 30 min | **TOTAL TIME:** 30 min, plus 1 h marinating | **YIELD:** 2 servings | **OPTION:**

Before I talk about the taste of this recipe, I want to touch on the quality. I highly encourage you to purchase sustainable, wild-caught tuna fillets, not only because they are more nutritious, but also because tuna is overfished, and several types of tuna are actually endangered. Take some time to inquire about the sourcing of your tuna from the fishmonger before you purchase. With that said, this recipe is absolutely divine, if I do say so myself! Marinating the fillets makes them practically fall-apart tender, and it infuses every bite with flavor. I love pairing creamy tuna with the toasty, nutty crunch of sesame seeds. This is a great dish to make if you want to impress someone (including yourself), because it looks like your favorite highfalutin' restaurant dish. But it's probably half the price when you cook it at home!

In a shallow casserole dish, whisk together tamari, sesame oil, garlic, ginger, vinegar, and maple syrup. Add tuna fillets side-by-side and refrigerate for 30 minutes. Flip and marinate on the other side for another 30 minutes.

While tuna is marinating, place macadamia nuts in a food processor or high-powered blender, and pulse until a fine crumble forms. (Don't let it turn to nut butter!) Transfer to a bowl, and add sesame seeds, 1 tablespoon arrowroot starch, salt, and pepper. Whisk to evenly combine.

Preheat oven to 350° F.

Remove tuna fillets from the marinade, and place on a plate, saving the leftover marinade. Press crumble mixture onto the top and bottom of the tuna fillets, using approximately one-quarter of the crumble per side. It should almost become a paste consistency. Depending on the size of your fillets, you may have some crumble leftover. If you do, press it into the sides of the fillets.

Heat a cast-iron or other nonstick skillet over medium-high heat, and add 1 tablespoon avocado oil. (If you are not using a nonstick pan, add an extra tablespoon avocado oil). When oil moves quickly around the pan and a splash of water sizzles when it hits the pan, it's ready for searing. Carefully place fillets in the pan, leaving 1 to 2 inches between each. Sear for 3 to 4 minutes. Fillets will be ready to flip when you can easily get a

(continued on next page)

¼ cup low-sodium tamari

2 teaspoons toasted sesame oil

2 cloves garlic, finely minced

¾-inch piece of ginger, peeled and grated (sub ¼ teaspoon ground ginger)

1 tablespoon apple cider vinegar (sub lime juice)

1 tablespoon maple syrup (K sub stevia drops to taste)

2 4- or 5-ounce sushi-grade tuna fillets (fresh or thawed-from-frozen)

¾ cup raw macadamia nuts (sub blanched almonds)

3 tablespoons sesame seeds, plus more for garnish (white or black seeds will work)

1 tablespoon plus 1 teaspoon arrowroot starch (sub cornstarch), divided

¼ teaspoon sea salt

¼ teaspoon black pepper

1 tablespoon avocado oil, plus more if not using a nonstick skillet

½ cup plus 1½ teaspoons water, divided

NOTE

We use avocado oil in this recipe, even with a nonstick skillet, because it helps create a crispy crust.

spatula underneath without the flesh sticking to the pan. You're looking for a golden-brown crust. Flip and sear another 2 minutes.

If you want to cook the tuna longer, place skillet in the oven for 3 to 10 minutes, or until the fish reaches your desired doneness (no oven: bright pink/raw center; 3 minutes: medium pink center; 7 minutes: very light pink center; 10 minutes: fully cooked center). This will depend on the thickness of your fillets as well.

Allow the fillets to rest for 10 minutes before slicing. While fillets are resting, strain leftover marinade through a fine mesh strainer into a small saucepan. Add ½ cup water, and heat over medium heat. Allow to simmer for 5 minutes. Taste marinade. If it seems too salty, add a few more tablespoons water until it reaches your desired flavor.

Combine the remaining 1 teaspoon arrowroot starch and 1½ teaspoons water in a small bowl. Stir to dissolve, then add starch liquid to the marinade. Cook for another 30 seconds or so, stirring occassionally until sauce noticeably thickens.

Slice tuna against the grain (approximately ½-inch thick), and serve immediately with marinade and an extra sprinkle of sesame seeds.

Leftovers will keep tightly sealed in the refrigerator up to 3 days. I don't recommend freezing.

SUGGESTED SIDES

Miso Coconut Roasted Eggplant
(page 159)

Italian Green Bean & Toasted
Quinoa Salad (page 160)

5-Ingredient Kimchi Coleslaw
(page 163)

Pistachio Pesto Crab Cakes

GF K | **HANDS-ON TIME:** 40 min | **TOTAL TIME:** 50 min | **YIELD:** 8 crab cakes | ⏱ ⊕ | **OPTION:** DF

I'm not sure I can ever make pesto without pistachios now that I have tasted the magic. It's key to use the store-bought roasted and salted ones—I've tried recreating them at home, and it's just not the same. That said, these crab cakes don't even need a condiment, they are so lovely! Slightly crispy on the outside, light and mildly sweet on the inside, they're an homage to my childhood in Baltimore, Maryland (yep, I spent my first twelve years in "Salty Balty"!). Do not skimp on the quality of your crab here; it makes all the difference in the world. "Jumbo lump" and "wild-caught" are your ticket to recreating this classic seafood dish, even in a landlocked area.

Make the Pistachio Pesto: Combine all pesto ingredients except olive oil (and mayonnaise, if using) in a food processor. Pulse until it forms a fine crumble. While machine is running, slowly pour in olive oil until it reaches your desired consistency. Taste for seasoning, and add more salt and pepper if you like. If you want to make the pesto creamier, first set aside 2 tablespoons to go inside the crab cakes, then stir mayonnaise into the rest.

Make the Crab Cakes: Heat a cast-iron or other nonstick skillet over medium heat, and add 1 tablespoon oil. When oil moves quickly around the pan, add shallots. Cook, stirring every minute or so, until softened and translucent, 3 to 4 minutes. Allow to cool for 5 minutes.

Drain crabmeat, and gently squeeze out excess liquid. Place in a mixing bowl, along with cooked shallots, salt, pepper, mustard, eggs, almond flour, mayonnaise, 2 tablespoons Pistachio Pesto, and lemon juice. No need to clean the pan you used for the shallots. Use your hands to evenly incorporate. This is quite a wet mixture. Line a baking sheet with parchment paper. Scoop ¼ cup crab mixture, and place on baking sheet. Repeat with remaining mixture, so you have 8 scoops.

Turn on exhaust fan. Heat the same skillet over medium-high heat, and add remaining 2 tablespoons oil. When oil moves quickly around the pan and is shimmering, add several crab cakes (I can usually get 3 or 4 in the pan), leaving a few inches between each. Gently press them

(continued on next page)

PISTACHIO PESTO:

2 ounces fresh basil, (2 cups, packed)

¾ cup roasted, salted pistachios

Juice from 1 lemon (2 tablespoons)

1 large or 2 small cloves garlic, roughly chopped

¼ cup freshly grated parmesan cheese (DF sub 2 tablespoons nutritional yeast)

1 teaspoon mild, white miso paste

Pinch black pepper

½ cup extra virgin olive oil

2 to 4 tablespoons mayonnaise (optional, but recommended)

CRAB CAKES:

3 tablespoons avocado oil, divided

1 medium shallot, diced into ¼-inch pieces (⅓ cup)

12 ounces jumbo lump wild-caught crabmeat

1 teaspoon sea salt (feel free to start with ½ teaspoon and add to taste)

½ teaspoon black pepper

1½ teaspoons Dijon mustard

2 large eggs

½ cup blanched almond flour

2 tablespoons mayonnaise

2 tablespoons Pistachio Pesto

1 teaspoon lemon juice

PISTACHIO PESTO CRAB CAKES *(continued)*

down to approximately 3 inches in diameter. Cook until golden brown and crusty on the bottom, 4 to 5 minutes. When you can slide a spatula under the crab cakes easily, flip and cook for another 2 to 3 minutes to achieve the same color and crust.

Place on a serving platter or a large plate. Repeat cooking process with remaining crab cakes. (Note that cooking time might be less, as the pan gets hotter. You also might need to turn the heat down a bit.) Allow final batch to cool for 5 minutes before serving with Pistachio Pesto.

Leftovers will keep sealed in the refrigerator for 3 days or in the freezer for 2 months. Store pesto and crab cakes separately.

Ideas for
LEFTOVER PISTACHIO PESTO

Toss leftover pesto with cooked noodles of choice and a little more olive oil for an easy vegetarian pasta. Use it as a spread for avocado toast or fried or scrambled egg toast. Use it as a dip for roasted veggies. (I particularly love broccoli and Brussels sprouts with pesto.) For a low-carb snack, dollop a little pesto onto some high-quality deli meat with a slice of cheese and roll up.

SUGGESTED SIDES

Mediterranean Spaghetti
Squash Bake (page 173)

Macadamia & Roasted Grapefruit
Salad with Lemony Vinaigrette
(page 295)

Chickpea, Avocado & Goat Cheese
Salad with Grainy Mustard Dressing
(page 286)

NOTE

I have used both canned wild crab and thawed-from-frozen wild crab, and both have worked.

BBQ Blackened Salmon

   | HANDS-ON TIME: 20 min | TOTAL TIME: 25 min | YIELD: 4 servings | OPTION: (K)

If you don't enjoy salmon, either 1) you're not buying fresh, wild-caught salmon or 2) you haven't discovered the proper cooking techniques. In addition to flavor, the former is important for both the environment and your health, and the latter is important because we want to really taste our food! My foolproof method for cooking salmon is to start with a good sear, which caramelizes the top and adds a nice crust. Then I pop it into a hot oven just long enough to firm it up without losing the juiciness. Once you've practiced this a few times, you can switch up the spices (try the Cajun Seasoning on page 334) or just use salt and pepper and top with pesto. In the meantime, you can't go wrong with my BBQ Seasoning.

Make the BBQ Seasoning: Place all seasoning ingredients in a small bowl, and whisk to combine, or place in a sealable jar or container and shake.

Make the Salmon: Preheat oven to 350° F. Place salmon fillets on a baking sheet, flesh side up, and drizzle ½ teaspoon avocado oil over each. Rub in oil to coat, then top each fillet with 1 teaspoon BBQ Seasoning. (You'll have leftover seasoning.) Press gently to help seasoning stick.

Heat a cast-iron or other nonstick skillet over medium-high heat. (If you don't have a nonstick pan, add 2 tablespoons avocado oil to the pan.) Test to see if pan is ready by adding a splash of water. If it sizzles, the pan is ready (this is true with either pan). I suggest turning on your exhaust fan at this point.

Place salmon fillets in the pan, flesh side down. Depending on the size of your pan, you might need to do this in two batches. Crowding the fish may prevent blackening.

Sear for 2 to 5 minutes (this will depend on the thickness of the fillets). They are ready to flip when you can easily get a spatula underneath without the flesh sticking to the pan. Flip and sear for another 2 to 3 minutes. If you want your salmon more well-done, place it on a parchment-lined baking sheet. Bake for 3 to 7 minutes, or until fillets reach desired color (less pink = more well-done). Allow fillets to rest 5 minutes before enjoying.

Store leftover BBQ Seasoning in a tightly sealed plastic bag or jar. Leftover salmon will keep tightly sealed in the refrigerator for 3 days. I don't recommend freezing.

BBQ SEASONING:

¼ cup coconut sugar ((K) sub monkfruit sweetener)

2 tablespoons paprika

1 tablespoon chili powder

1 tablespoon garlic powder

4 teaspoons onion powder

1 tablespoon sea salt (can start with less and add to taste)

1 teaspoon ground cumin

½ teaspoon ground cinnamon

½ teaspoon black pepper

SALMON:

4 6-ounce salmon fillets (I buy skin-on fillets then remove the skin after cooking)

2 teaspoons avocado oil

SUGGESTED SIDES

Tahini Brussels Sprouts with Pistachios & Dates (page 133)

"Hot" Honey Cheddar-Stuffed Sweet Potato Skins (page 130)

Broccoli Gorgonzola Salad with Miso Maple Dressing (page 147)

NOTE

Check your fillets for tiny pin-bones by running your finger along the flesh in several directions. If you feel bones, use a tweezer to remove them.

Honey Walnut Shrimp

Confession: I don't remember ever actually ordering Honey Walnut Shrimp at a Chinese restaurant, so I guess I can't say for sure that my version is accurate. I *can* say that it is absolutely scrumptious! I can also say that I feel like I'm enjoying indulgent takeout whenever I make my Honey Walnut Shrimp, and I often reserve it for "Sunday Scaries." Frozen wild-caught shrimp is easy to find and more affordable than other types of high-quality seafood, so I like to keep a few extra bags around for just lazy weekends. Plus, this recipe comes together in a snap! While they're not fried shrimp, these lil' guys have a nice crunch from coating them in arrowroot starch and giving them a hot sear. I love serving them with a cooked grain, thinly sliced scallions, and a generous drizzle of sauce. They're also amazing in tacos or on salads.

Make the Roasted Walnuts: Preheat oven to 350° F. Line a baking sheet with parchment paper. Spread walnuts on baking sheet in an even layer. Place butter and honey in a microwave-safe bowl, and microwave for 20 to 30 seconds, until melted (butter might not look melted, but stir for a bit and it should liquify). Pour mixture over walnuts, and use a spatula to stir, coating the walnuts evenly. Roast for 12 minutes, or until fragrant and slightly darkened in color, then set aside to cool. As they harden, a delectable butter honey film will form between the walnuts—don't discard this!

Make the Honey Sauce: Place all the sauce ingredients in a mixing bowl, and whisk until smooth and creamy. (I like to mash the miso against the side of the bowl with a fork to thin it out, making it easier to incorporate.) Set aside at room temperature.

Make the Shrimp: Pat shrimp with a dish towel to remove excess liquid. Place arrowroot starch, salt, and onion powder in large sealable plastic bag or marinating container, and gently stir or shake to combine. Add shrimp, seal tightly, and shake to evenly coat.

Heat a large sauté pan over medium-high heat, and add butter. When butter is bubbling, add half of the shrimp in an even layer. Don't stir! Allow shrimp to cook until golden brown on the bottom, 3 to 4 minutes (okay, you can peek to check), before using tongs to flip. Cook without stirring, until shrimp is opaque throughout, approximately 2 minutes.

(continued on page 214)

ROASTED WALNUTS:

1 tablespoon butter
   (DF sub avocado oil)

1 tablespoon honey

⅔ cup raw walnuts

HONEY SAUCE:

3 tablespoons mayonnaise

2 tablespoon honey

1 tablespoon sriracha

1 teaspoon lemon juice

½ teaspoon mild, white miso paste

¼ teaspoon sea salt

SHRIMP:

1 pound raw shrimp, fresh or thawed-from-frozen, peeled and deveined (I also get them with tails removed, but that's up to you)

¼ cup arrowroot starch (sub cornstarch)

½ teaspoon sea salt

½ teaspoon onion powder

2 tablespoons butter (DF sub avocado oil)

1 8-ounce can sliced water chestnuts, drained and rinsed (sub bamboo shoots or baby corn) (optional)

HONEY WALNUT SHRIMP *(continued)*

Transfer shrimp to a large heatproof mixing bowl, then repeat with remaining shrimp. You might need to add a little more butter and turn the heat down a bit. This batch should take a minute or so less than the first.

When all of your shrimp are cooked and in the same bowl, fold in walnuts with their honey-butter film, and water chestnuts, if using. Add Honey Sauce to taste, and gently toss. (I use all of the sauce.)

Leftover shrimp will keep tightly sealed in the refrigerator for 2 days. I don't recommend freezing.

SUGGESTED SIDES

Broccoli Gorgonzola Salad with Miso Maple Dressing (page 147)

Sour Cream & Onion Cauliflower Risotto (page 152)

LUNCH + DINNER ENTRÉES

Italian Marinated Shrimp & Fluffy Shallot Rice

GF | **HANDS-ON TIME:** 45 min | **TOTAL TIME:** 1 h, plus 4 h marinating | **YIELD:** 4 servings

This dish was inspired by an "Italian Dressing Chicken" my mama used to make and which I simply adored. Who would have thought salad dressing would make a lovely marinade for various proteins? Well, it does, and shrimp is my favorite centerpiece of choice. It's also another way to use my homemade Italian Dressing. I pretty much always keep a batch around and use it in various ways (ideas on page 217). This recipe will also teach you how to make perfect stovetop rice every time—soft, fluffy, and without a crunchy burned layer to clean off of your pot. Adding buttery shallots just takes it over the top!

Make the Italian Dressing: Place all dressing ingredients in a blender, and purée until smooth and creamy.

Prepare the Shrimp: Drain excess liquid from shrimp if using thawed-from-frozen.

Place shrimp and ½ cup Italian Dressing in a sealable plastic bag or marinating container, shake gently to coat, and marinate for 4 hours in the refrigerator. Do not marinate any longer than 4 hours, as the acid in the dressing will start to break down the shrimp too much. (No one wants mushy shrimp.)

Make the Fluffy Shallot Rice: While shrimp is marinating, place rice in a fine-mesh sieve, and rinse with running cold water for 15 to 20 seconds until the water runs clear.

Add 2 cups of water to a small saucepan, and bring it to a boil over medium-high heat. While water is coming to a boil, place 1 tablespoon butter in a separate medium saucepan over medium heat. When butter is melted and moves quickly around the pan, add rice and salt. Cook, stirring constantly, until rice has a toasted fragrance and is leaving some sticky residue on the bottom of the pan, 3 to 4 minutes. Pour boiling water over rice, then bring to a simmer over low heat. Cover, and cook for 18 minutes. Resist temptation to look at the rice while cooking.

While rice is cooking, use the pan you used for boiling water to cook the shallots. Place the remaining 1 tablespoon butter in the pan over medium-low heat. When butter has melted and moves quickly around

(continued on page 217)

ITALIAN DRESSING:

- ½ cup extra virgin olive oil
- ⅓ cup white balsamic vinegar
- 2 cloves garlic, minced
- ¾ teaspoon sea salt (feel free to start with ½ teaspoon and add to taste)
- ½ teaspoon black pepper
- 1 teaspoon dried oregano
- ½ teaspoon onion powder
- 2 tablespoons freshly grated parmesan cheese (sub nutritional yeast)
- 2 teaspoons maple syrup or honey (sub liquid stevia, to taste)

SHRIMP:

- 1 pound raw shrimp, fresh or thawed from frozen, peeled and deveined
- 1 batch Italian Dressing

FLUFFY SHALLOT RICE:

- 1 cup medium-grain white or arborio rice
- 2 cups water
- 2 tablespoons butter
- ½ teaspoon sea salt
- 1 medium shallot, minced (⅓ cup) (sub ¼ medium red onion, diced into ¼-inch pieces)

LUNCH + DINNER ENTRÉES

ITALIAN MARINATED SHRIMP
& FLUFFY SHALLOT RICE *(continued)*

the pan, add shallots. Cook, stirring every 30 seconds or so, until softened and translucent, 4 to 5 minutes.

Once rice has simmered for 18 minutes, remove from the heat, and allow to sit for another 10 minutes, covered. After 10 minutes, uncover and fluff with a fork, then stir in shallots. Set rice aside.

Cook the Shrimp: Heat a cast-iron or other nonstick skillet over medium heat. Place the shrimp and marinade in the skillet. We're not trying to sear the shrimp, so it doesn't matter if the pan is fully heated when you add them. Cook, stirring and flipping, until shrimp is completely opaque throughout, 4 to 6 minutes.

Serve immediately over Fluffy Shallot Rice with remaining Italian Dressing and pan juices.

Leftover shrimp will keep tightly sealed in the refrigerator for 2 days. Leftover rice will keep in the refrigerator for 4 days. I don't recommend freezing.

SUGGESTED SIDES

Carrot & Zucchini Ribbons with
Lemony Pistachio Pesto (page 151)

Roasted Romaine with
Basil Caesar Hummus Dressing
(page 298)

Buttery Lemon Pepper Leeks
(page 148)

NOTE

Make a double batch of Italian Dressing, and use half for the shrimp and half for my Italian Green Bean & Toasted Quinoa Salad (page 160).

LUNCH + DINNER ENTRÉES

Poultry Entrées

The outline for this chapter came together quickly. I love chicken and turkey, but they're not always the most flavorful protein, so I am constantly brainstorming ways to jazz them up. As a result, I was bursting with recipe ideas to bring to life, such as Chicken Parmesan with Sun-Dried Tomato Marinara, Creamy Cajun Chicken Pasta, Pineapple Paprika Fajitas, and more! You'll notice a handful of "one pot" dishes here, which was a happy challenge to take on, for y'all and selfishly for myself. While creating my Bakery and Dessert recipes, I often made my Go-To Rotisserie Chicken or BBQ Turkey Hashbrown Casserole for simple lunches throughout the week. The recipes in this section have been tested and approved by picky-eater kiddos, and I'm hopeful for the same experience in your kitchen if you struggle to find meals that make everyone happy. While I included my recipe for Buffalo Chicken Dip with this main-course chapter, it's also a major hit as a game-day or party appetizer.

Chicken Parmesan

with SUN-DRIED TOMATO MARINARA

GF K │ **HANDS-ON TIME:** 50 min │ **TOTAL TIME:** 1 h, 25 min, plus 2 to 24 h marinating

YIELD: 6 to 8 servings ⊕ ⬇

Even after several specific requests for a Chicken Parmesan recipe, I hesitated, simply because there are so many recipes out there. However, when I did a little internet search, I didn't see any that used grain-free flours, but still included dairy. And I personally can't imagine Chicken Parmesan without a little cheesy goodness. So here you go, my loves—I hope it lives up to your expectations! In addition to welcoming those gooey cheese-pulls, I add piquant sun-dried tomatoes and bright, fresh basil to the marinara sauce. The result is a richer and, dare I say, more sophisticated twist on this family favorite. I know this recipe has quite a few steps, so feel free to substitute your favorite store-bought marinara for mine. It will still be fantastic.

Prepare the Chicken: Place chicken breasts between two pieces of parchment paper, and pound until ½-inch thick, using the smooth side of a meat mallet or other blunt heavy object. Slice breasts crosswise into 3 pieces each. Place chicken in a sealable plastic bag or marinating container along with 1 cup almond milk and vinegar. Marinate for at least 2 hours and up to 24.

While chicken is marinating, place almonds in a high-powered blender or food processor, and pulse until a fine crumble forms—chunkier than flour but fine enough so you can't see large pieces of almond. Transfer to a mixing bowl along with almond flour, ½ cup parmesan, garlic powder, onion powder, paprika, pepper, and ¼ teaspoon salt. Stir to combine, then refrigerate until use.

Make the Sun-Dried Tomato Marinara: Combine all marinara ingredients, in the order listed, in a food processor, and purée until smooth. Transfer to a saucepan, and bring to a simmer over medium

(continued on next page)

CHICKEN:

2 pounds boneless, skinless chicken breasts

1 cup plus 2 tablespoons unsweetened almond milk, divided

2 tablespoons apple cider vinegar (sub lemon juice)

1 cup roasted, unsalted almonds

1¼ cups blanched almond flour

1 cup freshly grated parmesan cheese, divided

1 teaspoon garlic powder

1½ teaspoons onion powder

1 teaspoon paprika

½ teaspoon black pepper

¼ teaspoon sea salt, plus more for sprinkling

2 to 4 tablespoons avocado oil, plus more for greasing

2 large eggs, beaten

1 batch Sun-Dried Tomato Marinara

6 ounces mild cheddar cheese, shredded (1½ cups)

(continued on next page)

Ideas for

LEFTOVER ALMONDS

Use as a salad topping, in my Strawberry Almond Cobbler (page 101), or instead of pecans in my Gooey Pecan Cinnamon Rolls (page 104). Or eat by the handful 'cause they're scrumptious!

CHICKEN PARMESANWITH
SUN-DRIED TOMATO MARINARA *(continued)*

heat. Cook for 10 minutes, stirring every minute or so. If it's splashing, reduce the heat. Set aside to cool, then refrigerate until time to assemble the recipe.

Assemble and Cook the Casserole: Line a baking sheet with parchment paper. Remove the chicken from the marinade, shaking off excess, and lay the pieces side by side on the parchment. Pat dry on both sides.

Preheat oven to 425° F. Grease a 13 × 9 × 2-inch baking dish with avocado oil.

In a small shallow bowl, whisk together eggs and remaining 2 tablespoons almond milk. Dip each piece of chicken into the egg wash, then the almond mixture. Place pieces back onto the baking sheet, wait a minute, then dredge pieces again in the almond mixture, pressing firmly. You might need to wash your hands a few times during the process.

Heat a large cast-iron or other nonstick skillet over high heat, and turn on exhaust fan. Add avocado oil. Test if pan is ready by touching a piece of chicken to the pan. When it sizzles, it's ready. Add a few pieces of chicken to the pan without crowding, and lightly sprinkle with salt. Cook until golden brown and crispy, 2 to 3 minutes. (You can peek underneath to check). Flip and sear for another minute, then place chicken in the baking dish. Repeat with remaining chicken. If necessary, add more oil to prevent sticking. (Even with a nonstick surface, the dredging can sometimes stick.)

Top each piece of chicken with a few tablespoons of marinara (exact amount to your personal taste). Cover evenly with cheddar and remaining ½ cup parmesan.

Bake for 12 minutes, then broil for 3 to 4 minutes, until cheese is golden brown and bubbling. Serve with any leftover Sun-Dried Tomato Marinara.

Leftovers will keep tightly sealed in the refrigerator for 4 days or in the freezer for 3 months.

SUN-DRIED TOMATO MARINARA:

- 1 15-ounce can no-salt-added diced tomatoes
- ½ cup firmly packed sun-dried tomatoes in olive oil, plus 1 tablespoon of the oil
- ½ ounce fresh basil (½ cup, packed)
- 5 cloves garlic, roughly chopped (This will have a pretty noticeable garlic flavor. Use 2 to 3 if you don't want that.)
- ½ teaspoon sea salt
- ½ teaspoon dried oregano
- ¼ cup tomato paste (sub ketchup)

SUGGESTED SIDES

Roasted Romaine with
Basil Caesar Hummus Dressing
(page 298)

Mediterranean Spaghetti Squash
Bake (page 173)

Ideas for
LEFTOVER
DREDGING MIXTURE

You may have leftover dredging mixture. You can freeze it, and use in the future for seared chicken, shrimp, eggplant, or zucchini rounds (just make sure to cook thoroughly, as it will have touched raw chicken).

LUNCH + DINNER ENTRÉES

One-Pot Creamy Cajun Chicken Pasta

(DF) | **HANDS-ON TIME:** 1 h, 5 min | **TOTAL TIME:** 1 h, 5 min, plus 6 to 24 h marinating | **YIELD:** 4 to 6 servings

  OPTION: (GF)

One of my favorite dishes growing up was a penne pasta dish at a restaurant my family frequented often. It had a vodka-style red sauce, and the chicken was seasoned with the perfect "kick" for my nine-year-old-palate. I wanted to recreate this dining experience for y'all, and I think my Creamy Cajun Chicken Pasta is the ticket! The spice is complementary but not overwhelming, and the "cheesy" cashew sauce adds just the right amount of creamy-gooey-ness without making the noodles heavy. If you really want to mimic my childhood favorite, use penne noodles, and throw in some frozen green peas near the end.

Use the short- or long-soak method to soak cashews (see page 44). Drain and rinse.

Slice chicken breasts against the grain into thin strips, approximately ¼-inch wide. Place in a sealable plastic bag or marinating container along with almond milk and lemon juice. Seal tightly, and shake or massage to ensure all pieces are coated. Marinate chicken for at least 6 hours or up to 24. (If your cashews finish soaking before the chicken, rinse and drain, and keep them in the fridge).

Make the Cajun Seasoning: Place all seasoning ingredients in a small bowl, and whisk to combine, or place in a sealable jar or container and shake.

Make the Pasta and Chicken: Once chicken has marinated, cook the pasta al dente according to package directions, 1 to 2 minutes less than shortest suggested time. Drain and rinse. Toss with some avocado oil if noodles are sticking. Set aside.

Drain and rinse cashews, and place them in a high-powered blender, along with water, nutritional yeast, and miso. Blend until completely smooth and creamy. Set aside.

Remove chicken from the marinade, shaking off excess, and place in a large mixing bowl. Toss with Cajun Seasoning (the whole batch).

Turn on your exhaust fan. Heat a large saucepan over medium-high heat, and add avocado oil. When oil moves quickly around the pan

(continued on next page)

PASTA AND CHICKEN:

1 cup raw cashews

2 pounds boneless, skinless chicken breasts

½ cup unsweetened almond or cashew milk

Juice from 1 lemon (2 tablespoons)

8 ounces pasta of choice ((GF) sub gluten-free pasta)

1 cup water

¼ cup nutritional yeast

1 teaspoon mild, white miso paste

1 tablespoon plus 1 teaspoon sea salt, plus more to taste

1 batch Cajun Seasoning

2 tablespoons avocado oil

Black pepper, to taste

1½ cups frozen green peas (optional)

CAJUN SEASONING:

1 tablespoon paprika

2 teaspoons garlic powder

2 teaspoons onion powder

1½ teaspoons sea salt (feel free to start with 1 teaspoon if you're salt-sensitive)

1 teaspoon black pepper

1 teaspoon dried oregano

1 teaspoon crushed red pepper flakes (use ½ teaspoon if you're heat-sensitive)

1 tablespoon coconut sugar (sub monkfruit sweetener)

ONE-POT CREAMY CAJUN CHICKEN PASTA *(continued)*

and is shimmering, add half of the chicken, quickly spreading it around the pan so pieces aren't overlapping (as much as possible). Cook until golden brown on the bottom, 4 to 5 minutes, then flip. You know it's ready when the chicken easily releases from the pan. (I find tongs helpful in making sure you get each piece.) Sear for another 2 minutes. Transfer chicken to a heatproof bowl. Repeat with remaining chicken. If necessary, add more oil to prevent sticking. The second batch might take a little less time.

Add cashew sauce and first batch of chicken to the saucepan. Turn to medium-low heat, scraping up any caramelized bits for additional flavor. Cook, stirring, until it is warm throughout. Add pasta, toss to coat, and cook for another minute. Feel free to add splashes of water (2 tablespoons at a time) if you want to thin the sauce. If using, add peas and cook until just warmed through. Taste for seasoning, and add more salt and pepper if you like. Serve immediately.

Leftover pasta will keep tightly sealed (once completely cooled) in the refrigerator for 4 days or in the freezer for 2 months if you have used wheat-based noodles. Chickpea- or veggie-based noodles do not keep well. To reheat leftovers, place them in a saucepan with a few splashes of water, and heat over medium heat.

SUGGESTED SIDES

LL's Sweetgreen Order Salad (page 275)

Carrot & Zucchini Ribbons with Lemony Pistachio Pesto (page 151))

Ideas for
LEFTOVER CAJUN SEASONING

Although you'll use the whole batch of Cajun Seasoning in this recipe, you might want to make a double batch so that you'll have leftovers to use on roasted potatoes, roasted or broiled salmon, as a grilling rub for steak or chicken, as an add-in for cooked rice or other grain, or as a sprinkle for popcorn. You can also mix it with full-fat plain yogurt to make a veggie dip.

LUNCH + DINNER ENTRÉES

One-Pot Pineapple Paprika Fajitas

DF P | **HANDS-ON TIME:** 45 min | **TOTAL TIME:** 45 min, plus 4 to 8 h marinating | **YIELD:** 6 servings | | **OPTION:** GF

I started making this dish when my cooking classes expanded from eight to fourteen attendees. I needed recipes that could be doubled or tripled easily and which could be prepped in advance. Enter, fajitas! But not just any fajitas. I like to pump up mine with finely chopped jalapeño and tangy, sweet pineapple. The pineapple doubles as a tenderizer in your marinade, resulting in soft, juicy chicken. By the time the chicken hits the pan, it's already infused with so much flavor! Feel free to play around with the veggies you use, and don't forget about our frozen friends—I've thrown in frozen green beans, broccoli, and corn.

Make the Marinade: Place all marinade ingredients in a blender, and purée until smooth. Pour into a marinating container or sealable plastic bag.

Slice chicken breasts against the grain into ¼-inch strips—the thinner, the better. Add to marinating container or bag. Seal and wipe with a soapy sponge to remove bacteria. Marinate in the refrigerator for 4 to 8 hours.

Make the Fajitas: When you're ready to cook, turn on the exhaust fan, and place a large bowl near the stove. Heat a large sauté pan over high heat, and add avocado oil. When oil moves quickly around the pan and is shimmering, add chicken, shaking off excess marinade as you remove it from the container or bag. Save leftover marinade. Note that some of your chicken will overlap or won't touch the pan, and that's okay. Allow chicken to cook, without stirring, until any liquid has evaporated and there are brown bits on the bottom of the pan, 5 to 6 minutes. Flip chicken, and cook for another 2 to 3 minutes. Remove chicken from the pan, and transfer to the bowl.

NOTE

About 1 in 10 jalapeños is spicier than others. Taste a tiny piece, and if it seems particularly hot, reduce the amount used in this recipe to ½ jalapeño.

MARINADE:

1 cup frozen chopped pineapple, thawed

Juice from 1 lime (2 tablespoons)

2 tablespoons low-sodium tamari

1 medium jalapeño, stems, seeds, and white pith removed, then diced into ¼-inch pieces

2 cloves garlic, diced into ¼-inch pieces

1½ teaspoons paprika

1 teaspoon chili powder

½ teaspoon onion powder

½ teaspoon ground cumin

FAJITAS:

1½ pounds boneless, skinless chicken breasts

2 tablespoons avocado oil

⅓ cup water

1 medium red bell pepper, sliced into ½-inch strips

1 medium yellow bell pepper, sliced into ½-inch strips

½ medium yellow onion, sliced into ¼-inch half moons (¾ to 1 cup)

1¼ cups frozen chopped pineapple

Salt, to taste

12 tortillas of choice (GF sub gluten-free tortillas)

(continued on next page)

Reduce heat to medium. Deglaze with a splash of water (2 tablespoons), scraping up any brown bits from the bottom of the pan. Add bell peppers and onions, cover with a lid, and steam until veggies are fork-tender, 4 to 5 minutes. Add chicken back to the pan, along with pineapple and any leftover marinade.

Cook fajita mixture until pineapple is warmed through and no liquid remains in the bottom of the pan, another 5 to 7 minutes. Taste for seasoning, and add salt to taste.

Serve with tortillas and whatever toppings you like. Leftovers will keep tightly sealed in the refrigerator for 5 days or in the freezer for 4 months.

SUGGESTED TOPPINGS:

Sour cream, shredded cheddar cheese, avocado slices, shredded lettuce, salsa, cilantro, and lime wedges

SUGGESTED SIDES

5-Ingredient Kimchi Coleslaw
(page 163)

Broccoli Gorgonzola Salad with
Miso Maple Dressing (page 147)

Chickpea, Avocado & Goat Cheese
Salad with Grainy Mustard Dressing
(page 286)

Ideas for
LEFTOVER FROZEN PINEAPPLE

If you have leftovers, use the rest of the bag in smoothies, such as Coconut Lime Macadamia Smoothie (page 50).

Go-To Rotisserie Chicken

GF K P | **HANDS-ON TIME:** 30 min | **TOTAL TIME:** 1 h, 45 min (Instant Pot); 8 h, 30 min (Crock-Pot

YIELD: 6 to 8 servings | **OPTION:** DF

This recipe alone might make owning an Instant Pot worthwhile. Just a quick spin in this glorious multi-cooker, and you have fall-apart-tender, juicy rotisserie-style chicken. Cooking whole chickens at home is a fantastic way to save money as well! While many grocery stores sell whole roasted chickens, very few use high-quality birds, and often they've been injected with a fake sodium solution. While it looks like we're using a lot of spice rub here, remember that 1) we're covering an entire bird and 2) a good bit falls into the liquid. If you don't own an Instant Pot, I got you: There's a Crock-Pot alternative, as always!

Both Versions: Place an 18-inch piece of parchment paper on the countertop. Place the chicken on top, and use parchment as your prep surface. Alternately, you can prep the chicken in a clean sink. Remove the giblets from inside the chicken, if any. Rinse the chicken with room temperature water, making sure to rinse out the cavity. Pat thoroughly dry with paper towels or a dish towel.

In a small bowl, combine salt, paprika, pepper, oregano, onion powder, and garlic powder.

In another small bowl, mash together 1 tablespoon spice mixture and 1 tablespoon softened butter to make a paste (you can microwave for 10 seconds to help combine). Starting at the cavity, carefully loosen the skin of the chicken breasts, separating it from the meat. You can usually do this with your fingers, but you may need a paring knife to make some small cuts to loosen things up. Rub paste evenly under the breast skin.

Rub remaining tablespoon butter, then remaining spice mixture, over the entire outside of the chicken. It's okay if some of the spice mixture falls off.

Stuff chicken cavity with half of the onion chunks, garlic head halves, and 2 lemon quarters. If some of it doesn't fit, just set aside.

Instant Pot Version: If you can, plug in the Instant Pot close to your stove (with the stove off), and turn on exhaust fan. Place avocado oil in the canister, and press "Sauté" on "High" or "More." Once the oil is shimmering, add chicken, breast side down, and sear for 5 to 7 minutes. Flip chicken by grabbing the cavity with tongs in your dominant hand and turning the chicken. Use a fork in your nondominant hand to help

(continued on next page)

Ingredients

- 4-pound whole chicken
- 1 tablespoon sea salt (less if you prefer)
- 2½ teaspoons paprika
- 2 teaspoons black pepper
- 2 teaspoons dried oregano
- 2 teaspoons onion powder
- 2 teaspoons garlic powder
- 2 tablespoons softened butter, divided (DF sub coconut oil)
- ½ medium sweet yellow onion, chopped into 1-inch chunks (¾ to 1 cup)
- 1 head garlic, sliced in half crosswise, excess peel removed (it's okay if some of the cloves fall apart)
- 1 lemon, cut into quarters, divided
- 1 tablespoon avocado oil (sub coconut oil)
- 1 cup low-sodium chicken stock

SUGGESTED SIDES

Macadamia & Roasted Grapefruit Salad with Lemony Vinaigrette (page 295)

"Hot" Honey Cheddar-Stuffed Sweet Potato Skins (page 130)

Creamy Corn & Chive Farro (page 156)

Buttery Lemon Pepper Leeks (page 148)

Bacon-y Cabbage & Onions (page 164)

LUNCH + DINNER ENTRÉES

lift and turn. Sear for another 5 minutes, then press "Cancel." Add broth, remaining onion chunks, remaining lemon quarters, and anything else that didn't fit in the cavity. Try not to pour broth directly on top, which can wash off spices. Cover and turn to seal, then set to "Manual" 24 minutes. Each pound of chicken takes about 6 minutes to cook in the Instant Pot, so adjust accordingly if your chicken is larger or smaller than 4 pounds.

When the Instant Pot beeps to signal the end of the cooking time, allow it to release pressure naturally, approximately 15 minutes. Remove chicken carefully (I use tongs and a fork again), and allow to cool for 10 to 15 minutes before enjoying. If you like, you can transfer chicken to a heatproof dish, and broil for several minutes to get crispier skin.

Crock-Pot Version: Turn on your exhaust fan. Heat a large sauté pan over high heat, and add avocado oil. When the oil moves quickly around the pan and is shimmering, add chicken, breast side down, and sear for 3 to 4 minutes. Flip chicken by grabbing the cavity with tongs in your dominant hand and turning the chicken. Use a fork in your nondominant hand to help lift and turn. Sear for another 5 minutes, then carefully transfer chicken, breast-side up, to the Crock-Pot. Try not to transfer the leftover oil with it, since it will likely have burned spices in it.

Add broth, remaining onion chunks, remaining lemon quarters, and anything else that didn't fit in the cavity to the Crock-Pot. Try not to pour broth directly on top, which can wash off spices. Cover and turn Crock-Pot to low. Cook for 6 to 7 ½ hours, carefully flipping chicken halfway through the cooking time. The closer to 7 ½ hours, the more fall-of-the-bone tender, which may or may not be your goal. (I do 6 hours if I want to eat the chicken in pieces or 7 ½ if I'm going to use it for chicken salad.)

Both Versions: I like to use tongs to remove the garlic halves, and squeeze the cloves out. Enjoy them with the chicken or with roasted veggies, on avocado toast, or in scrambled eggs. I also like to strain the leftover liquid through a fine-mesh sieve into a heatproof bowl, and refrigerate overnight. In the morning, I skim off and compost the fat on top (you can save it for cooking if you like, but the flavor is too strong for me). I then pour the liquid into a glass jar, and keep it in the freezer to use as a broth in other recipes. Be sure to leave room in the jar, as liquid expands when it freezes.

Leftover chicken will keep tightly sealed in the refrigerator for 4 days or in the freezer for 4 months.

Ideas for
LEFTOVER CHICKEN

I love turning leftovers into a super quick chicken salad. I just remove any skin, chop the chicken finely (or pulse it in the food processor), and mix with some mayonnaise, a touch of Dijon mustard, thinly sliced celery, roasted chopped walnuts, and halved red grapes.

Buffalo Chicken Dip

GF DF P | **HANDS-ON TIME:** 20 min | **TOTAL TIME:** 1 h, 50 min (Instant Pot); 6 h, 20 min (Crock-Pot)

YIELD: 8 servings | | **OPTION:** K

Man, am I glad I decided to make buffalo sauce a theme here. When the mild heat and acidic bite of Frank's RedHot pairs with something creamy, such as coconut milk, the result is absolutely irreplaceable and addictive. I considered including this dish in the Snack-itizer chapter, but I truly prefer it as dinner throughout the week. I've used this dip all sorts of ways: spooned into tacos with shredded lettuce and a dollop of sour cream or yogurt, over a big crunchy salad, in a bowl with white rice and my Vegan Tomato-y Collard Greens (page 155), or just scooped up with my favorite chips.

Use the short- or long-soak method to soak cashews (see page 44). Drain and rinse.

Place coconut milk, soaked cashews, Frank's RedHot, honey, garlic, nutritional yeast, miso, salt, and half of the red peppers in a high-powered blender, in the order listed. Purée until completely smooth. Taste for seasoning, and add more salt and nutritional yeast if you like.

Instant Pot Version: Combine the chicken, remaining red peppers, and onions in the canister of an Instant Pot, then pour coconut milk mixture on top. Stir to incorporate evenly. Secure lid and set Instant Pot to "Manual" 55 minutes. Once the Instant Pot beeps to signal the end of the cooking time, allow to release pressure naturally, 15 to 20 minutes. Open lid, shred chicken with two forks, and stir everything together until creamy and incorporated.

Crock-Pot Version: Combine the chicken, remaining red peppers, and onions in the Crock-Pot, then pour coconut milk mixture on top. Stir to incorporate evenly. Turn to low heat, and cook 6 hours. Open the pot, shred chicken with two forks, and stir everything together until creamy and incorporated.

Leftovers will keep tightly sealed in the refrigerator for 5 days or in the freezer for 4 months.

¾ cup raw cashews

¾ cup canned full-fat coconut milk

¾ cup original Frank's RedHot sauce

3 tablespoons honey (K sub monkfruit sweetener)

5 cloves garlic, roughly chopped

¼ cup nutritional yeast

1 teaspoon mild, white miso paste

1½ teaspoons sea salt (feel free to start with less and add to taste)

1 medium red bell pepper, chopped into ½-inch pieces (1½ cup) (sub yellow or orange pepper)

3 pounds boneless, skinless chicken thighs

½ medium yellow onion, chopped into ½-inch pieces (¾ to 1 cup)

SUGGESTED SIDES

"Hot" Honey Cheddar-Stuffed Sweet Potato Skins (page 130)

Bacon-y Cabbage & Onions (page 164)

LUNCH + DINNER ENTRÉES

Turkey Cheddar Lasagna

HANDS-ON TIME: 55 min | **TOTAL TIME:** 2 h, 20 min | **YIELD:** 12 to 15 servings | **OPTION:** GF

Y'all, I'm not going to lie. Putting this lasagna together is a pain in the butt. It requires a couple of hours and a lotta dishes. That said, I promise you it is worth the trouble! The key to a really special lasagna is infusing flavor into each and every layer; hence, the extra steps of sautéing onions and shallots, stirring in molasses, blending fresh basil, puréeing eggs into the ricotta mixture, and more. Plus, this recipe hides cauliflower among each scrumptious bite, so it's basically a "one-pot wonder." (Sort of.) This recipe also makes a ton of food, and it freezes beautifully, so your labor is not in vain! Next time you have a rainy Sunday afternoon to play with, give this lasagna a try, and pat yourself on the back for covering at least a week's worth of dinners.

Preheat oven to 375° F. Grease a 15 × 10 × 2-inch (or similar size) casserole dish with avocado oil. (Note: since prep takes some time, feel free to wait until half or three-quarters of the way through the recipe to preheat the oven.)

Make the Tomato Sauce: Place all sauce ingredients in a blender or food processor, and purée until smooth. Pour into a mixing bowl, and set aside.

Make the Meat Layer: Heat a large saucepan over high heat, and add 2 tablespoons avocado oil. You might want to turn on your exhaust fan. When the oil moves quickly around the pan and is shimmering, add ground turkey. Use a spatula to break it up into an even layer, then cook without stirring for 8 to 10 minutes. (If you want to multitask, you can start on the ricotta layer during this time). Flip meat, and cook for another 5 minutes or so. It's okay if there is still some pink—we're just going for caramelization. Break up meat again using your spatula, then scrape meat out of the saucepan into a heatproof bowl.

Reduce the heat to medium, and deglaze with a splash of water (2 tablespoons), scraping up any brown bits from the bottom of the pan. Add onions and shallots, and cook, stirring every minute or so, until softened and translucent, 3 to 4 minutes. Add garlic, and cook another 30 seconds, then add turkey back into the pan. Add salt, pepper, and molasses, and stir to incorporate, continuing to break up the meat. You might add a splash of water to help mix it all together. Turn off heat, and set saucepan aside.

(continued on page 236)

TOMATO SAUCE LAYER:

2 14½-ounce cans no-salt-added diced tomatoes

1 6-ounce can tomato paste

1 ounce fresh basil (1 cup, packed; sub 1 tablespoon dried basil)

2 teaspoons dried oregano

1 teaspoon onion powder

1 teaspoon sea salt

¼ teaspoon black pepper

MEAT LAYER:

2 tablespoons avocado oil

2 pounds ground turkey (mix of dark and light meat)

⅓ cup water

½ medium yellow onion, chopped into ½-inch pieces (¾ to 1 cup)

1 large or 2 small shallots, diced into ¼-inch pieces (½ cup)

4 cloves garlic, minced

1 teaspoon sea salt

¼ teaspoon black pepper

2 tablespoons molasses (sub aged balsamic vinegar)

(continued on page 236)

SUGGESTED SIDES

Roasted Romaine with Basil Caesar Hummus Dressing (page 298)

Carrot & Zucchini Ribbons with Lemony Pistachio Pesto (page 151)

LUNCH + DINNER ENTRÉES

234   SIMPLY LAURA LEA

Make the Ricotta Layer: Place water in a medium saucepan, and bring to a boil. While water is coming to a boil, remove the base and leaves from cauliflower, and chop into 1½-inch florets (3½ to 4 cups). When the water is boiling, add florets. Boil until knife-tender, 3 to 4 minutes, then drain and rinse with cold water until they reach room temperature.

Place cauliflower, ricotta, eggs, coconut milk, salt, and pepper in a blender or food processor. Purée until smooth. Pour into a large mixing bowl, and stir in parmesan cheese and 2 cups cheddar.

Assemble the Lasagna: Make layers in the following order: 4 to 6 tablespoons sauce; lasagna noodles (can break them if needed); one-third of the sauce (approximately 1 rounded cup); one-third of the ricotta mixture (approximately 1¼ cups); one-half of the meat; lasagna noodles; one-third of the sauce; one-third of the ricotta mixture; remaining meat; lasagna noodles; remaining ricotta mixture; remaining cheddar, and a thin layer of parmesan.

Cover lasagna with tented aluminum foil. (If the foil touches the top it will pull the cheese off when you remove it.) Bake for 30 minutes. Remove foil, and bake for another 30 minutes, until golden brown and bubbling. Allow to cool for at least 25 minutes before slicing.

Leftovers will keep tightly sealed in the refrigerator for 5 days or in the freezer for 2 months.

RICOTTA LAYER:

6 cups water

½ medium head cauliflower

15 ounces whole-milk ricotta

2 large eggs

1½ cups canned full-fat coconut milk (sub 1 cup unsweetened almond milk)

1 teaspoon sea salt

½ teaspoon black pepper

½ cup freshly grated parmesan cheese, plus more for topping

12 ounces mild cheddar cheese, shredded (3 cups), divided

ASSEMBLY:

Avocado oil for greasing

16 to 20 ounces no-boil lasagna noodles (GF sub gluten-free noodles)

Grated parmesan cheese for topping

NOTES

Shred the cheddar cheese on top of the piece of aluminum foil you'll use to cover and bake the lasagna. No clean up, and any extra cheese can go on top of the lasagna.

Instead of the ricotta, you can use 8 ounces full-fat cream cheese, then increase the coconut milk to about 2 cups (a full 15-ounce can).

The amount of lasagna noodles you need will depend on the shape of the lasagna, so I recommend buying 20 ounces and having leftovers.

LUNCH + DINNER ENTRÉES

BBQ Turkey Hashbrown Casserole

| **HANDS-ON TIME:** 30 min | **TOTAL TIME:** 1 h, 35 min | **YIELD:** 6 servings | ⊕

I have no idea where the inspiration came from for this recipe. Perhaps I couldn't decide if I was in a brunch-y or BBQ-y mood at the time, so I meshed them together? Regardless, I'm grateful for the lightbulb moment that led to my hashbrown casserole creation! If you already have the spice rub made (and it only takes a minute), putting this together is a cinch, and no one will notice that it contains half a head of cauliflower. Sliceable, packable, and freezable, it's a versatile meal cold or warm. Feel free to use ground beef or a mixture of dark and light ground chicken, if you prefer.

Make the BBQ Seasoning: Place all seasoning ingredients in a small bowl, and whisk to combine, or place in a sealable jar or container and shake.

Make the Quick BBQ Sauce: Whisk all sauce ingredients together in a small bowl. Leftovers will keep tightly sealed in the refrigerator for 5 days.

Make the Casserole: Remove base and leaves from cauliflower, and chop into approximately 1½-inch florets (3½ to 4 cups). If using frozen cauliflower rice, place in a microwave-safe bowl, and microwave for 2 to 3 minutes, until thawed. Allow to cool until you can handle it, then press a dish towel on top to absorb excess liquid.

Preheat oven to 400° F. Turn on your exhaust fan. Heat a cast-iron or other nonstick skillet over medium-high heat, and add 1 tablespoon avocado oil. When oil moves quickly around the pan and is shimmering, add onions and hashbrowns, and spread into an even layer. Cook without stirring until golden brown and crispy underneath, 5 to 7 minutes (you can peek to check).

Reduce heat to medium-low. Deglaze with ½ cup water, scraping up any brown bits from the bottom of the pan and stirring into the hashbrowns. Cook, stirring frequently, until water is completely evaporated, another 2 to 3 minutes. Add garlic and ¼ cup BBQ Seasoning, and cook, stirring, another 30 seconds. Add another splash of water (2 tablespoons) to prevent burning. Transfer mixture to a large heatproof mixing bowl, and set aside to cool for at least 5 minutes. Do not clean skillet.

Add cauliflower florets to a food processor, and blend until they form a paste consistency, like wet cornmeal. (Note: there's no need to do this if using cauliflower rice.)

Add cauliflower to hashbrown mixture, along with nutritional yeast, eggs, mayonnaise, mustard, almond flour, and ground turkey. Combine thoroughly. (I suggest using clean hands.) This mixture will be quite wet.

(continued on on page 239)

BBQ SEASONING:

¼ cup coconut sugar (sub 3 tablespoons monkfruit sweetener)

2 tablespoons paprika

1 tablespoon sea salt

1 tablespoon chili powder

1 tablespoon garlic powder

4 teaspoons onion powder

1 teaspoon ground cumin

½ teaspoon ground cinnamon

½ teaspoon black pepper

QUICK BBQ SAUCE:

6 tablespoons ketchup

1½ teaspoons molasses

1 tablespoon maple syrup or honey

1 tablespoon low-sodium tamari

1 tablespoon apple cider vinegar

CASSEROLE:

½ medium head cauliflower (sub 12 ounces frozen cauliflower rice)

3 tablespoons avocado oil (sub olive oil), divided

½ sweet yellow onion, diced into ¼-inch pieces (approximately 1 cup)

3 cups frozen hashbrowns

½ cup water

6 cloves garlic, minced

¼ cup BBQ Seasoning

(continued on page 239)

BBQ TURKEY HASHBROWN CASSEROLE *(continued)*

Place remaining 2 tablespoons avocado oil in the same cast-iron skillet, and turn heat to high. Make sure exhaust fan is on. When oil moves quickly around the pan and is shimmering, add cauliflower-hashbrown-turkey mixture to the pan, and spread in an even layer. Allow to cook for 2 minutes, then carefully (it's heavy!) place in the oven.

Bake for 40 minutes, or until firm to touch and edges are slightly pulling away from the sides.

Allow to cool for 20 minutes before slicing and using a flat spatula to remove wedges. Top with Quick BBQ Sauce to taste.

Leftovers will keep tightly sealed in the refrigerator for 5 days or in the freezer for 2 months.

Ideas for
LEFTOVER HASHBROWNS

Brown leftover hashbrowns in a hot cast-iron skillet, then stir with scrambled eggs, pinches of salt and pepper, and grated parmesan cheese. Or defrost potatoes, and add to a mixing bowl, along with 1 to 2 eggs (depends how much you have left), diced bell pepper, a dash of chili powder, salt and pepper, and some shredded cheddar cheese. Scoop into nonstick cupcake tins, and bake at 400° F until crispy (could take up to 45 minutes). Or place hashbrowns on a parchment-lined baking sheet in an even layer, brush with avocado oil, toss with any of my spice rubs, and bake at 350° F until crunchy, then allow to cool completely before breaking up.

3 tablespoons nutritional yeast

2 large eggs

2 tablespoons mayonnaise

1 tablespoon Dijon mustard

½ cup blanched almond flour

1 pound ground turkey (use a mixture of light and dark meat)

1 batch Quick BBQ Sauce, to taste

NOTES

If you don't have a nonstick pan, use 3 tablespoons oil to cook the onions and hashbrowns, making the recipe total 4 tablespoons.

Double the recipe for the Quick BBQ Sauce if you like to dip things!

When buying hashbrowns, look for ones that have only potatoes and maybe citric acid for preserving as ingredients.

SUGGESTED SIDES
Vegan Tomato-y Collard Greens
(page 155)

Best Potato Salad
(page 167)

Charred Green Bean & Farro Salad
with Avocado Ranch Dressing
(page 293)

Veggie Entrées

B efore I began writing this book, I did a poll to see what kind of content y'all were looking for. The number one request I received was for more vegan and vegetarian recipes. I absolutely loved this response. While I think animal proteins and dairy can be an important part of a healthy lifestyle, I also think we all need to be eating more plants. Plants are packed with the micronutrients that help us sustain long-term vitality, as well as soluble and insoluble fiber to aid in digestion. I highly recommend using the Environmental Working Group's "Dirty Dozen" list when deciding where to splurge on organic produce. And don't forget that frozen organic veggies are a fantastic, nutritious option as well.

I developed this chapter with omnivores in mind, creating plant-based spins on classic favorites. You'll see better-than-takeout Orange Ginger Tofu, BBQ "Baked" Lentils that remind me of Sloppy Joe filling (in a good way!), Buffalo Tempeh Wraps, and much more. All except one recipe can be made vegan, but I certainly won't judge if you want to add a little parmesan cheese to my Roasted Red Pepper Pasta alla Vodka or a slice of sharp cheddar cheese to my Sweet Potato, Peanut & Black Bean Burgers. Regardless of where you fall on the plant-meat spectrum, I think you'll find something you love in this section!

Orange Ginger Tofu

  | **HANDS-ON TIME:** 18 min | **TOTAL TIME:** 48 min | **YIELD:** 3 to 4 servings ⏱ ⊕

This recipe alone was worth introducing tofu into my repertoire. I love to make a batch and enjoy it throughout the week—on a kale salad, with rice, in my favorite Buddha bowl, in tacos . . . yep, you name it! You'll have enough leftover sauce to coat a side veggie like roasted broccoli, which makes for an amazing companion to this tofu. It's totally cool if you want to swap tofu for shrimp or bite-sized chunks of chicken. Just watch the baking time, and adjust as needed (both should take less time).

Preheat oven to 400° F. Line two baking sheets with parchment paper.

Rinse tofu and pat dry. Cut into approximately 1-inch cubes. Place cubes side by side on the baking sheet, leaving a bit of space between each. Roast tofu for 40 minutes, flipping halfway.

While tofu is roasting, place orange zest, orange juice, garlic, maple syrup, ginger, salt, and ½ cup water in a small saucepan. Whisk to incorporate, then bring to a boil over medium-high heat. Boil sauce, whisking occassionally until it has reduced in volume by approximately one-third, 5 to 7 minutes. Reduce heat to low. Place arrowroot starch and remaining 2 teaspoons water in a small bowl, and whisk to dissolve. Pour into orange juice mixture, stirring constantly for 20 to 30 seconds. Simmer for another minute, stirring, then remove from the heat.

When tofu is done, transfer it to a heatproof bowl, and pour on enough sauce to coat. (I like to save a bit of the sauce to serve alongside the tofu.)

Tofu will keep tightly sealed in the refrigerator for 5 days and sauce will keep for 7. You can freeze the sauce for 3 months. I don't recommend freezing the tofu.

Ingredients

24 to 30 ounces extra firm tofu, ideally sprouted

Zest from 1 medium navel orange (1 tablespoon packed)

Juice from 2 medium navel oranges (½ cup)

2 cloves garlic, finely minced

3 tablespoons maple syrup

¾-inch piece ginger, peeled and grated

¾ teaspoon sea salt (feel free to start with ½ teaspoon and add to taste)

½ cup plus 2 teaspoons water

2 teaspoons arrowroot starch (sub cornstarch)

NOTE

Sprouted tofu is tofu made from sprouted soybeans—soybeans from seeds that have been germinated for several days. It can be easier to digest and is richer in bioavailable nutrients.

SERVING SUGGESTION

My favorite way to serve this is with my Baked Coconut Rice: Preheat oven to 375° F. Grease an 8-inch square baking dish with 1 teaspoon butter or coconut oil. Place 1½ cups uncooked medium-grain white rice in the dish.

In a small saucepan, place 1½ cups canned full-fat coconut milk, 1 cup water, and 1 teaspoon sea salt. Stir to combine. Cover and heat over medium-high heat. As soon as liquid comes to a rapid simmer, pour over rice. Stir and cover dish tightly with aluminum foil. Bake rice 65 minutes. Remove and uncover, fluffing with a fork. Stir in ⅓ cup toasted coconut flakes, and serve immediately. Rice will keep tightly sealed in the refrigerator for 5 days.

SUGGESTED SIDES

Cashew Kimchi Lettuce Cups (page 137)

Broccoli Gorgonzola Salad with Miso Maple Dressing (page 147)

Sheet Pan Sesame Tofu & Bok Choy

VG GF DF | **HANDS-ON TIME:** 18 min | **TOTAL TIME:** 45 mins, plus 4 to 24 h marinating | **YIELD:** 4 servings

This recipe is very much inspired by one of the more popular vegan recipes on my blog. It is a favorite of mine as well, and I still make it regularly. In the original version, I paired the nutty roasted tofu with eggplant, but I decided I wanted something green with a bit more texture for this recipe. However, feel free to try it with eggplant or whatever veggies you're craving. Cruciferous or starchy vegetables will need to be diced into fairly small pieces so they cook thoroughly. Oh, and for those of you who have my first book, this sauce might look familiar—it is indeed a variation on my beloved peanut sauce.

In a large sealable plastic bag or other marinating container, combine tamari, maple syrup, sriracha, tahini, sesame oil, garlic, and ginger. Whisk to roughly incorporate (doesn't have to mix perfectly). If you're using a plastic bag, you should be able to sit it upright on the counter and hold it while you whisk. Add tofu, seal tightly, and shake to evenly coat. Allow to marinate at least 4 hours, ideally overnight or up to 24 hours.

Preheat oven to 400° F. Line a large baking sheet with parchment paper.

Remove the base of the bok choy so that the individual stalks separate. Rinse and pat dry. If using regular-sized bok choy, slice stalks in half crosswise. Remove base and top 1 inch of the scallions, then rinse and pat dry. Slice crosswise into approximately 1 ½-inch pieces.

Place bok choy and scallions on the baking sheet, and sprinkle with salt and pepper.

Open the bag or container, and use a slotted spoon or tongs to remove tofu, shaking off and reserving excess liquid. Place tofu on the baking sheet, trying not to let it overlap with the veggies. Bake for 30 to 35 minutes, flipping tofu halfway to brown evenly. (I find tongs best for this.)

Place remaining marinade in a small saucepan. Add water, and bring to a simmer over medium-low heat. Simmer, stirring frequently, until marinade is slightly thickened.

Serve tofu and veggies with a drizzle of sauce and sesame seeds. (I love serving this with regular or cauliflower rice, in tacos, or over noodles.)

Tofu and sauce will keep tightly sealed in the refrigerator for 4 days. I don't recommend freezing.

⅓ cup low-sodium tamari

2 tablespoons maple syrup (sub monkfruit sweetener)

1 tablespoon sriracha (sub 1 teaspoon maple syrup if you don't want spice)

2 tablespoons tahini or unsweetened, unsalted almond or peanut butter

1 tablespoon toasted sesame oil

3 cloves garlic, finely minced

1-inch piece ginger, peeled and grated (sub ¼ teaspoon ground ginger)

12 to 15 ounces extra firm tofu, cut into 1-inch cubes (will vary by brand, but anything in this range works)

1 bunch baby bok choy (sub ½ large bunch regular-sized bok choy)

1 bunch scallions

Pinches salt and black pepper

⅓ cup water

Sesame seeds for garnish

SUGGESTED SIDES

Miso Coconut Roasted Eggplant (page 159)

Charred Green Bean & Farro Salad with Avocado Ranch (page 293)

Sun-Dried Tomato & Basil Falafel

with GREEN TAHINI SAUCE

V GF DF | **HANDS-ON TIME:** 35 min | **TOTAL TIME:** 1 h, 5 min | **YIELD:** approximately 16 falafels | ⊕ | **OPTION:** VG

Falafel is one of my all-time favorite foods. In fact, a falafel pita was the culinary highlight of my last trip to Paris, beating out chocolate croissants and cheesy baguettes. It took multiple tries to create a baked version that compares to the real deal, but the effort was worth it!

Preheat oven to 375° F. Line a baking sheet with parchment paper.

Make the Falafels: Heat a small saucepan over medium heat, and add olive oil. When oil moves quickly around the pan, add shallots. Cook, stirring every minute or so, until softened and translucent, 3 to 4 minutes. Reduce heat to low, add garlic, and stir constantly for another minute. Set aside to cool for 5 minutes.

Combine sun-dried tomatoes, basil, mayonnaise, cumin, pepper, salt, and chickpea flour in a food processor, and process until a chunky paste forms, approximately 5 seconds. Add chickpeas and cooled shallots to processor. Pulse until incorporated but some texture remains, stopping and scraping the sides if necessary. This is a fairly wet mixture.

Use lightly dampened fingers to form balls with 2 tablespoons batter per falafel. Place on the baking sheet at least 2 inches apart. Flatten into approximately ½-inch-thick disks.

Bake falafels for 18 minutes, then flip and bake for another 8 minutes, until golden brown. Allow to cool for 10 minutes before enjoying.

Make the Green Tahini Sauce: While falafel is baking, combine all sauce ingredients, in the order listed, in a blender, and blend until smooth and creamy. Sauce will thicken in the refrigerator. You can stir in a tablespoon or two of water when you use leftovers, if you want to thin it.

To serve, drizzle falafels with Green Tahini Sauce.

Leftover falafels will keep tightly sealed in the refrigerator for 5 days or in the freezer for 6 months.

FALAFELS:

2 tablespoons extra virgin olive oil

1 medium shallot, diced into ¼-inch pieces (⅓ cup)

4 cloves garlic, minced

¼ cup packed sun-dried tomatoes, excess oil squeezed off

½ ounce fresh basil, roughly chopped (½ cup, packed)

2 tablespoons mayonnaise (VG sub vegan mayonnaise)

¼ teaspoon ground cumin

¼ teaspoon black pepper

½ teaspoon sea salt

¼ cup chickpea flour

1 15-ounce can chickpeas, drained, rinsed, and patted dry

GREEN TAHINI SAUCE:

⅓ cup water

¾ ounce fresh basil (¾ cup, packed)

Juice from 1 lemon (2 tablespoons)

¼ cup tahini

1 teaspoon mild, white miso paste

1 clove garlic, roughly chopped

Pinches salt, black pepper, and onion powder

SERVING SUGGESTION

Stuff falafel in a whole-wheat pita. Or serve it over arugula with fresh lemon juice and olive oil (in addition to Green Tahini Sauce) and a side of salted avocado.

SUGGESTED SIDE

Italian Green Bean & Toasted Quinoa Salad (page 160)

Buffalo Tempeh Wraps
with AVOCADO RANCH DRESSING

V | HANDS-ON TIME: 30 min | TOTAL TIME: 1 h, plus 2 to 8 h marinating | YIELD: 5 wraps

OPTIONS: Vg GF DF

Why is everything more satisfying in a wrap? Sure, you can make these Buffalo Tempeh strips, dip them in my Avocado Ranch Dressing, and you'll be a happy camper. But when you throw those goodies in a wrap with some crunchy slaw and extra slices of creamy avocado? Well, it just hits the spot! There are a few great healthy wraps on the market, including low-carb ones made from coconut and gluten-free ones made with brown rice. If gluten doesn't bother you, I suggest looking for the ones made from sprouted wheat. They're quite pliable and totally delicious. Wrap or no, this buffalo tempeh is a fabulous plant-based protein to keep around for your meals or snacks throughout the week.

Make the Avocado Ranch Dressing: Place 2 tablespoons minced chives and all remaining ingredients in a blender, and blend until smooth and creamy. Transfer to a mixing bowl, and stir in remaining 2 tablespoons chives. Makes about 1 cup.

Make the Buffalo Tempeh: Slice each block of tempeh in half crosswise, then slice each half lengthwise into 5 rectangular pieces.

In a sealable plastic bag or marinating container, whisk together ¼ cup Frank's RedHot, tahini, tamari, maple syrup, and pepper. Add sliced tempeh, and gently toss to coat. Marinate in the refrigerator for at least 2 hours and up to 8.

Preheat oven to 400° F. Line a baking sheet with parchment paper. Shake off excess marinade, then place tempeh slices on the baking sheet in an even layer, leaving at least 1 inch between each. Bake for 30 minutes, then drizzle on remaining 2 tablespoon Frank's RedHot. Toss to coat. Serve as is or make wraps.

Assemble the Wraps: Place the wraps, one at a time, in the still-warm oven for 30 seconds before you roll each wrap. (If your wraps feel

(continued on page 250)

AVOCADO RANCH DRESSING:

¼ ounce chives, minced (¼ cup), divided

1 clove garlic, minced

1 teaspoon mild, white miso paste

1 ripe avocado, mashed (½ cup)

½ cup sour cream or plain full-fat yogurt (Vg DF sub dairy-free yogurt)

1½ tablespoons apple cider vinegar

1 teaspoon onion powder

½ teaspoon sea salt

½ teaspoon black pepper

½ cup unsweetened almond milk

BUFFALO TEMPEH:

16 ounces (2 8-ounce blocks) tempeh

¼ cup plus 2 tablespoons original Frank's RedHot, divided

2 tablespoons tahini

1 tablespoon low-sodium tamari

1 tablespoon maple syrup

¼ teaspoon black pepper

ASSEMBLY:

Wraps or tortilla of choice (GF gluten-free wraps)

½ batch 5-Ingredient Kimchi Coleslaw (page 163)

1 batch Avocado Ranch Dressing

Avocado slices

BUFFALO TEMPEH WRAPS
WITH AVOCADO RANCH DRESSING *(continued)*

soft and pliable, you can skip this step.) Spread a layer of Avocado Ranch Dressing on wrap, leaving approximately 1 inch free around the edges. Add 4 Buffalo Tempeh strips to the middle of the wrap. Top with approximately ⅓ cup Kimchi Coleslaw, followed by a few slices of fresh avocado. Fold the "east and west" sides of the wrap towards the center, to form a wrap. Tuck the "north and south" sides in toward the filling to secure the wrap. Enjoy immediately.

If only one wrap is being enjoyed at a time, I suggest making them à la carte when you want them, instead of all at once, as they will get soggy. You can keep the components separate and tightly sealed in the refrigerator for 4 days. I don't recommend freezing.

SUGGESTED SIDES

Charred Green Bean & Farro Salad
with Avocado Ranch Dressing
(page 293)

Miso Mushroom & Rice Soup
(page 282)

Buffalo Cauliflower Hummus
(for dipping) (page 134)

Ideas for
LEFTOVER CHIVES

Stir into scrambled eggs, sprinkle on roasted potatoes,
use in pesto, or stir into soup.

LUNCH + DINNER ENTRÉES

Artichoke, Leek & White Bean Gratin

(V) (GF) | **HANDS-ON TIME:** 35 min | **TOTAL TIME:** 1 h, 55 min | **YIELD:** 8 to 10 servings

This dish is my go-to entrée when I teach my Vegan and Vegetarian Dinners class. It feeds a lot of mouths and freezes beautifully. If you're looking for something flavorful, cozy, and crowd-pleasing, this gratin is just the ticket. I've also made a double batch and added diced chicken sausage to one gratin, when I add cooked quinoa near the end of the recipe.

Place quinoa in a fine-mesh sieve, and rinse under running water until there are no small foamy bubbles and the water runs clear, approximately 1 minute. Drain well.

Combine quinoa and 2 cups stock in a medium saucepan. Bring to a boil over medium-high heat, then reduce to the lowest possible setting. Cover pot with a lid, and simmer until the liquid has evaporated, 15 to 20 minutes. Remove from the heat, but keep covered 5 minutes. Uncover, fluff with a fork, and set aside.

Preheat oven to 375° F. Grease a 9 × 13 × 2-inch baking dish with 1 teaspoon butter.

Remove bottom ½ inch from the base of each leek, as well as almost all of the dark leafy top. (I leave approximately 1 inch and compost the rest.) Slice leeks in half lengthwise and remove the outer layer of each half. (If all of this seems confusing, the point is: we want to keep the light colored inner parts of the leeks because they're tender.)

Place leeks in a large mixing bowl full of room temperature water. Gently rinse and separate the leaves, then allow to sit 5 minutes. Skim the leaves off the top of the water, making sure not to stir up any dirt that has fallen to the bottom of the bowl. Pat leeks mostly dry, then slice into ½-inch-thick half-moons.

In a blender, combine remaining 1 ½ cups stock, yogurt, eggs, mustard, miso, salt, onion powder, and pepper. Blend until smooth. You can also thoroughly whisk together in a mixing bowl.

(continued on page 253)

1 cup dried quinoa

3½ cups low-sodium vegetable stock, divided

2 tablespoons plus 1 teaspoon softened butter, divided

2 medium leeks

½ cup plain full-fat yogurt or sour cream

2 large eggs

1 tablespoon plus 1 teaspoon Dijon mustard

1½ teaspoons mild, white miso paste

2 teaspoons sea salt (feel free to start with less and add to taste)

1 teaspoon onion powder

¼ teaspoon black pepper

1 14-ounce can artichoke hearts

6 cloves garlic, minced

1 15-ounce can no-salt-added cannellini beans, drained and rinsed

2 tablespoons arrowroot starch (sub cornstarch)

2 tablespoons water

8 ounces sharp cheddar cheese, shredded (2 cups), divided

ARTICHOKE, LEEK & WHITE BEAN GRATIN *(continued)*

Open artichoke hearts, and drain excess liquid, then roughly chop into approximately ¾-inch pieces. Remove any pieces that feel tough to your fingers.

Heat a large sauté pan over medium heat, and add remaining 2 tablespoons butter. When butter has melted and has small bubbles, add leeks. Cook, stirring, until leeks are softened, 3 to 4 minutes. Add minced garlic, and cook, stirring, another 30 seconds.

Add cooked quinoa, artichoke hearts, beans, and vegetable stock mixture. Gently and carefully stir everything together. Simmer for 3 to 4 minutes, adjusting heat as necessary, just to let the flavors come together. You may notice that the yogurt looks like it's curdling, but it's fine! Taste for seasoning, and add more salt if you like.

In a small bowl, place arrowroot starch and water, and stir to dissolve. Add to the pan, and stir until the mixture noticeably thickens, approximately 30 seconds. Add 1 cup shredded cheese, and carefully stir until melted.

Transfer gratin mixture to the baking dish, and sprinkle with remaining cup of cheese. Bake for 45 minutes, until edges are crispy and golden brown. Allow to cool for 10 minutes before serving.

Leftovers will keep tightly sealed in the refrigerator for 5 days or in the freezer for 3 months.

SUGGESTED SIDE

Tahini Brussels Sprouts with Pistachios & Dates (page 133)

Oil-Free Broccoli & Cheddar Pasta

VG DF | **HANDS-ON TIME:** 45 min | **TOTAL TIME:** 1 h, 50 min, plus overnight soaking

YIELD: 8 servings **OPTION:** GF

I know, I know, there's nothing new under the sun here. Or, is there? I'll let you decide. For my version of a vegan "mac," I use several of my favorite plant-based "cheese" sauce sources: cashews, carrots, and potatoes. The combination creates a rich sauce that will please any dairy-cheese lover. Roasting the veggies adds a heavenly complexity that only comes from caramelization. I think you and your family will love this nutritious alternative to the famous blue box!

Use the short- or long-soak method to soak cashews (see page 44). Drain and rinse.

Cook pasta al dente according to package directions (1 to 2 minutes less than the shortest suggested time). Drain and rinse. Toss with some avocado oil if you're worried that the pasta will stick together. Set aside. Preheat oven to 400° F. Line a baking sheet with parchment paper.

Place carrots and potatoes on the baking sheet, and toss with 1 teaspoon avocado oil and ¼ teaspoon salt. Spread in an even layer, and roast for 40 minutes, then allow to cool for 5 minutes.

While veggies are roasting, heat a small sauté pan over medium heat. Add remaining tablespoon avocado oil. When oil moves quickly around the pan and is shimmering, add onions. Cook, stirring every minute or so, until softened and translucent, 4 to 5 minutes. Reduce heat to low, and add garlic, stirring constantly for another 30 seconds. Set aside to cool for 5 minutes.

Place the cooled veggies in a high-powered blender along with cashews, remaining ½ teaspoon salt, miso, onion powder, garlic powder, turmeric, pepper, nutritional yeast, and almond milk. Blend until smooth, using a tamper as needed to keep it moving.

Combine cooked pasta, "cheese" sauce, and broccoli in a large pot over medium-low heat. Cook, stirring, until broccoli has thawed and pasta is warm throughout. Taste for seasoning, and add more salt if you like. (I add another ¼ teaspoon.) Serve immediately.

Leftovers will keep tightly sealed in the refrigerator for 4 days if you have used wheat-based noodles. Chickpea- or veggie-based noodles do not keep well. I don't recommend freezing.

½ cup raw cashews

16 ounces pasta noodles of choice (GF sub gluten-free noodles)

2 medium carrots, peeled and sliced into ¾-inch rounds (1 cup)

1 pound Yukon Gold potatoes, peeled and chopped into 1-inch pieces (2½ cups)

1 tablespoon plus 1 teaspoon avocado oil

¾ teaspoon sea salt, plus more to taste, divided

½ yellow onion, diced into ¼-inch pieces

4 cloves garlic, minced

1 teaspoon mild, white miso paste

½ teaspoon onion powder

¼ teaspoon garlic powder

¾ teaspoon ground turmeric

½ teaspoon black pepper

¼ cup nutritional yeast

1¼ cup unsweetened almond milk

12 to 16 ounces frozen broccoli

SUGGESTED SIDES

Vegan Tomato-y Collard Greens (page 155)

Buffalo Tempeh Wraps with Avocado Ranch Dressing (page 248)

LUNCH + DINNER ENTRÉES

Cauliflower Walnut Tacos

This is another recipe that originated on my blog, before weaseling its way into this book. I welcomed this vegan "taco meat" into the hardcover-recipe family because it is addictively delectable! As much as I love my classic 5-Minute Taco Meat (in my first cookbook), it's nice to have a high-fiber, plant-based alternative—especially one that can easily trick you into thinking it's the real deal. Umami-rich mushrooms and walnuts recreate the savoriness of ground beef, and my Taco Seasoning has the yumminess but none of the preservatives, vegetable oils, and excessive sodium found in store-bought packets. I also love to enjoy this "meat" on taco salads, in a bowl with my Fluffy Shallot Rice (page 343) as a nacho topping, or simply scooped with chips.

Make the Taco Seasoning: Place all seasoning ingredients in a small bowl, and whisk to combine, or place in a sealable jar or container and shake.

Make the Taco Filling: Preheat oven to 350° F. Place walnuts on a baking sheet. Roast for 10–12 minutes, until fragrant and slightly darkened in color. Set aside to cool 5 minutes. Increase oven temperature to 400° F.

Remove the base and leaves from the cauliflower, and chop into 1-inch florets (approximately 5 ½ cups). Line a baking sheet with parchment paper. Place cauliflower florets and mushrooms on the baking sheet. Drizzle with avocado oil, and toss to coat, then spread veggies in an even layer. Roast the veggies for 25 to 30 minutes, until florets are knife-tender with golden-brown edges. Allow to cool for 5 minutes.

Place ¼ cup Taco Seasoning, cooled walnuts, and nutritional yeast in a food processor. Pulse for 5 seconds, just to break up the walnuts. Add cooled veggies, and pulse a few more times, until mixture is incorporated but still chunky. Taste for seasoning, and add more if you like. (I use the rest of the batch.) If your "meat" needs a little reheating, place it in a 300° F oven until warmed through.

Assemble the Tacos: Fill taco shells with filling, and serve with whatever garnishes you like—I highly recommend diced tomatoes topped with fresh lime juice, salt, and pepper.

Leftovers will keep tightly sealed in the refrigerator for 5 days. I don't recommend freezing.

TACO SEASONING:

- 1 tablespoon coconut sugar (sub monkfruit sweetener)
- 2½ teaspoons chili powder
- 2¼ teaspoons paprika
- 2 teaspoons onion powder
- 1¼ teaspoon sea salt
- 1¼ teaspoon ground cumin
- 1 teaspoon garlic powder
- 1 teaspoon dried oregano

TACO FILLING:

- 1 cup raw walnuts
- 1 small head cauliflower
- 8 ounces pre-sliced baby bella mushrooms
- 1½ tablespoons avocado oil
- 1 batch Taco Seasoning
- 2 tablespoons nutritional yeast

ASSEMBLY:

- 12 to 16 6-inch taco shells
- Diced tomatoes drizzled with lime juice, salt and pepper, avocado, shredded lettuce, regular or vegan shredded cheese, and sriracha for garnish

SUGGESTED SIDES

5-Ingredient Kimchi Coleslaw (page 163)

Broccoli Gorgonzola Salad with Miso Maple Dressing (page 147)

Chickpea, Avocado & Goat Cheese Salad with Grainy Mustard Dressing (page 286)

LUNCH + DINNER ENTRÉES

BBQ "Baked" Lentils

Vg GF DF | **HANDS-ON TIME:** 7 min | **TOTAL TIME:** 1 h, 7 min (Instant Pot) to 4 h, 7 min (Crock-Pot)

YIELD: 8 to 10 servings

I'm a sucker for baked beans, and this BBQ lentil dish is my take on it. Green lentils hold up beautifully in an Instant Pot, and they are a mild backdrop for the sweet and savory BBQ Seasoning. This is an awesome "base" recipe to create different types of meals throughout the week. You can enjoy these lentils in tacos with shredded lettuce and a dollop of plain yogurt or sour cream . . . or add them to a bowl of quinoa and roasted broccoli with a generous drizzle of tahini . . . or stuff them in a burrito with some grass-fed cheddar cheese, a handful of fresh corn, and some thinly sliced red onion. I also love to serve them with my Creamy Corn & Chive Farro (page 156), in a Buddah bowl with rice and some fresh veggies, or Sloppy Joe-style on grilled buttered buns. You get the idea.

Make the BBQ Seasoning: Place all seasoning ingredients in a small bowl, and whisk to combine, or place in a sealable jar or container and shake.

Instant Pot Version: Place all ingredients for the lentils except salt and pepper, in the order listed, in the canister of an Instant Pot. Stir to evenly distribute ingredients, then seal Instant Pot. Set to "Manual" 35 minutes. When the Instant Pot beeps to signal the end of cooking time, allow it to release pressure naturally for at least 15 minutes, then turn to "Venting" to release remaining pressure. Remove lid, stir, and add salt and pepper to taste. You can add an extra splash of stock as well, if you want thin it out a bit.

Crock-Pot Version: Place all ingredients for the lentils except salt and pepper, in the order listed, in the Crock-Pot. Stir to evenly distribute ingredients, then cook on low heat for 3 ½ to 4 hours, until lentils are tender but not mushy. Remove lid, stir, and add salt and pepper to taste. You can add an extra splash of stock as well, if you want thin it out a bit.

Leftover lentils will keep tightly sealed in the refrigerator for 5 days or in the freezer for 6 months.

Ideas for
LEFTOVER BBQ SEASONING

Make a double batch of BBQ Seasoning and use it to prepare BBQ Sweet Potato Tofu Tacos (page 81), BBQ Blackened Salmon (page 211), or BBQ Turkey Hashbrown Casserole (page 237).

BBQ SEASONING:

¼ cup coconut sugar (sub monkfruit sweetener)

2 tablespoons paprika

1 tablespoon chili powder

1 tablespoon garlic powder

4 teaspoons onion powder

1 tablespoon sea salt (feel free to use less and add to taste)

1 teaspoon ground cumin

½ teaspoon ground cinnamon

½ teaspoon black pepper

LENTILS:

1½ cups dried green lentils, rinsed for 10 to 15 seconds in cold water

3 cups low-sodium vegetable stock, plus more for thinning

6 tablespoons BBQ Seasoning

2 tablespoons ketchup

1 tablespoon molasses

Salt and black pepper, to taste

SUGGESTED SIDES

5-Ingredient Kimchi Coleslaw
(page 163)

Creamy Corn & Chive Farro
(page 156)

Vegan Tomato-y Collard Greens
(page 155)

LUNCH + DINNER ENTRÉES

Roasted Red Pepper Pasta alla Vodka

 | **HANDS-ON TIME:** 50 min | **TOTAL TIME:** 1 h, 15 min | **YIELD:** 6 to 8 servings | **OPTIONS:**

Don't be intimidated by the ingredient list for this pasta; it's pretty much all pantry staples. The hummus is the secret source for this dish's creamy, dreamy texture. And even omitting the vodka, this dish is something to look forward to after a long day. I prefer it simple without *accoutrement*, but you could totally top it with chickpeas, roasted veggies, black olives, or an animal protein of choice. Once you try this, you might find yourself sneaking hummus into all of your pasta sauces!

Preheat oven to 415° F. Line a baking sheet with parchment paper.

Slice the tops and bottoms off of each bell pepper, remove the core and any seeds, and trim any extra white pith. Slice into 2-inch strips. Place strips on the baking sheet, along with the top and bottom pieces, leaving space between each. Roast peppers for 40 minutes, flipping halfway through.

While the peppers are roasting, cook the pasta al dente according to package directions (1 to 2 minutes less than the shortest suggested time). Drain, rinse, and return to the pot. If noodles are sticking, drizzle with a bit of oil from the jar of sun-dried tomatoes, but make sure to save at least 1 tablespoon.

Heat a small sauté pan over medium heat, and add 1 tablespoon oil from sun-dried tomato jar. When oil moves quickly around the pan and is shimmering, add onions. Cook, stirring every minute or so, until onions are softened and translucent, 4 to 6 minutes. You can add splashes of water (2 tablespoons) as necessary to prevent sticking or burning. Once onions are cooked, turn off the heat, and add minced garlic. Stir constantly 30 seconds. Allow veggies to cool for at least 5 minutes.

Once peppers are cool, place them in a high-powered blender along with cooled onion mixture and all remaining ingredients. Purée until smooth and creamy. Taste for seasoning, and add more salt if you like.

Place pot with pasta back on stove, and add as much of the sauce as you like. (I use almost all except ½ cup, which I save to add to leftovers.) Stir to combine, then cook over low heat until warmed through, 3 to 4 minutes. Serve immediately.

Pasta will keep tightly sealed (once completely cooled) in the refrigerator for 5 days or in the freezer for 2 months if you have used wheat-based noodles. Chickpea- or veggie-based noodles do not keep well. To reheat leftovers, place them in a saucepan with a few splashes of water or extra sauce, and heat over medium heat.

2 medium red bell peppers

16 ounces penne noodles
(GF sub gluten-free noodles)

1 to 2 tablespoons olive oil from jar of sun-dried tomatoes

½ medium yellow onion, diced into ¼-inch pieces (¾ to 1 cup)

6 cloves garlic, minced

½ cup canned full-fat coconut milk

⅓ cup sun-dried tomatoes in olive oil, excess oil shaken off

½ cup plain hummus

1½ teaspoons mild, white miso paste

2 tablespoons vodka (optional)

¼ cup nutritional yeast

1 tablespoon plus 1 teaspoon honey (Vg sub maple syrup)

½ teaspoon paprika

¾ to 1½ teaspoons sea salt (I use the full amount)

⅛ teaspoon black pepper

Ideas for
LEFTOVER HUMMUS

Use leftover plain hummus to make Roasted Romaine with Basil Caesar Hummus Dressing (page 298).

SUGGESTED SIDES

LL's Sweetgreen Order Salad (page 275)

Sweet Potato, Peanut & Black Bean Burgers

VG DF | **HANDS-ON TIME:** 35 min | **TOTAL TIME:** 1 h, 35 min | **YIELD:** 6 burgers | **OPTION:** GF

I actually created these veggie burgers right after I turned in my first cookbook, and I loved them so much I almost tried to add them in! But the book already had a veggie burger recipe (which I still adore), so I decided to wait as patiently as possible to share later, and here we are! So many of my favorite flavors come together in these "meaty" patties, and of course, they pass the test of actually holding together throughout the eating process. These veggie burgers are freezer-friendly, so I recommend doubling the batch and keeping some stored for a rainy (busy/lazy) day. They're awesome over mixed greens with my Peanut Sesame Sauce and half an avocado. I've also sliced them in half vertically and used them as taco fillings. Delicious.

Preheat oven to 350° F. Line a large baking sheet with parchment paper.

Place oats, almond flour, paprika, garlic powder, cumin, and salt in a food processor or high-powered blender. Set aside without blending.

Heat a large saucepan over medium heat, and add olive oil. When oil moves quickly around the pan and is shimmering, add sweet potatoes and onions. Once you hear the veggies sizzling, cook approximately 2 minutes without stirring. Stir briefly, then cook another 2 minutes without stirring. Add shallots and a splash of water (2 tablespoons) to the pan. Cook, stirring constantly, another minute. Reduce heat to lowest setting, add another splash of water, then cover with a lid. Cook until sweet potatoes are easily pierced with a knife but not mushy, 8 to 10 minutes. Remove from the heat, and allow to cool for 5 minutes.

While veggies are cooling, combine beans, peanut butter, and tamari in a large mixing bowl. Use a fork to mash into a paste and blend ingredients evenly. (You should still see some chunks of bean, but it should all stick together.)

Add cooled sweet potato mixture to the food processor or high-powered blender. Pulse until ingredients are incorporated into a sticky "dough." If you use a blender, it will likely require some stopping and scraping down. It's okay if there are still some small veggie chunks.

Add sweet potato mixture to bean mixture, then add corn (still frozen is okay) and peanuts. Use a fork or clean hands to combine ingredients

(continued on page 264)

Ingredients

- 1 cup rolled oats (GF sub gluten-free oats)
- ½ cup blanched almond flour
- 1 teaspoon paprika
- ½ teaspoon garlic powder
- ¼ teaspoon ground cumin
- 1 teaspoon sea salt (feel free to start with less and add to taste)
- 2 tablespoons olive oil
- ⅔ medium sweet potato, peeled and chopped into ½-inch cubes (1 cup)
- ½ large yellow onion, diced into ¼-inch pieces (1 cup)
- 1 medium shallot, diced into ¼-inch pieces (⅓ cup)
- 1 15-ounce can no-salt-added black beans, drained and rinsed
- ⅓ cup unsweetened, unsalted peanut butter (creamy or crunchy)
- 1 tablespoon low-sodium tamari
- ½ cup frozen corn kernels
- ½ cup roasted salted peanuts, roughly chopped
- Bibb lettuce, thinly sliced tomato, cheddar cheese, Dijon mustard, and ketchup for garnish

evenly. This will be a sticky dough. Taste for seasoning, and add more salt if you like. (I add an extra ½ teaspoon.)

Prepare a bowl of lukewarm water, and grab a ½-cup measure. Dip measuring cup into water, shaking off excess, then scoop ½ cup packed burger mixture. (I like to hold the measuring cup with one hand and shake it with the other hand to loosen, but you can also scrape it out with a spoon.) Place scooped mixture on the baking sheet, then repeat with the rest of the burger mixture until you have 6 patties. (Be sure to wet the cup between patties). If there is any mixture leftover, evenly distribute among the burgers.

Rinse and lightly dampen hands. Smooth each burger into a ball, then flatten into an approximately 3½-inch-wide patty. Leave at least 1 inch between each patty. (I like to smooth out the sides as well with dampened fingers.)

Bake burgers for 35 minutes, carefully flipping after 20 minutes. Burgers should be firm to touch with golden-brown tops and edges when done. Allow to cool for 5 minutes, then place on a cooling rack for another 5 minutes before enjoying with garnishes of choice.

Leftovers will keep tightly sealed in the refrigerator for 6 days or in the freezer for 6 months.

Ideas for
LEFTOVER FROZEN CORN

Considering making the Creamy Corn & Chive Farro (page 156) with any leftover corn.

SUGGESTED SIDES

Creamy Corn & Chive Farro (page 156)

5-Ingredient Kimchi Coleslaw (page 163)

Picnic Macaroni Salad with Italian Dressing (omit salami for vegetarian) (page 189)

Ideas for
LEFTOVER SWEET POTATO

You'll have about one-third of a medium sweet potato left over. You might buy a few extra, chop them and the leftovers into 1-inch chunks, and toss with avocado oil and any of my spice rubs or just salt and pepper. Roast at 415° F on a parchment-lined baking sheet until tender.

Tomato & Spinach "Ricotta" Lasagna

Ve DF | **HANDS-ON TIME:** 45 min | **TOTAL TIME:** 1 h 25 min, plus overnight soaking

YIELD: 10 servings 🔸 **OPTION:** GF

Here's the deal: vegan lasagna is a labor of love! Each layer requires its own TLC! That said, this recipe is significantly simpler than the original version on my blog. Thank goodness for store-bought marinara, because "doctoring it up" instead of making it from scratch is a game-changer here. As with any of my more time-intensive recipes, this makes a ton of food, and oh, is it divine! I find this vegan lasagna just as indulgent as my Turkey Cheddar Lasagna (page 234), and I've witnessed several carnivores go nuts for it (pun intended).

Preheat oven to 350° F. Grease a 15 × 10 × 2-inch (or similar size) casserole dish with olive oil. (Note: prep takes some time, so feel free to wait until half or three-quarters of the way through recipe to preheat oven.)

Use the short-soak method to soak cashews (see page 44).

Make the Tomato Sauce Layer: Place all tomato sauce ingredients in a blender, and purée until smooth. Transfer to a mixing bowl, and set aside. Rinse blender; no need to wash.

Make the Spinach "Ricotta" Layer: Heat a medium saucepan over medium heat, and add olive oil. When oil moves quickly around the pan and is shimmering, add onions and cook, stirring every minute or so, until softened and translucent, 4 to 6 minutes. Reduce heat to low, add garlic, and cook for another minute, stirring constantly. Allow to cool 5 minutes.

Place remaining spinach ricotta layer ingredients in a high-powered blender or food processor. Add cooled onion mixture, and blend until completely smooth and creamy. You will need to use a tamper to get everything to mix properly. Transfer to a mixing bowl, and set aside. If you used a blender, give it a rinse; no need to wash.

Make the Cashew Bechamel Layer: Combine soaked cashews and all remaining cashew béchamel layer ingredients in the high-powered blender, and purée until smooth. Transfer to a mixing bowl (or you can keep it in the blender, but remove it from the base, and be careful of the blade). The consistency is thin, but it will thicken as it bakes. As you begin to make your layers, the béchamel may blend with the other layers. It's okay!

(continued on page 267)

TOMATO SAUCE LAYER:

48 ounces store-bought marinara sauce (I like Rao's Homemade Original)

¼ cup ketchup (sub 3 tablespoons coconut sugar or monkfruit sweetener)

½ ounce fresh basil, roughly chopped (½ cup, packed)

1 teaspoon red pepper flakes (optional)

SPINACH "RICOTTA" LAYER:

2 tablespoons olive oil

½ medium yellow onion, diced into ¼-inch pieces (¾ to 1 cup)

2 cloves garlic, roughly chopped

12 to 15 ounces extra firm tofu, drained and crumbled

¼ cup nutritional yeast

2 cups frozen organic chopped spinach

½ ounce fresh basil, roughly chopped (½ cup, packed)

1 teaspoon mild, white miso paste

1½ teaspoons sea salt

2 tablespoons tahini (pourable consistency)

Juice from 1 lemon (2 tablespoons)

(continued on page 267)

Assemble the Lasagna: Layer your lasagna in the following order: one-third of the spinach ricotta (approximately 1 rounded cup); lasagna noodles (can break them if needed); one-third of the tomato sauce (approximately 2 cups); one-quarter of the cashew béchamel (approximately 1 rounded cup); lasagna noodles; one-third of the spinach ricotta; one third of the tomato sauce; one-quarter of the cashew béchamel; lasagna noodles; remaining spinach ricotta; remaining tomato sauce; lasagna noodles; remaining cashew béchamel (make sure it covers all of the noodles).

Bake lasagna for 50 to 55 minutes, until firm to touch and "crackly" looking on top with golden-brown edges. To get more golden-brown color on top, place it under the broiler for a few minutes. Allow to cool for at least 20 minutes before serving. To reheat, place individual servings in the oven at 350° F until warmed through.

Leftovers will keep tightly sealed in the refrigerator for 5 days or in the freezer for 2 months.

NOTES

Look for a marinara sauce that uses only olive oil, no vegetable oils, and has less than 400 mg sodium per ½ cup.

The amount of lasagna noodles you'll need depends on the shape of the pan, so I recommend buying 20 ounces and having leftovers.

CASHEW BECHAMEL LAYER:

2 cups raw cashews, soaked and drained (see page 44)

2½ cups room temperature water

⅓ cup arrowroot starch (sub cornstarch)

2 tablespoons nutritional yeast

2 teaspoons apple cider vinegar

1 teaspoon sea salt

½ teaspoon garlic powder

ASSEMBLY:

16 to 20 ounces no-boil lasagna noodles (GF sub gluten-free noodles)

Olive oil for greasing

SUGGESTED SIDES

Roasted Romaine with
Basil Caesar Hummus Dressing
(page 298)

Carrot & Zucchini Ribbons with
Lemony Pistachio Pesto (page 151)

Chapter 9

SOUPS + SALADS

*I*s there any cozier combination than soup and salad? While I don't always pair the two, I decided to include them in the same chapter, in case you do. For example, my French Onion & Kale Lentil Soup with my Roasted Romaine, or my chilled Cucumber Cantaloupe Gazpacho with my Macadamia & Roasted Grapefruit Salad are perfect matches. The contrast in textures and temperatures when you pair soup and salad just creates a more interesting eating experience. That said, if you prefer to keep these categories separate, you can enjoy my Cozy Chunky Minestrone soup with some grilled French bread instead, or you can slurp up my Miso Mushroom & Rice Soup with a side of your favorite kimchi. This is also a fantastic section to refer to when you're looking for easy, make-ahead meals. Whether it's whipping up a batch of creamy Cajun Cauliflower Potato Soup or prepping the components of LL's Sweetgreen Order Salad, there's something for every craving and season to get you through the week.

Orange Balsamic Beef & Farro Stew

DF | **HANDS-ON TIME:** 15 min | **TOTAL TIME:** 1 h, 25 min (Instant Pot); 8 h, 15 min (Crock-Pot)

YIELD: 6 servings | | **OPTION:** GF

I know this might sound like an odd combination, but the flavors really do come together in the loveliest way! The sweetness and acidity of orange and balsamic vinegar cut through the rich meat and chewy farro. This recipe also includes a very underrated vegetable—turnips. Low in carbohydrates and packed with fiber and micronutrients such as B vitamins, iron, calcium, and much more, turnips have a horseradish-like flavor that becomes milder when cooked. As with most Instant Pot or Crock-Pot recipes, there's very little work involved in creating a piping hot, succulent dinner. A crusty baguette with a little gruyère cheese broiled on top is a dreamy companion to this comforting meal.

Instant Pot Version: Place stew meat and arrowroot starch in the Instant Pot canister, and toss to evenly coat. Add all remaining ingredients in the order listed, then stir to evenly incorporate. Secure lid and set to "Manual" 35 minutes. When the Instant Pot beeps to signal the end of cooking time, allow pressure to release naturally for 20 minutes, then turn to "Venting" to release any remaining pressure. Open lid, taste for seasoning, and add more salt if you like. Stir in more broth to thin as desired.

Crock-Pot Version: Place stew meat and arrowroot starch in a Crock-Pot, and toss to evenly coat. Add all remaining ingredients in the order listed, then stir to evenly incorporate. Cook on low for 6 ½ to 7 hours, until meat is tender but not falling apart. Taste for seasoning, and add more salt if you like. Stir in more broth to thin as desired.

Stew will keep tightly sealed in the refrigerator for 5 days or in the freezer for 4 months.

NOTES

If you don't want to use turnips, feel free to sub another root vegetable, like carrots, parsnips, potatoes, or even beets.

Always zest an orange before slicing and juicing. It's easier in that order.

You may want to add a bit more stock or water when you reheat this stew, as it will thicken in the fridge.

- 1½ pounds stew meat, cut into 1½-inch pieces (I buy pre-diced, but sometimes I need to cut up some bigger pieces)
- 1 tablespoon arrowroot starch (sub cornstarch)
- 1½ cups low-sodium chicken or beef broth, plus more to thin as desired
- ½ medium sweet yellow onion, diced into ¼-inch pieces (¾ to 1 cup)
- 2 medium or 3 small turnips, peeled and chopped into 1-inch pieces (1½ cups)
- 6 cloves garlic, minced
- Zest from 1 navel orange (1 tablespoon)
- Juice from 2 navel oranges (¾ cup)
- ¼ cup aged balsamic vinegar
- 1½ teaspoons sea salt, plus more to taste (feel free to start with less)
- ½ teaspoon garlic powder
- ½ teaspoon paprika
- 1 teaspoon onion powder
- ¾ cup uncooked farro, rinsed and drained (GF sub medium-grain brown rice)

SERVING SUGGESTION

I love to top servings of this stew with some freshly grated parmesan cheese and a sprinkle of fresh herbs.

Creamy Corn & Shrimp Chowder

This is the second-to-last recipe I added to the cookbook, but now I can't imagine this "baby" without it. Why? In part, because I just really wanted to share a chowder (chowdah?) with you! A chowder is simply a soup that has a few elements: 1) something creamy, 2) potatoes or corn or seafood or a mixture, and 3) broken crackers or biscuits for thickening. So I'm pretty sure this recipe counts, but it's fabulous regardless! While my chowder isn't quite as thick as a traditional version, it's equally soothing and satisfying, without feeling heavy. Plus, this is a two-fer, because I also show y'all how to make a versatile veggie stock (hint: it's really easy). Feel free to add some potato to this chowder, but you might need to increase the simmering time at the end. It's also wonderful with pre-cooked and chopped kielbasa thrown in.

To make sure you've removed all the silky hairs from the corn, wrap a dish towel around each ear, and twist in opposite directions. Hold one ear upright in a medium-sized mixing bowl with your non-dominant hand. Using a sharp knife in your dominant hand and moving vertically, slice off kernels into the bowl. Repeat with remaining ears, then snap all cobs in half. Set kernels aside for use in the chowder.

Make the Vegetable Stock: Heat a stockpot or large soup pot over medium-high heat, and add avocado oil. When oil moves quickly around the pot and is shimmering, add corn cob halves, onions, carrots, fennel, garlic, and jalapeño. Cook, stirring every minute or so, until veggies are start to soften, 6 to 8 minutes. Add water, and use a spatula or wooden spoon to scrape any brown bits from the bottom of the pan into the liquid. Bring to a boil, then reduce heat to low, and simmer 1 hour, uncovered.

Carefully strain stock through a large fine-mesh sieve into a large heatproof bowl. (I gently press the veggies to get a little more liquid out, then let the strainer sit a full minute before removing.) If you only have a small fine-mesh sieve, you can strain the stock in batches, discarding or composting the leftover veggies as you go. You should have approximately 4½ cups veggie stock.

(continued on page 274)

VEGETABLE STOCK:

4 ears of corn, husks removed

2 tablespoons avocado oil

1 medium sweet or Vidalia onion, unpeeled and roughly chopped into 1½-inch pieces

2 medium carrots, peeled and roughly chopped into 1½-inch pieces (1½ cups)

1 fennel bulb with fronds, rinsed and roughly chopped into 1½-inch pieces (including fronds)

1 head garlic, unpeeled and sliced in half crosswise

1 medium jalapeño, seeds removed and chopped into ½-inch pieces

7 cups water

CHOWDER:

1 batch Vegetable Stock

1 teaspoon salt, plus more to taste (feel free to start with less)

½ teaspoon black pepper

1 medium red bell pepper, diced into ¼-inch pieces (1¼ cups)

2 cups frozen edamame beans, ideally non-GMO and organic; no need to thaw (16 ounces)

Kernels from 4 ears corn (above)

1 pound raw shrimp, peeled and deveined (thawed-from-frozen or fresh works)

1 15-ounce can full-fat coconut milk (sub 1½ cups half & half)

Soup or oyster crackers, for serving

SOUPS + SALADS

Make the Chowder: Clean and dry your pot, and place it back on the stove, then return the stock to the pot. Bring to a simmer over medium-low heat, then add salt, pepper, bell peppers, edamame, and corn kernels. Simmer 10 minutes, stirring every few minutes, then add shrimp. Simmer *just* until shrimp is pink all the way through, another 3 to 6 minutes (time will depend on the size of the shrimp, and you may need to turn the heat up a bit to get it back to a simmer). Stir in coconut milk.

Taste for seasoning, and add more salt if you like. (I add another ½ teaspoon). Serve chowder with a handful of crushed crackers.

Chowder will keep tightly sealed in the refrigerator for 3 days or in the freezer for 2 months.

NOTES

I compost the strained veggies leftover from making stock. They have very little nutrition or flavor left in them.

General Cooking Tip: If you want a thicker soup or stew, leave the lid off during cooking, as more liquid will evaporate. For brothier soups, keep the lid on during cooking.

LL's Sweetgreen Order Salad

VG GF DF | **HANDS-ON TIME:** 50 min | **TOTAL TIME:** 1 h, 25 min | **YIELD:** 4 servings |

Whenever I travel, I make a point to see if my destination city has a Sweetgreen. This grab-n-go salad restaurant defies all expectations of a chain. The ingredients are locally sourced and incredibly high-quality. Perhaps even more importantly, whoever is creating the Sweetgreen menu knows flavor, because their toppings, proteins, and dressings are delicious and creative. After countless Sweetgreen visits, I've solidified my favorite combination, and y'all always ask about it. So I decided to recreate this dreamy salad for you (and myself). Sweetgreen hasn't made its way to Nashville yet, but I'm keeping my fingers and toes crossed! This is a fantastic recipe if you don't love leftovers, because you can keep all of the components separate and throw them together for a fresh meal each day.

Make the Ginger Tahini Dressing: Combine all dressing ingredients in a mixing bowl, and whisk until creamy and incorporated (start with 2 tablespoons water). You can also purée everything in a blender. Add more water as you like to achieve desired consistency. (I use 4 tablespoons total.)

Make the Salad: Make sure both of your oven racks are close to the middle of the oven. Preheat oven to 400° F. Line 2 baking sheets with parchment paper.

Place sweet potatoes and tofu on one baking sheet. Drizzle with 2 teaspoons oil, and sprinkle with ¼ teaspoon salt, then gently toss to coat. Spread in an even layer, trying not to overlap pieces. Set aside.

In a small bowl, combine red pepper flakes, chili powder, onion powder, garlic powder, pepper, and ¼ teaspoon salt. Stir to evenly incorporate.

Place broccoli on the other baking sheet, and toss with 1 teaspoon oil and 1½ teaspoons spice mixture. Spread in an even layer.

Place both pans in the oven. Roast broccoli for 20 minutes, until tender with crispy edges, and sweet potatoes and tofu for 35 to 40 minutes, until potatoes are tender and tofu has light golden-brown edges. Don't forget to set two timers.

While veggies are roasting, place kale in a large mixing bowl along with remaining teaspoon oil and a pinch of sea salt. Use clean hands to massage oil and salt into the kale, until it has noticeably reduced in volume and softened in texture. Cover and refrigerate.

(continued on page 277)

GINGER TAHINI DRESSING:

¼ cup runny tahini (pourable consistency)

¼ cup avocado oil

Juice from 1 large or 2 small limes (3 tablespoons)

1½ teaspoons mild, white miso paste

1-inch piece ginger, peeled and grated (sub ¼ teaspoon ground ginger)

2 cloves garlic, finely minced

1 tablespoon honey

2 to 6 tablespoons filtered water

Pinch salt

SALAD:

1 medium sweet potato, cut into 1-inch cubes (2 to 2½ cups)

12 to 15 ounces extra firm tofu, cut into 1-inch cubes, patted dry

4½ teaspoons avocado oil

½ teaspoon plus a pinch sea salt

½ teaspoon red pepper flakes

1 teaspoon chili powder

½ teaspoon onion powder

¼ teaspoon garlic powder

¼ teaspoon black pepper

1 medium head broccoli, chopped into 1½-inch florets (4½ to 6 cups)

2 bunches lacinato kale, stems removed and sliced into ¼-inch thick ribbons (see page 45)

⅓ cup raw sunflower seeds

Sliced avocado and kimchi (optional)

1 batch Ginger Tahini Dressing

Place sunflower seeds, remaining spice mixture, and ½ teaspoon oil in a small oven-safe sauté pan. Toss to coat, and spread in an even layer. After the potatoes, tofu, and broccoli are finished roasting, remove them from the oven, and place sunflower seeds in the oven. Roast for 10 minutes, until slightly golden brown in color. Set aside to cool.

Assemble the Salad: Once everything is cool, you can either place all items in separate airtight containers (I keep tofu and sweet potatoes together) and store in the refrigerator for 5 days, or you can assemble 4 salads, using roughly one-quarter of each of your components per salad. (Note: this is approximately 1 ½ tablespoons sunflower seeds per salad; they're harder to eyeball). Cover servings, and pull them out throughout the week. Add avocado and kimchi, if using, just before serving. Add dressing liberally to each serving. I don't recommend freezing any of the components of this salad.

NOTE

If I'm using an organic sweet potato, I don't bother with peeling it.

SOUPS + SALADS

Cajun Cauliflower Potato Soup

Vg GF DF P | **HANDS-ON TIME:** 25 min | **TOTAL TIME:** 1 h, 10 min | **YIELD:** 10 servings |

First things first: if y'all have gotten this far in the book, you know that I don't do a lot of spicy food. So here's one for my spice lovers, who might be looking for a little kick! While this soup contains an entire head of cauliflower, you'd never know it. In addition to some serious nutrient density, puréed cauliflower contributes to the silky texture of this soup. And I do love the beautiful Yukon Golds in here, because potatoes are delicious and a great source of potassium, vitamin C, vitamin B6, and more. Don't be afraid to enjoy potatoes, y'all! While this recipe is vegan-friendly, it's also fabulous with some cooked Italian sausage stirred in or topped with a little grass-fed cheddar cheese.

Make the Cajun Seasoning: Place all seasoning ingredients in a small bowl, and whisk to combine, or place in a sealable container and shake.

Make the Soup: Heat a stockpot or large soup pot over medium heat, and add avocado oil. When oil moves quickly around the pot and is shimmering, add shallots. Cook, stirring, until shallots are softened and translucent, 3 to 4 minutes. Reduce heat to low, and add Cajun Seasoning and water, continuously stirring for another 30 seconds. Add all remaining ingredients except nutritional yeast, salt, and pepper. Stir to combine.

Bring soup to a simmer, cover, and simmer until cauliflower and potatoes are fork-tender, approximately 30 minutes. Add nutritional yeast, and cook, stirring, for another minute. Remove from the heat, and allow to cool for 15 minutes.

Grab your largest mixing bowl. Carefully add soup to the blender (I can get usually get half of it in), and purée until smooth. Make sure to use safe blending techniques, starting with the power on low and holding a dish towel over the top. Pour puréed soup into the mixing bowl. Repeat with remaining soup.

When it is all puréed, return soup to the pot over low heat. Taste for seasoning, and add more salt, pepper, and red pepper flakes if you like. (I add 1 teaspoon of salt and ½ teaspoon pepper). Serve immediately. I love serving this soup with thinly sliced roasted potatoes and a drizzle of olive oil.

Leftovers will keep tightly sealed in the refrigerator for 6 days or in the freezer for 3 months.

CAJUN SEASONING:

1 tablespoon paprika

2 teaspoons garlic powder

2 teaspoons onion powder

1½ teaspoons sea salt (start with 1 teaspoon if you're salt-sensitive)

1 teaspoon black pepper

1 teaspoon dried oregano

1 teaspoon crushed red pepper flakes (use ½ teaspoon if you're heat-sensitive)

1 tablespoon coconut sugar (sub monkfruit sweetener)

SOUP:

2 tablespoons avocado oil

2 medium shallots, diced into ¼-inch pieces (⅔ cup)

1 batch Cajun Seasoning

4 cups water

4 cups low-sodium vegetable stock

1 pound Yukon Gold or other yellow potatoes, peeled and chopped into ½-inch pieces (2½ cups)

1 medium head cauliflower, chopped into 1½-inch florets (6 to 7 cups)

1 15-ounce can no-salt-added white beans (cannellini or great northern), drained and rinsed

1 tablespoon coconut sugar (sub monkfruit sweetener)

⅓ cup nutritional yeast

Salt, black pepper, and red pepper flakes, to taste

SOUPS + SALADS

Cozy Chunky Minestrone Soup

HANDS-ON TIME: 30 min | **TOTAL TIME:** 1 h, 10 min | **YIELD:** 8 to 10 servings | **OPTIONS:** Vg DF GF V

Don't be off-put by the long ingredient list for this soup. If you have my recommended pantry staples, then you have what you need aside from perishables. Plus, this soup is simply worth the shopping and the few steps you have to take to bring it together. It hits all the cozy, warming notes, and it's a one-pot meal, since it is packed with veggies, which you can also switch up based on your preference. In addition to the serving suggestion in the recipe, I love topping this soup with a dollop of goat cheese and a swirl of pesto.

Combine basil, onion powder, salt, and pepper in a small bowl. Set aside.

Heat a stockpot or large soup pot over medium heat, and add olive oil. When oil moves quickly around the pan and is shimmering, add shallots and carrots, and cook, stirring, until shallots are softened and translucent, 5 to 7 minutes. Add splashes of water (2 tablespoons each) as necessary to prevent sticking or burning. Add green beans and spices, and cook, stirring constantly, for another 3 to 4 minutes. Add garlic, and cook, stirring constantly, for another 30 seconds.

Add stock, diced tomatoes, tomato paste, sun-dried tomatoes, parmesan cheese, and molasses, and stir to incorporate. Bring to a boil, then reduce heat to low, and simmer, covered, for 15 minutes.

Stir in chickpeas, sausage, and pasta, and simmer, covered, until the pasta cooks and vegetables are butter-knife tender, 12 to 15 minutes. Serve immediately. I like to serve the soup with extra grated parmesan and a drizzle of any leftover olive oil from the sun-dried tomato jar.

Leftovers will keep tightly sealed in the refrigerator for 5 days or in the freezer for 2 months.

1 teaspoon dried basil

½ teaspoon onion powder

1 to 2 teaspoons sea salt (start with 1 and add more to taste; I use 2)

½ teaspoon black pepper

2 tablespoons olive oil from jar of sun-dried tomatoes, plus more for garnish (sub avocado oil)

2 large or 3 medium shallots, diced into ¼-inch pieces (1 cup)

2 medium-large carrots, peeled and sliced into ½-inch rounds or half-moons for thicker ends (1½ cups)

2 cups frozen green beans, cut into 1½-inch pieces

6 cloves garlic, minced

8 cups low-sodium chicken stock (V Vg sub vegetable stock)

2 14½-ounce cans no-salt-added diced tomatoes

1 6-ounce can tomato paste

½ cup sun-dried tomatoes in olive oil, drained and sliced into ¼-inch ribbons

¼ cup grated parmesan cheese, plus more for garnish (Vg DF sub 3 tablespoons nutritional yeast)

1 tablespoon molasses

1 15-ounce can no-salt-added chickpeas, drained and rinsed

12 ounces precooked Italian chicken sausage links, sliced into ½-inch rounds (V Vg sub an additional can chickpeas)

8 ounces dried pasta of choice (GF sub gluten-free pasta)

Miso Mushroom & Rice Soup

 | **HANDS-ON TIME:** 30 min | **TOTAL TIME:** 1 h | **YIELD:** 8 servings |

When I was in college, one of my best friends (heyyy, Allie!) and I would go to the local Japanese restaurant and order a "meal deal" that included miso soup, ginger salad, and two sushi rolls. At the time, miso soup was simply a way to fill my insatiable twenty-year-old appetite, and I never paid it much mind. Fast forward to a bitterly cold NYC winter a few years later, and miso soup became the highlight of any sushi dinner. My favorite way to enjoy miso soup is with a big ole' scoop of white rice stirred in, so I decided to include that in my version of this magical, healing dish. I omit traditional nori strips, because I find that the flavor overpowering, but feel free to add them to yours. I love the way this recipe makes me feel, and I often take it to postpartum mamas or sick friends.

1 cup white jasmine rice

10 cups cold water

1½-inch piece ginger, peeled and grated

¼ cup low-sodium tamari, plus more to taste and for garnish

8 to 10 ounces sliced baby bella mushrooms

½ cup mild, white miso paste (extra important to remember to use mild white)

¼ cup hot tap water

15 ounces extra firm tofu, drained, rinsed, and cut into 1-inch cubes

1 bunch scallions, base and 1-inch of the top removed, sliced into 1-inch long pieces (I like to slice mine on the diagonal)

1 8-ounce can water chestnuts, drained and rinsed

Rinse rice in a fine-mesh sieve until running water until water is clear, approximately 30 seconds. Drain well.

Place cold water in a stockpot or large soup pot, and bring to a boil over medium-high heat. As soon as water is boiling, add rice, stir, and reduce heat to low. Simmer, covered, until rice is tender but not mushy, approximately 20 minutes. Add ginger, tamari, and mushrooms, and simmer for another 10 minutes with the lid off. You might need to increase the temperature to get it back to a simmer.

While the soup is simmering, place miso in a mixing bowl, and top with the hot water—it doesn't need to be boiling. Gently stir into a creamy paste. (I use the back of a spoon to break it down, then a whisk to smooth it out.)

Add tofu, scallions, and water chestnuts to the soup, and simmer for 10 minutes. Remove pot from the heat, and stir in miso mixture.

Taste for seasoning, and add more tamari if you like. (I add another tablespoon. I also drizzle my servings with a bit more tamari.)

Leftover soup will keep tightly sealed in the refrigerator for 6 days. I don't recommend freezing.

French Onion & Kale Lentil Soup

GF | **HANDS-ON TIME:** 40 min | **TOTAL TIME:** 1 h, 45 min | **YIELD:** 6 to 8 servings | ⊕ | **OPTION:** Vg

I went out of my comfort zone big time in this cookbook's soup section. 1) I'm not a huge soup person, and 2) when I am, I usually go for creamy over brothy. But I was determined to create a few soups that I absolutely craved, which would also appease my broth lovers. My French Onion & Kale Lentil Soup did the trick and then some! Using caramelized onions, hearty lentils, and beef broth, this soup is rich, satisfying, and layered with flavor, while still remaining light. Note that is is still fabulous veganized with vegetable broth and sans cheese!

Make the Caramelized Onions: Turn on exhaust fan. Heat a large stock or soup pot over medium-high heat, and add avocado oil. When oil moves quickly around the pan and is shimmering, add onions. Allow to cook without stirring until it looks like the onions are burning, 4 to 6 minutes. Add ½ cup water to deglaze, scraping up any brown bits from the bottom of the pan. (Be careful as this will create hot steam.) Stir onions briefly, reduce heat slightly, and repeat burning and deglazing process once more, using the remaining ½ cup water (another 4 to 6 minutes).

Reduce heat to medium-low (you can turn off exhaust fan), and cook onions, stirring every 5 minutes or so, until they are a dark, jammy consistency, approximately 35 minutes. Feel free to add splashes of water to prevent sticking or burning as they cook.

Make the Soup: While onions caramelize, whisk together balsamic vinegar, mustard, tamari, molasses, salt, and pepper in a small bowl.

Once onions are caramelized, add garlic to the same pot, and cook, stirring, until softened and fragrant, 30 seconds to 1 minute. Add vinegar mixture, lentils, broth, and water. Stir and bring to a simmer.

Cover pot with a lid, leaving it slightly ajar to allow some steam to escape. Simmer until lentils are tender, approximately 35 minutes. Stir in kale and cheese, and cook until kale is wilted and cheese is melted, another 2 to 3 minutes. Taste for seasoning, and add more salt and cheese if you like. I also like to add some cheese on each serving and broil until golden brown before serving with some crusty bread.

Leftover soup will keep tightly sealed in the refrigerator for 5 days or in the freezer for 3 months.

CARAMELIZED ONIONS:

1 tablespoon avocado oil

2 medium yellow onions, sliced into ¼-inch half-moons

1 cup water

SOUP:

2 teaspoons aged balsamic vinegar

1 tablespoon Dijon mustard

1 tablespoon low-sodium tamari

1 tablespoon molasses

1 teaspoon sea salt, plus more to taste

½ teaspoon black pepper

5 cloves garlic, minced

1 cup dried green lentils

4 cups low-sodium beef broth (sub chicken or Vg vegetable broth, but I prefer beef)

4 cups filtered water

½ bunch lacinato kale, stems removed and sliced into ½-inch thick ribbons (3 cups, packed) (see page 45)

4 ounces sharp cheddar cheese, shredded (1 cup), plus more to taste (Vg omit for vegan)

> ### NOTE
>
> It's important to keep the onion slices even and thin to make sure they all cook at the same rate.

Chickpea, Avocado & Goat Cheese Salad
with GRAINY MUSTARD DRESSING

 | HANDS-ON TIME: 15 min | TOTAL TIME: 15 min, plus 1 to 8 h chilling | YIELD: 4 to 6 servings |

This is such an incredibly simple dish, and it's one I find myself making when I'm low on energy and time. Creamy, hearty, and bursting with spring flavors, this is my kind of a "happy" meal. Just thinking about it reminds me of warm, sunny Nashville afternoons! Don't skip the dollop of mayo in my Grainy Mustard Dressing; it really brings the dish together and reminds me of an updated take on classic southern salads.

Make the Grainy Mustard Dressing: Combine all dressing ingredients in a small bowl, and whisk until creamy.

Make the Salad: Peel and chop the avocados into 1-inch pieces. Place in a large mixing bowl along with the chickpeas and cucumber. Pour approximately three-quarters of the dressing over the top, and toss to coat. Cover with plastic wrap, pressing it right onto the ingredients to prevent avocados from browning. Refrigerate at least 1 hour or up to overnight. After salad has chilled, gently fold in goat cheese and basil. Taste for seasoning, and add more salt, pepper, and dressing if you like. Serve immediately.

With plastic wrap pressed right onto the salad, leftovers will keep in the refrigerator for 2 days. The avocado might brown a bit, but it's fine to eat! I don't recommend freezing.

NOTES

Feel free to peel the cucumber or not. I usually peel when the cucumber is not organic. Remove the seeds by scooping them out with a spoon.

Taste your cucumber skin to make sure it's not bitter; that happens to some cucumbers. Peel if so.

If you think you'll have leftovers, I recommend adding basil to each individual serving instead of to the whole batch.

GRAINY MUSTARD DRESSING:

¼ cup extra virgin olive oil

1½ tablespoons apple cider vinegar

1 tablespoon mayonnaise

1 tablespoon whole-grain mustard (sub 2 teaspoons Dijon mustard)

¼ teaspoon sea salt

¼ teaspoon onion powder

Pinch garlic powder

1 drop stevia, or to taste (sub honey or maple syrup, to taste) (optional)

SALAD:

2 medium ripe avocados

1 15-ounce canned no-salt-added chickpeas, rinsed and drained

1 medium cucumber, sliced in half lengthwise, seeds removed, and sliced into ½-inch half moons (1½ cups)

1 batch Grainy Mustard Dressing

2 ounces goat cheese, crumbled

½ ounce fresh basil, sliced into ¼-inch thick ribbons (½ cup, packed) (sub roughly chopped cilantro or parsley)

Salt and black pepper, to taste

Classic Egg Salad My Way

(V) (GF) (DF) | **HANDS-ON TIME:** 25 min | **TOTAL TIME:** 35 min, plus 1 hr chilling | **YIELD:** 3 servings | ❄

I'm pretty sure this recipe title is an oxymoron, but it just feels right! My first book has chicken and tuna salad recipes, so I felt compelled to complete the southern-salad trifecta with my go-to egg version! Plus, I genuinely make this all the time when I'm running low on food. I usually have the necessary ingredients, it comes together quickly, and it tastes absolutely incredible on toast, scooped with crackers, thrown on top of greens, or even straight-up with a fork. There's nothing fancy or unpredictable about my egg salad, but I have spent years crafting just the right ratio of mayo to mustard to sweet to salt. Oh, and lots of pepper is absolutely crucial—I often end up adding another pinch to each serving.

Place eggs (gently!) and 1 teaspoon vinegar in a medium saucepan, and cover with room temperature water by approximately 1 inch. Bring to a boil over medium-high heat. As soon as water starts boiling, remove pan from the heat, and cover with a lid. Allow to sit 12 minutes.

While eggs are sitting, combine remaining teaspoon vinegar and all remaining ingredients in a mixing bowl, and stir until creamy and incorporated.

After 12 minutes, carefully drain water out of saucepan, leaving eggs, then run cold water over eggs for 1 minute. Remove eggs from saucepan, and place in a heatproof mixing bowl, then run cold water over them for another minute. Pat eggs dry and peel. You might need to rinse and pat them dry after peeling if some small pieces of shell remain.

Using the large holes of a box grater, grate eggs into the mayonnaise mixture. (You can also chop the eggs or smash them with a fork, but I prefer the ease and texture provided by a box grater.) Fold everything together to form a creamy salad. Refrigerate for at least 1 hour before enjoying.

Leftovers will keep tightly sealed in the refrigerator for 4 days. I don't recommend freezing.

6 large eggs, preferably on the older side, 4 to 5 days from the expiration date (they're easier to peel when they're older)

2 teaspoons white or apple cider vinegar, divided

4 to 6 tablespoons mayonnaise (I use 6)

1 tablespoon Dijon mustard

1 teaspoon honey or 2 tablespoons sweet pickle relish

¼ teaspoon sea salt, plus more to taste

½ teaspoon black pepper

¼ teaspoon onion powder

2 tablespoons finely minced shallots (optional)

2 tablespoons thinly sliced scallions (optional)

¼ cup finely chopped dill pickles (optional)

2 to 3 tablespoons minced chives (optional)

NOTE

If you're using dill pickles as optional add-in, you can sub the teaspoon vinegar for a teaspoon pickle juice.

SOUPS + SALADS

Cucumber Cantaloupe Gazpacho

Ve GF DF | **HANDS-ON TIME:** 15 min | **TOTAL TIME:** 15 min, plus 4 to 8 hours chilling | **YIELD:** 4 servings ❄

Every summer as a child, I could expect gazpacho to start showing up on the patio dinner table. My mother's gazpacho was inspired by the classic Silver Palate recipe: a tomato and red-wine-vinegar base, filled with crunchy diced vegetables. While I loved the bright freshness of this chilled soup, I didn't love the texture—I never quite knew whether to slurp or chew! I decided to play around with the gazpacho concept, using my preferred summer flavors and puréeing the lot into an absolutely slurpable consistency. Throwing this together couldn't be easier, and the result will cool you down from head to toe after a long day in the sun. Gazpachos are very forgiving, so definitely use this as a template to do some experimenting of your own; I think seedless watermelon would sub beautifully for the cantaloupe.

- ½ medium cantaloupe, peeled, seeded, and chopped into 1½-inch chunks (3½ to 4 cups)
- ½ large English cucumber or 1 medium slicing cucumber, peeled and chopped into 1-inch chunks (2 rounded cups)
- ½ ounce cilantro, plus more for garnish (½ cup, packed)
- 1 small or ½ medium shallot, diced into ¼-inch pieces (¼ cup)
- ¼ cup olive oil
- 2 tablespoons white balsamic vinegar (sub white wine vinegar)
- 1 tablespoon honey (sub maple syrup)
- ¼ teaspoon salt, plus more to taste
- Pinch black pepper
- ¼ teaspoon red pepper flakes
- Chopped cilantro, dollop of yogurt, and pumpkin or sunflower seeds for garnish

Place cantaloupe and cucumber in a high-powered blender, and purée until it forms a "chunky" liquid, approximately 20 seconds. You may need to use the tamper to get it started. Add all remaining ingredients, and purée until smooth and creamy, approximately 1 minute.

Pour soup into a large bowl, taste for seasoning, and add more salt if you like. Cover and chill at least 4 hours or up to overnight before serving. Serve with suggested garnishes or whatever else you fancy!

Gazpacho will keep tightly sealed in the refrigerator in for 3 days. I don't recommend freezing.

NOTE

To prep the cantaloupe, slice a disk off the top and bottom to expose the flesh. Set it upright on the counter. Hold cantaloupe with your non-dominant hand, and use a sharp knife to slice off the peel in vertical strokes with your dominant hand. Use a metal spoon to scoop out seeds.

Ideas for
LEFTOVER CANTALOUPE

I like to make this recipe and my Cantaloupe Lemon Sherbet Popsicles (page 330) recipe in the same week, since each calls for half of a cantaloupe.

Charred Green Bean & Farro Salad

with AVOCADO RANCH DRESSING

HANDS-ON TIME: 20 min | **TOTAL TIME:** 1 h, 15 min, plus 1 to 8 h chilling | **YIELD:** 6 to 8 servings

❄ ⊕ | OPTIONS:

This recipe is straight-up inspired by one of my local Nashville faves, Cafe Roze. If you ever get a chance to visit Music City, you must add Cafe Roze to your bucket list. Not only is the interior an Instagram (and life) dream, the menu is gorgeous, healthy, creative, and consistently mouth-watering. I am particularly smitten with their farro and green bean salad. The textural combination of chewy farro and lightly crisp green beans is divine, and their house-made avocado ranch takes it over the top. While I don't have the original recipe, I think I came pretty close in my knockoff!

Make the Green Bean & Farro Salad: Place farro in a shallow bowl, and check for any husks (tough hay-like shells). Remove any that you see. Rinse farro with cold water in a fine-mesh sieve, drain, and place in a large (at least 4-quart) pot, along with ¼ teaspoon salt and chicken stock. (Note: if you missed any husks, they will likely bob to the surface, and you can remove them). Stir, bring to a boil over medium-high heat, then reduce heat to low, and simmer, covered, until farro is soft but still chewy, 25 to 30 minutes. Drain off any excess stock. Transfer farro to a large mixing bowl.

While farro is cooking, preheat oven to 415° F. Line a baking sheet with parchment paper. Trim the ends off green beans, and rinse in a colander, then drain well. Add remaining salt, avocado oil, and pepper (while beans are still in the colander), and toss to coat. Spread green beans in an even layer on the baking sheet, and roast for 20 minutes. Turn to broil, and broil until beans have some charred brown spots, 2 to 6 minutes depending on the oven. Watch closely. Allow to cool for 10 minutes.

Make the Avocado Ranch Dressing: Place 2 tablespoons minced chives and all remaining dressing ingredients in a blender, and blend until smooth and creamy. Transfer to a small bowl, and stir in remaining 2 tablespoons chives. (Note: if using fresh parsley or dill, blend ¼ cup of the herbs with the remaining ingredients in the blender. Roughly chop the remaining ¼ cup herbs, and stir into dressing.) Makes 1 cup.

(continued on next page)

GREEN BEAN & FARRO SALAD:

1¾ cups uncooked farro

½ teaspoon sea salt, divided

4 cups low-sodium chicken stock (🟢 sub low-sodium vegetable stock)

½ pound green beans

1 tablespoon avocado oil

¼ teaspoon black pepper

1 batch Avocado Ranch Dressing

½ cup roasted, salted pistachios

Freshly grated parmesan cheese, for garnish

AVOCADO RANCH DRESSING:

¼ ounce chives, minced (¼ cup) (sub ½ cup dill or parsley, minced), divided

1 clove garlic, roughly chopped

1 teaspoon mild, white miso paste

1 medium ripe avocado, mashed (½ cup)

½ cup sour cream (sub plain full-fat yogurt or 🟤 🟢 dairy-free yogurt)

1½ tablespoons apple cider vinegar

1 teaspoon onion powder

½ teaspoon sea salt

½ teaspoon black pepper

½ cup unsweetened almond milk

SOUPS + SALADS

CHARRED GREEN BEAN & FARRO SALAD
WITH AVOCADO RANCH DRESSINGR *(continued)*

Assemble the Salad: Once green beans have cooled, chop into approximately 2-inch pieces and add to farro. (I like to cut the green beans with kitchen scissors.) Stir in Avocado Ranch Dressing to taste (I use the whole batch). If you're planning to add parmesan cheese, hold off on any extra salt. If not using parmesan, stir in another ¼ teaspoon salt or to taste.

Cover with plastic wrap, making sure that it is presses against the salad to prevent the avocado from browning. Refrigerate for at least 1 hour and up to 8 hours before serving. When it's time to serve, add any leftover Avocado Ranch Dressing if you like. Then chop pistachios, and fold into salad along with parmesan cheese, if using.

Leftovers will keep tightly sealed with plastic wrap in the refrigerator for 3 days. If leftovers look a little "dry," drizzle with the juice from one lemon and a few tablespoons of avocado or olive oil, then toss to coat. I don't recommend freezing.

Macadamia & Roasted Grapefruit Salad

with LEMONY VINAIGRETTE

GF | **HANDS-ON TIME:** 20 min | **TOTAL TIME:** 1 h, 5 min | **YIELD:** 4 servings | ⊕ | **OPTION:** **V**

Hello, flavor bomb! While some of my salads take a bit of creative license with the meaning of "salad," this one is a traditional trifecta: crisp greens, bold toppings, and a zippy vinaigrette. Sometimes there's nothing better! I love how the richness of macadamia nuts and blue cheese cuts through the generous amount of citrus in this salad. Peppery arugula is crucial to hold up against the other components, and it's a dream with crunchy bacon, which is optional but . . . bacon. I love serving this salad with seafood entrées or just adding some blackened salmon or grilled shrimp on top.

Make the Macadamia & Roasted Grapefruit Salad: Make sure both of your oven racks are close to the middle of the oven. Preheat oven to 375° F. Line a large baking sheet with parchment paper. Place grapefruit segments on the baking sheet, and drizzle with maple syrup. Toss to coat.

Place macadamia nuts in a small baking dish or ovenproof sauté pan, and drizzle with avocado oil. Add a pinch of salt, and toss to coat.

Place grapefruit and macadamia nuts in the oven on separate racks. Roast macadamia nuts until light golden brown around the edges, approximately 12 minutes. Allow to cool until you can handle them, 5 to 10 minutes, then roughly chop. Don't forget to set two timers.

Roast grapefruit for 45 minutes, then turn the oven to broil. Broil grapefruit until golden brown around the edges, approximately 2 minutes. Watch closely. Allow grapefruit to cool for at least 5 minutes before using.

Make the Lemony Vinaigrette: While grapefruit is roasting, combine all vinaigrette ingredients in a glass jar with a lid or other sealable container, and shake until smooth and creamy.

(continued on next page)

MACADAMIA & ROASTED GRAPEFRUIT SALAD:

2 medium-sized grapefruits, peeled, segmented, and large seeds removed (5 cups)

1 tablespoon maple syrup

¾ cup raw macadamia nuts (sub roasted, salted macadamia nuts and skip the instructions for roasting them)

½ teaspoon avocado oil

¼ teaspoon plus a pinch sea salt

5 ounces baby arugula

3 to 4 ounces blue cheese, crumbled

4 slices cooked bacon, crumbled (**V** omit for vegetarian)

Lemony Vinaigrette, to taste

LEMONY VINAIGRETTE:

½ cup avocado oil

Zest from 1 lemon (1 tablespoon)

Juice from 2 lemons (¼ cup)

1 teaspoon Dijon mustard

2 tablespoons finely minced shallot

¼ teaspoon sea salt

1 tablespoon maple syrup (sub liquid stevia)

Assemble the Salad: Place arugula in a large mixing or serving bowl. Top with roasted grapefruit, macadamia nuts, crumbled blue cheese, and bacon, if using. Toss with Lemony Vinaigrette to taste. If you add the grapefruit while it is still slightly warm, it will soften the arugula. If you plan to have leftovers, make sure the grapefruit is completely cool before adding to the salad. Also if you want leftovers, toss the vinaigrette on individual servings to prevent sogginess.

The salad will keep undressed and tightly sealed in the refrigerator for 3 days. I don't recommend freezing.

Ideas for
LEFTOVER BLUE CHEESE

If you have leftover blue cheese, use it in my Broccoli Gorgonzola Salad with Miso Dressing (page 147) or as a topping for my Steak Bites (page 190)—delicious!

NOTES

If you bake up a whole batch of bacon, you can plan to make my Best Potato Salad (page 167) or Bacon-y Cabbage & Onions (page 164) the same week. To cook the bacon, follow the instructions in the B.E.C. Freezeritos recipe (page 75).

Instead of the grapefruit, feel free to use other fruits, like apples, peaches, pears, plums, oranges, or strawberries. Just be sure to watch the roasting time.

Roasted Romaine

with BASIL CAESAR HUMMUS DRESSING

(V) (GF) (K) (P) | **HANDS-ON TIME:** 20 min | **TOTAL TIME:** 1 h, 20 min | **YIELD:** 6 servings ⊕ ❄ | **OPTIONS:** (Vg) (DF)

I seriously debated whether to include this recipe, because my first cookbook also contains a Caesar Dressing recipe. But I was enamored with this hummus-based version, and I thought y'all would appreciate a new way to treat romaine lettuce, the reliable workhorse of greens. Plus, you can absolutely use another dressing or sauce of choice to garnish your roasted romaine. But I implore you to give this version a try first, as I think it will feel unique and special to you! Broiling the romaine creates a light char that is both delectable and a lovely contrast to the cool, crunchy inner leaves. I find myself drawn to this salad on warmer days in particular, so you could also throw them on the grill for a BBQ side dish.

Make the Basil Caesar Hummus Dressing: Place all dressing ingredients in a blender, and purée until smooth and creamy. Refrigerate at least 1 hour and up to 24 hours before serving. Note that the dressing will thicken a bit in the fridge, so you can stir in water one tablespoon at a time to reach desired consistency.

Make the Roasted Romaine: Turn the oven to broil, and place a rack in the upper-third of your oven (one rung above the middle). Line a baking sheet with parchment paper.

Remove the base of each romaine head (approximately 1 ½ inch). Trim off any funky-looking leaves. Slice romaine heads in half lengthwise. The halves will start to fall apart a bit, and that's okay; just try to keep them in their natural bunches as you place them side by side on the baking sheet. It's also okay that it may be a tight squeeze. Evenly drizzle with avocado oil, then sprinkle with salt and pepper. Gently rub to coat the leaves. A pastry brush works well.

Place romaine in the oven, and broil until each half has a nice golden-brown char on top but is still green on the sides, 3 to 4 minutes. Watch closely.

Serve immediately topped with Basil Caesar Hummus Dressing and garnishes of choice.

Leftovers will keep tightly sealed in the refrigerator for 2 days. If you want them to stay crunchy, don't dress the romaine until just before serving. I don't suggest re-broiling the leftovers; I just eat them cold. I don't recommend freezing.

BASIL CAESAR HUMMUS DRESSING:

¼ cup filtered water

½ cup plain hummus

2 tablespoons tahini

Juice from ½ lemon (1 tablespoon)

¾ ounce fresh basil, roughly chopped (¾ cup, packed)

1 clove garlic, roughly chopped

½ teaspoon onion powder

½ teaspoon black pepper

¼ teaspoon garlic powder

¼ teaspoon sea salt

2 teaspoons Dijon mustard

1 teaspoon low-sodium tamari

1 teaspoon mild, white miso paste

1 to 2 teaspoons maple syrup (start with 1 and add to taste, or sub stevia drops to taste)

ROASTED ROMAINE:

1 12-ounce bag romaine (usually contains 3 heads)

1½ tablespoons avocado oil

¼ teaspoon sea salt

¼ teaspoon black pepper

Basil, for garnish

Freshly grated parmesan cheese ((Vg) (DF) sub nutritional yeast)

Ideas for
LEFTOVER HUMMUS

Make my Roasted Red Pepper Pasta alla Vodka (page 261) to use up the rest of your hummus.

SOUPS + SALADS

Chapter 10

DESSERTS

*H*ere we are, friends! We have arrived at my absolute favorite chapter: dessert! Anyone who knows me well knows that I have an aggressive sweet tooth. As I discussed in the introduction, I successfully tackled my sugar cravings recently by increasing my intake of healthy fats and decreasing my intake of carbohydrates. As a result, I no longer feel the need for something sweet after every meal. However, I cannot imagine a world without dessert, and I still often treat myself to a little somethin' sweet. Of course, my desserts are made with protein- and fiber-rich flours, natural sweeteners (and much less of them than traditional goodies), and healthy fats, instead of harmful vegetable oils, so I feel great enjoying them. I feel even better serving them to loved ones . . . and y'all! I adore every single recipe in this chapter, from my Lemon Almond Pound Cake and Chocolate Chip Cookie Dough Ice Cream to my 5-Layer Magic Bars and Cantaloupe Lemon Sherbet Popsicles. My wish is for these desserts to serve as a form of community and connection among family and friends. Because at the end of the day, is there anything sweeter?

Chai-Spiced Cake Donuts

(V) (GF) (DF) | **HANDS-ON TIME:** 25 min | **TOTAL TIME:** 2 h, 20 min | **YIELD:** 9 donuts

Want to get to know someone quickly? Ask if they're a cake or yeast donut person. I'm not going to assign right or wrong here, but um, cake donuts all the way (with rare exceptions). I far prefer the experience of biting into a moist, slightly crumbly cake-like donut than a puff of chewy air (again, with exceptions). As such, these baked donuts are right up my alley. The natural fats found in almond flour, coconut flour, and egg yolks come together for a divinely tender and rich donut experience. Since I've been on a chai tea kick, I thought the warming spices would be a welcome addition. Truthfully, these donuts are nutritious enough to enjoy for breakfast or as a snack, as well as dessert!

Place 1 cup water in a small saucepan, and bring to a boil. Place chai tea bag in a heatproof mug. When water is boiling, immediately pour over tea bag, and place mug in the refrigerator. Steep for at least 20 minutes and up to overnight in the fridge (longer for stronger flavor; I suggest overnight).

Preheat oven to 350° F. Grease a silicone donut mold with avocado oil. (Greasing is an extra precaution even with the nonstick mold). Place mold on a baking sheet.

In a large mixing bowl, combine almond flour, coconut flour, baking powder, baking soda, salt, cinnamon, ginger, and nutmeg. Whisk to incorporate.

In a smaller mixing bowl, combine whole eggs, egg yolk, coconut sugar, ¼ cup avocado oil, and vanilla. Remove chai tea from the refrigerator, and measure out ¾ cup (this should be most of the liquid). Test the temperature with your finger. If it is lukewarm or cooler, it can be added to the wet ingredients. If not, place back in the fridge for another 5 to 10 minutes, until cooled to at least lukewarm. When tea is ready, add it to the wet ingredients. Whisk to evenly incorporate.

Add wet ingredients to dry, and whisk until creamy. Pour a slightly rounded ¼ cup batter into each donut mold (approximately ¼ cup plus 1 tablespoon), then gently shake mold to spread in an even layer. Batter should come about two-thirds of the way up the mold. If you have a standard 6-donut mold, you should have approximately 1 cup batter left. Keep leftover batter at room temperature.

(continued on next page)

SPECIAL EQUIPMENT:
Silicone donut mold

INGREDIENTS:
1 cup water

1 chai tea bag

¼ cup avocado oil, plus more for greasing

1 cup blanched almond flour

½ cup plus 2 tablespoons coconut flour

1½ teaspoons baking powder

1 teaspoon baking soda

¼ teaspoon sea salt

1½ teaspoons ground cinnamon

½ teaspoon ground ginger

½ teaspoon ground nutmeg

2 large eggs, room temperature

1 large egg yolk, room temperature (compost or save the white for another use)

⅔ cup coconut sugar

1 teaspoon vanilla extract

Melted coconut butter for glazing (optional)

Ideas for
LEFTOVER CHAI TEA

Use leftover tea bags to make my Almond Chai Latte (page 58) throughout the week.

DESSERTS

CHAI-SPICED CAKE DONUTS *(continued)*

Bake donuts for 22 minutes, until firm but "bouncy" to touch. They should have risen right to the edge of the mold.

Allow to cool for 20 minutes, then run a butter knife around the edge of each donut. Place a cooling rack on top of the donuts while still in the mold, and holding it tightly, flip everything upside down. You should be able to gently peel the mold away, releasing your donuts.

Clean and grease molds again, and repeat donut-making process with remaining batter. You should get 3 more. Note that batter will be a little thicker for the second round, so I use dampened fingers to smooth it into the molds.

Glaze cooled donuts with melted coconut butter, if using.

Leftover donuts will keep tightly sealed at room temperature for 2 days, in the refrigerator for 5 days, or in the freezer for 5 months.

NOTES

Egg whites can be drying in baked goods, so sometimes I like to just use yolks to increase the richness but maintain moisture.

Don't wait between donut rounds to bake, or your donuts won't rise as much.

Ideas for
LEFTOVER EGG WHITE

Store the egg white in the refrigerator, then add it to your next batch of scrambled eggs, stir it into hot oatmeal, or brush on loaf or muffin recipes before they bake for a glossy, brown top.

You can also use it to make a topping for baked fruit. Make the crumble from the Finally Banana Pudding recipe (page 322). Mix a few cups of fruit of your choice with a tablespoon of arrowroot starch, a drizzle of maple syrup, and a splash of vanilla extract. Place the fruit in a cast-iron skillet, then top with crumble. Bake at 350° F until fruit is bubbling and gooey.

DESSERTS

Pumpkin Spice Cake

with CREAM CHEESE FROSTING

 | **HANDS-ON TIME:** 15 min | **TOTAL TIME:** 2 h, 45 min | **YIELD:** 10 servings | **OPTION:**

I first used chickpea flour in a carrot cake recipe for my blog (it's still there if you want to check it out). I fell head over heels in love with the moisture and density that it adds. As a result, I knew it would be the ideal flour for this pecan-studded, spice-infused pumpkin cake. I love this cake so much that it's one I hoard for myself, instead of giving away leftovers. I'll eat it for breakfast, lunch, dinner, or as a snack . . . in addition to dessert. If you're a Carrot Cake or Hummingbird Cake fan, you will adore this rustic Pumpkin Spice Cake with Cream Cheese Frosting!

Grease a 9-inch nonstick springform pan with oil of choice.

Preheat oven to 375° F. Place pecans on a baking sheet, and roast for 8 to 12 minutes, until fragrant and slightly darkened in color. Set aside to cool.

Make the Pumpkin Spice Cake: Combine all dry ingredients (except pecans and optional ingredients) in a large mixing bowl, and whisk to evenly incorporate. Crack eggs into a separate mixing bowl, and add remaining wet ingredients. Whisk to evenly incorporate.

Add wet ingredients to dry, and carefully fold to evenly incorporate. You can use a whisk to break up any chunks of almond flour or coconut sugar. Roughly chop cooled pecans, and add ¾ cup to the batter, along with optional coconut, raisins, or chocolate chips. Fold into the batter, then pour batter into pan. Use a dampened spatula to spread in an even layer, then gently shake pan to remove any bubbles. Bake for 40 to 43 minutes, until a toothpick inserted in the center comes out with a bit of "goo"—don't worry; it will firm up.

Allow to cool for 10 minutes, then remove the sides of the springform pan, and allow cake to cool for another 1 hour. (I suggest making frosting during this hour.)

Slice the cake in half horizontally by pushing a sharp chef's knife into the center of the cake parallel to your counter. Then, gently turn the cake in a circle, keeping the knife steady, until you get all the way around. Grab a thin, flat cutting board or plate, and slide the top disk onto it. Set halves

(continued on next page)

Oil for greasing pan

DRY INGREDIENTS:

1 cup raw pecans (sub walnuts)

2 cups chickpea flour

1 cup blanched almond flour

1 cup coconut sugar (sub ¾ cup monkfruit sweetener)

2 tablespoons ground cinnamon

1 teaspoon ground nutmeg

1 teaspoon ground ginger

¼ teaspoon sea salt

1½ teaspoons baking powder

½ teaspoon baking soda

¾ cup unsweetened shredded coconut, raisins, or chocolate chips (optional)

WET INGREDIENTS:

3 large eggs, room temperature

1 cup canned pumpkin purée

1 cup unsweetened organic applesauce

½ cup coconut oil, melted, plus more for greasing (sub melted butter or avocado oil)

1 tablespoon vanilla extract

CREAM CHEESE FROSTING:

16 ounces cream cheese, straight from the refrigerator (DF sub vegan cream cheese)

½ cup (1 stick) butter, softened (DF sub semi-solid coconut oil)

¾ cup coconut sugar (sub 10 tablespoons monkfruit sweetener)

aside to cool for another 30 minutes, or until room temperature, before frosting. Frost cake with Cream Cheese Frosting or Dairy-Free Frosting, and garnish with remaining chopped pecans.

With dairy-based frosting, cake keeps tightly sealed at room temperature for 2 days or in the refrigerator for 4 days. With non-dairy frosting, cake must be refrigerated immediately, and it will keep for 4 days. Unfrosted cake will keep in the freezer for 3 months.

Cream Cheese Frosting: Combine all frosting ingredients in the bowl of a stand mixer or in a mixing bowl if using a hand-held mixer. Start on the lowest speed, and mix until ingredients are mostly incorporated. You might need to stop and scrape the bowl and paddles once or twice if the ingredients are clumping. Increase speed to high, and beat until soft and fluffy, approximately 1 minute. Set aside until cake is ready to be frosted. Don't refrigerate or it will be too hard to spread. When ready to frost, spread approximately one-third over the bottom cake layer. Gently place remaining cake layer on top. Use remaining frosting to coat the top and sides, starting with the top. (I love the rustic look of slightly "bare" sides, where you can see some of the cake peeking out.)

Dairy-Free Frosting: You can replace traditional cream cheese with a vegan cream cheese, but the result tends to be runnier. Also use semi-solid coconut oil in place of butter. You can add one tablespoon of arrowroot starch at a time until it thickens to the desired consistency. Even then, I suggest icing the bottom layer of the cake and refrigerating it for 5 to 10 minutes, then icing the top.

NOTE

Because of the coconut sugar, this frosting is more like a caramel color instead of white. If you want it to be white, use monkfruit sweetener or just regular white sugar. However, monkfruit doesn't dissolve as well as coconut sugar, so it might be a bit grainy.

Ideas for
LEFTOVER CANNED PUMPKIN

Add a few tablespoons of leftover pumpkin purée to LL's Daily Fruit-Free Green Smoothie (page 54) or my Almond Chai Latte (page 58), stir into oatmeal, stir into a chili or other hearty soup like my Cozy Chunky Minestrone Soup (page 281), or just freeze it in ice cube molds to thaw and use again for this cake.

DESSERTS

Lemon Almond Pound Cake

V GF DF | **HANDS-ON TIME:** 20 min | **TOTAL TIME:** 1 hour, 30 minutes | **YIELD:** 16 servings

I had the pleasure of traveling to Atlanta for a speaking engagement one crisp fall weekend. The lovely woman who coordinated the event greeted me with a healthier take on the classic pound cake. I was smitten, and I immediately earmarked something similar for this cookbook. My version deviates a bit from hers to accommodate my pantry, but I am so grateful for the bright, lemony inspiration. This cake is velvety, appropriately dense, and all kinds of indulgent, while still full of nutritious goodness!

Preheat oven to 350° F. Grease the Bundt pan liberally, making sure to saturate every nook and cranny. (Greasing is an extra precaution even wiht a nonstick mold.) Place pan on a baking sheet.

Combine all dry ingredients in a large mixing bowl, and whisk to incorporate. Crack eggs into a medium mixing bowl. Add remaining wet ingredients, and whisk until smooth. Add wet ingredients to dry, and whisk until batter is completely smooth.

Pour into the pan, and spread into an even layer. (I tap the baking sheet on the counter a few times.) Bake the cake for 47 minutes, until light golden brown around the edges.

Let cool 20 minutes. Place a large plate on top of the cake while still in the pan. Hold the plate with one hand, and place your other hand underneath the baking sheet, then flip. The cake should slide out.

If glazing, wait until the cake is completely cool, at least 1 hour, to make the glaze. Place all glaze ingredients in a mixing bowl, and whisk until smooth. It might look like it won't mix, but be gentle and patient and you'll get a nice creamy glaze. Drizzle over cake. If you don't use glaze, you can slice the cake after cooling an additional 25 minutes.

Cake will keep tightly sealed at room temperature for 3 days, in the refrigerator for 7 days, or in the freezer for 3 months.

NOTE

Instead of the glaze included here, try my Condensed Coconut Milk (page 345) as a frosting (there will be leftovers that you can drizzle on individual servings).

SPECIAL EQUIPMENT:

Silicon Bundt mold

Oil or butter for greasing Bundt pan

DRY INGREDIENTS:

1 cup chickpea flour

1 cup coconut flour

1 cup blanched almond flour

¼ teaspoon sea salt

¼ teaspoon baking soda

WET INGREDIENTS:

5 large eggs, room temperature

1 cup maple syrup

1 cup avocado oil

¾ cup unsweetened almond, coconut, or cashew milk (canned full-fat coconut milk is my preference)

2 teaspoons almond extract (sub 1 tablespoon vanilla extract)

Zest from 2 lemons (2 loosely packed tablespoons)

Juice from 1 lemon (2 tablespoons)

GLAZE:

¼ cup arrowroot starch (sub cornstarch)

Juice from 1 lemon (2 tablespoons)

1 tablespoon maple syrup

Grain-Free Java Pecan Pie

V GF P | **HANDS-ON TIME:** 35 min | **TOTAL TIME:** 2 h, 40 min, plus 2 h cooling

YIELD: 6 to 8 servigs | ❄ | **OPTION:** K

Boy, oh boy! Am I glad I fell in love with coffee again before I tested my first pecan pie recipe. Otherwise, I'd probably have created something good, but not nearly this good! Throwing some strong coffee into the mix adds just the right hint of bitterness to even out the ooey-gooey pecan filling. My buttery, flaky crust makes a gorgeous base for this Java Pecan Pie, and sometimes I'll add pinches of ground cinnamon and ginger to the crust. In the world of pies (um, take me there), pecan was never a favorite … until now. Regardless of the season, you can't go wrong with this pie. Plus, it'll put a little pep in your step!

Make the Perfect Pastry Crust: Combine all ingredients except water in a food processor. Pulse until it forms pieces the size of small peas. (Alternately, combine almond flour, coconut flour, arrowroot starch, and salt in a large mixing bowl. Whisk to incorporate, then add butter. Use fingers to rub butter into the flour until it forms pieces the size of small peas.) Add ice water, 1 tablespoon at a time, and either pulse or mix with your fingers just until it forms a shaggy dough. The amount of water will depend on the day's humidity. You want it to hold together but not feel sticky. Form dough into a disk approximately 2 inches high, then wrap with plastic wrap, and refrigerate for 20 minutes.

Preheat oven to 350° F. Grease a 10-inch pie pan thoroughly with melted butter or coconut oil.

After 20 minutes, remove dough from the fridge. Place an 18-inch piece of parchment on the counter, and sprinkle with a thin layer of arrowroot starch. Place dough on parchment, and sprinkle more starch on top. If your parchment is sliding, you can lightly grease the countertop to stabilize.

Using a rolling pin, roll dough into a 10-inch round shape (as close as you can get), less than ¼-inch thick. Dust with starch as necessary to prevent sticking. Turn pie pan upside down onto dough, and slice off excess dough around the edges. Place one hand under the parchment and flip so that dough covers the pie tin. Gently pat dough into the pan in an even layer. You should see approximately ½ inch of pie pan around the top edge. You can wet your fingers to smooth little cracks. Use a fork to prick holes all over the crust, sides included. (I space them approximately 1 inch

(continued on page 312)

SPECIAL EQUIPMENT:

Tape Measure

PERFECT PASTRY CRUST:

1 cup blanched almond flour

½ cup coconut flour

½ cup arrowroot starch, plus more for dusting (sub cornstarch)

¼ teaspoon sea salt

½ cup (1 stick) cold butter, diced into ½-inch cubes (sub ½ cup solid coconut oil)

2 to 6 tablespoons ice water

Melted butter or coconut oil for greasing pan

PIE FILLING:

2 cups raw whole pecans

2 large eggs, room temperature

½ cup strong brewed coffee, room temperature

6 tablespoons melted butter, cooled to room temperature (sub melted coconut oil)

2 tablespoons molasses

⅔ cup coconut sugar (K sub ½ cup monkfruit sweetener)

1½ teaspoons vanilla extract

1½ teaspoons instant espresso powder (optional)

Pinch sea salt

2 tablespoons arrowroot starch (sub cornstartch)

DESSERTS

GRAIN-FREE JAVA PECAN PIE *(continued)*

apart.) This helps prevent air bubbles from forming when you prebake your crust. If you like, you can also use a fork to make a pretty decoration around the edge.

Bake crust for 15 minutes, or until light golden brown around the edges. Allow to cool completely, approximately 40 minutes, before filling.

Make the Pie Filling: Preheat oven to 350° F (it will already be preheated, if you just made the crust). Place pecans on a baking sheet. Roast for 10 to 12 minutes, until fragrant and slightly darkened in color. Set aside to cool.

Crack eggs into a mixing bowl. Add brewed coffee, butter, molasses, coconut sugar, vanilla, espresso powder (if using), salt, and arrowroot starch. Whisk until smooth and creamy. It's okay if there are some little clumps of arrowroot; just break up any that are bigger than pea-size. When pecans have cooled enough to touch, stir them into the filling mixture.

Scrape filling into cooled crust, and spread in an even layer. Cover with aluminum foil so the crust edges aren't exposed, and bake for 35 minutes. Remove foil, and bake for another 15 minutes, or until crust is golden brown and the top is slightly firm to touch. Allow to cool for 2 hours at room temperature before slicing with a very sharp knife.

Leftovers will keep tightly sealed at room temperature for 2 days, in the refrigerator for 5 days, or in the freezer for 3 months.

NOTES

You can make this pie coffee-free. Just use unsweetened almond milk instead of the brewed coffee, and omit the optional espresso powder.

Grab the extra dough leftover from trimming, ball it up, and use that to press dough into the pie pan instead of your fingers. The warmth from your fingers can mess with the fat in your dough.

The photo on page 311 shows a crust rolled a bit thinner and placed in the pan so that it came up to the top.

DESSERTS

5-Layer Magic Bars

  HANDS-ON TIME: 25 min | **TOTAL TIME:** 1 h, 10 min, plus 3 h, 30 min cooling

YIELD: 9 to 12 bars ❄ ⊕ | **OPTIONS:** Ⓥ🄳🄵

These bars are one of my most-favorite in all the land. And by *land*, I mean this cookbook. I don't remember where I first experienced a classic 7-Layer Magic Bar, but I'll never forget the impression it made on me (which went something like *more, more, more*). I was intimidated by the thought of recreating it because recipes typically require sweetened condensed milk and butterscotch chips, which aren't the healthiest. But then I had two profound realizations: 1) I could make sweetened condensed coconut milk that is dairy-free and preservative-free and 2) who needs butterscotch chips when you have all this other goodness?! So here they are in all their gooey glory, and I hope you love them as much as I do.

Make the Condensed Coconut Milk: Pour coconut milk into a saucepan, and bring to a boil over medium-high heat. Watch closely; as soon as milk starts to boil, reduce heat to low, and stir in maple syrup or coconut sugar. If you're not watching it closely, it will bubble over and cause a mess! Bring to a simmer, and cook until mixture is reduced by approximately half and thickened significantly, 35 to 40 minutes. Stir in vanilla and salt. Pour into a heatproof bowl, and refrigerate at least 30 minutes. This makes about 1 ¼ cups condensed coconut milk.

Make the Bars: Preheat oven to 350° F. Line an 8-inch square baking dish with parchment paper, allowing at least ½ inch to overhang the sides.

Combine almond flour, dates, vanilla, and salt in a food processor. Blend until it forms a fine sticky crumble. You should be able to pinch it and have the dough stick together. Press evenly and firmly into the baking dish.

Place coconut, walnuts, and chocolate chips in a mixing bowl, and toss to evenly distribute. If you like, you can sprinkle on another pinch of sea salt (my preference).

Once the condensed milk has cooled to room temperature (approximately 30 minutes), drizzle ¼ cup over the dough in the baking dish. Evenly distribute the coconut mixture on top, then evenly drizzle on remaining condensed milk; it should cover the entire surface.

(continued on page 315)

CONDENSED COCONUT MILK:

1 15-ounce can full-fat coconut milk

¼ cup maple syrup or coconut sugar (the latter is my preference for a caramel flavor, but the color will be darker)

¾ teaspoon vanilla extract

⅛ teaspoon sea salt

BARS:

1 cup blanched almond flour

10 to 12 pitted medjool dates, (1 cup, packed)

¾ teaspoon vanilla extract

⅛ teaspoon sea salt, plus more for garnish

1¼ cups unsweetened coconut flakes

¾ cup raw walnuts, roughly chopped (sub pecans)

1 cup dark or semi-sweet chocolate chips (Ⓥ🄳 sub vegan chocolate chips)

DESSERTS

Bake for 30 minutes, until slightly golden brown and bubbling. If you want, broil for a few minutes, until edges of coconut flakes are golden brown. Watch carefully.

Allow to cool at room temperature for 30 minutes, then refrigerate for at least 2 hours. If the dish is still hot, I suggest putting it on top of a dish towel in your fridge. After 2 hours, remove bars from the baking dish, then refrigerate another hour before slicing and serving.

Leftover bars will keep tightly sealed in the refrigerator for 1 week or in the freezer for 3 months.

Ideas for
LEFTOVER UNSWEETENED COCONUT FLAKES

Use extra coconut in my Coconut Lime Macadamia Smoothie (page 50) or Miso Coconut Roasted Eggplant (page 159) or use as a topping for Orange Ginger Tofu (page 243).

NOTE

Condensed Coconut Milk is a great dairy-free icing option for recipes like my Lemon "Poppy" Chia Scones (page 113), Spiced Pear Sour Cream Loaf (page 124), Gooey Pecan Cinnamon Rolls (page 104), Maple Bourbon Baked Pears (page 321), and more! It's also great to keep on hand for subbing in recipes that require traditional condensed milk.

Hungry Girl Chocolate Chunk Cookies

(V) | **HANDS-ON TIME:** 25 min | **TOTAL TIME:** 1 h, 25 min | **YIELD:** 18 to 20 cookies | **OPTIONS:** (DF) (GF)

Oh, these cookies! These chunky little "trail mix" cookies were inspired by a multi-generation family recipe. I fell in love with them upon first bite and immediately asked for permission to tweak them LL Balanced-style. Not only did I receive permission, I received praise for my version, so I knew they were good enough for you! Hungry Girl Cookies taste indulgent enough to pass for dessert, but they're also full of filling goodness, and they make a fantastic school or hiking snack. I hope they become a tradition in your family as well!

Preheat oven to 375° F. Line a baking sheet with parchment paper.

Combine all dry ingredients in a large mixing bowl, and whisk to incorporate. Fold in all of the mix-ins.

Combine all wet ingredients in another mixing bowl, and whisk until the mixture becomes a slightly lighter color and fluffier texture, approximately 30 seconds.

Add wet ingredients to dry, and use clean hands or a spatula to incorporate into a dough. Dough will be dry.

Use approximately 2½ tablespoons of the dough to form balls, and place them on the baking sheet, with at least 2 inches between each. (I use a dampened 2-inch ice cream scoop; each cookie is a rounded scoop.) Flatten the balls to about 1 inch high.

Bake for 11 minutes (they will look underdone), then allow to cool for 10 minutes before carefully transferring to a cooling rack. Allow to cool for another 10 minutes before enjoying.

Repeat with remaining dough.

Allow cookies to cool completely before storing them in a sealed container. Cookies will keep at room temperature for 2 days, in the refrigerator for 5 days, or in the freezer for 3 months.

DRY INGREDIENTS:

1½ cups blanched almond flour

½ cup rolled oats ((GF) sub gluten-free oats)

1 teaspoon baking powder

½ teaspoon baking soda

½ teaspoon sea salt

MIX-INS:

¾ cup chopped semi-sweet chocolate (sub ¾ cup chocolate chips; (DF) sub vegan chocolate chips)

½ cup unsweetened shredded coconut

½ cup pecans, chopped into ¼-inch pieces (sub walnuts)

5 to 6 pitted medjool dates, diced into ¼-inch pieces (¼ cup, packed)

WET INGREDIENTS:

¾ cup coconut sugar (sub 10 tablespoons monkfruit sweetener)

1 large egg, room temperature

10 tablespoons melted butter ((DF) sub coconut oil)

1½ teaspoons vanilla extract

NOTE

If you want to decrease the fat in these cookies, sub 5 tablespoons unsweetened applesauce for half of the butter or coconut oil. Batter will be slightly more wet, but that's okay.

DESSERTS

Easiest Peanut Butter Macadamia Nut Cookies

 | **HANDS-ON TIME:** 15 min | **TOTAL TIME:** 45 min | **YIELD:** approximately 20 cookies | | **OPTION:** Ⓚ

This recipe stems from one that's still wildly popular on my blog. It's a dump-and-stir cookie, as easy as it gets, and you won't believe how this simple process yields such a delightful result! To take the original to another level, I added chopped roasted and salted macadamia nuts, which create the most divine texture and contrast to caramel-sweet coconut sugar. You could certainly play around with your add-ins, substituting another nut or chocolate chips or dried fruit. These cookies beg for irregular edges, little helping hands, and sneaking leftovers before bed.

Preheat oven to 350° F. Line a baking sheet with parchment paper.

Crack egg into a large mixing bowl. Add all remaining ingredients except macadamia nuts and salt. Whisk until evenly incorporated, then fold in chopped macadamia nuts.

Dollop approximately 2 tablespoons dough per cookie onto the baking sheet, leaving at least 1 inch between each. Sprinkle with a tiny bit of salt, if using.

Bake for 8 minutes for a more gooey cookie or 10 for a more firm cookie. Allow to cool for 2 to 3 minutes before transferring to a cooling rack. Cool another 10 minutes before enjoying.

Repeat with remaining dough.

Cookies will keep tightly sealed at room temperature for 2 days, in the refrigerator for 6 days, or in the freezer for 3 months.

1 large egg, room temperature

¾ cup runny unsweetened, unsalted peanut butter (creamy or crunchy)

1 teaspoon vanilla extract

¼ teaspoon baking soda

½ cup coconut sugar (Ⓚ sub 6 tablespoons monkfruit sweetener)

⅓ cup unsweetened almond milk

⅓ cup roasted, salted macadamia nuts, roughly chopped

Maldon or other large flake sea salt (optional)

NOTE

You can use raw macadamia nuts in the cookie dough, in which case I suggest adding ¼ teaspoon salt.

SERVING SUGGESTION

Make ice cream sandwiches with any flavor of ice cream you like.

DESSERTS

Maple Bourbon Baked Pears

V P | **HANDS-ON TIME:** 25 min | **TOTAL TIME:** 55 min | **YIELD:** 12 servings | ⏱ | **OPTIONS:**

This is one of those workhorse desserts that's perfect to keep in your back pocket when you need to entertain and impress on short notice. There's something so rustic and beautiful about roasted pears, with edges slightly charred and glazed in their own juices. Well, maybe not *just* their own juices, as we are drizzling these babies with a little fat, a little sweetness, and a little southern charm (aka *bourbon*). If alcohol concerns you, you can totally leave it out, but I suggest substituting a few tablespoons of fresh orange juice for that "pop" factor.

6 medium semi-ripe red anjou pears

2 tablespoons melted butter (**Vg DF** sub coconut oil)

2 tablespoons coconut sugar

2 tablespoons bourbon or whiskey

½ teaspoon maple extract

Pinch sea salt

Vanilla ice cream (optional)

NOTE

You can sub other pears of your choice. Just be sure your pears are firm to the touch, not hard, and have a light pear scent.

Preheat oven to 400° F. Line a baking sheet with parchment paper.

Slice pears in half vertically; try to keep the stem intact on one half. Lay halves flesh-side down on a cutting board, and create thin horizon,mtal cuts, ⅛- to ¼-inch apart. Cut approximately three-quarters of the way down; do not cut through to the bottom.

Carefully transfer pear halves to the baking sheet, using a spatula, flesh-side down.

In a small mixing bowl, whisk together all remaining ingredients. Pour approximately 1 teaspoon mixture over each pear, then evenly distribute whatever is left. Wait 1 or 2 minutes, then use a pastry brush to grab some of the mixture that's fallen onto the baking sheet, and coat the pears a second time. Most of it will fall off to the side again, and that's okay!

Roast pears for 25 to 30 minutes, until fork tender and golden brown around the edges. If you like, you can broil them for a few minutes to get a nice caramelization on top. Watch carefully. Allow to cool for 8 to 10 minutes before serving with a spoonful of the juices from the baking sheet and some vanilla ice cream. I also love serving this with my Condensed Coconut Milk (page 345).

Leftover pears will keep tightly sealed in the refrigerator for 4 days. I like to enjoy them cold. I don't recommend freezing.

Finally Banana Pudding

(V) (GF) | **HANDS-ON TIME:** 30 min | **TOTAL TIME:** 2 h, plus 4 to 24 h chilling | **YIELD:** 6 servings | ❄ | **OPTIONS:**

I honestly thought it wasn't possible—a healthy banana pudding, made with real food ingredients, that could truly stand up to its beloved classic counterpart. I tried multiple variations, and I realized that the key is not to incorporate bananas into the actual pudding. Boxed gelatin mixes have all sorts of preservatives and chemicals designed to keep them bright yellow, and you won't find any of that here! Instead, you'll find a lovely layer of fresh, tender bananas on the bottom, creamy vanilla pudding in the middle, and an addictive homemade crumble on top. This dish is the opposite of fussy, and it's perfect for casual evenings with friends, summer potlucks, or for loved ones going through a difficult time. If you adore this traditional dessert like I do, I think you will be plumb pleased by mine!

Make the Vanilla Pudding: Place egg yolks in a medium bowl, and whisk until smooth.

Place coconut milk and maple syrup in a small saucepan. Bring mixture to a light simmer over medium-low heat, stirring every 1 or 2 minutes. Once simmering, scoop out ½ cup of the milk mixture, and slowly pour it into the yolks, whisking constantly as you pour. (This tempers your eggs, so they don't scramble.) Slowly pour the egg yolk mixture back into the saucepan, whisking constantly as you pour.

In a small bowl, combine arrowroot starch and water, and stir to dissolve. Add to the milk mixture, whisking constantly as you pour, and then whisk another 30 seconds. Simmer, stirring every minute, until noticeably thickened, 3 to 4 minutes.

Remove saucepan from the heat, and stir in butter and vanilla until smooth and creamy. If you see little white chunks in your mixture, you probably scrambled the eggs a tiny bit. In that case, place the mixture in a blender, and blend until smooth. Or press through a fine-mesh sieve to remove any chunks.

Pour pudding into a medium to large heatproof bowl (so it cools faster), and refrigerate for 1 hour, stirring every 20 minutes.

Make the Crumble: Preheat oven to 325° F. Line a baking sheet with parchment paper.

(continued on page 324)

VANILLA PUDDING:

- 3 large egg yolks (save whites for crumble)
- 1 15-ounce can full-fat coconut milk
- ⅓ cup maple syrup (sub monkfruit sweetener)
- 1 tablespoon arrowroot starch (sub cornstarch)
- 1 tablespoon water
- 2 tablespoons butter ((DF) (P) sub coconut oil; doesn't matter if it's solid or melted)
- 1¼ teaspoons vanilla extract

CRUMBLE:

- 1½ cups blanched almond flour
- 2 tablespoons egg whites (leftover from the yolks)
- 2 tablespoons maple syrup (sub monkfruit, but add 1 tablespoon blanched almond flour)
- 2 tablespoons butter, melted ((DF) (P) sub coconut oil)
- ¼ teaspoon vanilla extract
- Pinch sea salt
- 3 medium-ripe bananas (some brown spots but not as ripe as you want for banana bread)

DESSERTS

FINALLY BANANA PUDDING *(continued)*

Combine all crumble ingredients in a medium mixing bowl. (I find it easiest to add the egg whites to a ¼-cup measure and then pour half of that into the bowl, rather than trying to measure with a tablespoon.) Whisk to incorporate. The mixture should be the texture of wet sand. Spread crumble in an even layer on the baking sheet, approximately ¼-inch thick. (I use a dampened spatula to do this.)

Bake 17 minutes, until edges are light golden brown, then allow to cool for 20 minutes before breaking up into a crumble—whatever size chunks you prefer.

Assemble the Pudding: Slice 2 bananas into ¼-inch-thick rounds. Place rounds in an even layer over the bottom of an 8-inch square or 10 × 6-inch dish. Top with vanilla pudding, and spread in an even layer. Make sure it covers all of the bananas. Evenly sprinkle crumble over the top. Refrigerate pudding, uncovered, at least 4 hours and up to overnight before serving.

Slice remaining banana into ¼-inch-thick rounds, and place them evenly over the crumble. Serve immediately.

Wrap leftovers in plastic wrap, pressing the plastic against the bananas, which will help prevent oxidizing. Leftovers will keep in the refrigerator up to 3 days. I don't recommend freezing.

NOTE

To separate eggs easily, crack the egg and pour it over your hand (palm facing up) with your fingers opened just enough to let the egg whites slip through into a bowl. Then add the yolk to a separate bowl.

Ideas for
LEFTOVER EGG WHITES

Store the egg whites in the refrigerator, then add them to your next batch of scrambled eggs, stir them into hot oatmeal, or brush on loaf or muffin recipes before they bake for a glossy, brown top. You can also use them to make a topping for baked fruit: Make the crumble (see recipe above) using the egg whites. Mix a few cups of fruit of your choice with a tablespoon of arrowroot starch, a drizzle of maple syrup, and a splash of vanilla extract. Place the fruit in a cast-iron skillet, then top with crumble. Bake at 350° F until fruit is bubbling and gooey.

DESSERTS

Chocolate Chip Cookie Dough Ice Cream

 HANDS-ON TIME: 35 min | **TOTAL TIME:** 2 h, 25 min, plus 8 h freezing and overnight soaking

YIELD: 8 servings | **OPTIONS:**

While chocolate ice cream was a top-five request, Chocolate Chip Cookie Dough was the resounding number-one choice. And for good reason! Who doesn't go gaga for a combination of buttery, chocolate-studded cookie batter and luscious vanilla ice cream? I know I do, so I was over-the-moon thrilled when this recipe turned out! I think the key was repurposing my Chocolate Chip Cookie Dough Bites as actual cookie dough chunks in the ice cream. They work perfectly folded into the thick, creamy vanilla base, and they stay soft and "bite-able" even after freezing. For all my diehard CCCD Ice Cream lovers out there, please let me know what you think of this LL Balanced spin!

Make sure your ice cream canister has been frozen for at least 24 hours.

Make the Chocolate Chip Cookie Dough: Place cashews and dates in a food processor, and pulse until they form a chunky crumble, 20 to 30 seconds. Add vanilla, baking soda, salt, and butter, and blend until mixture is sticky when pressed together, another 20 to 30 seconds. When it's ready, it should sound "clumpier" as it blends. Add chocolate chips, and pulse until chips are mostly incorporated. The dough will look "chocolatey," but you should still see chunks of chips. Transfer dough to a large mixing bowl. Form dough into balls using approximately 1 ½ teaspoons for each. Place on a baking sheet. Freeze for 25 minutes, or refrigerate at least 1 hour. We want the balls to be firm enough to fold into the ice cream without completely breaking down.

Make the Ice Cream: Use the short- or long-soak method to soak cashews (page 44). Drain and rinse.

Add ingredients to a high-powered blender in the following order: coconut milk, soaked cashews, maple syrup, vanilla, salt, and alcohol, if using. Blend until completely smooth and creamy.

Plug the base of your ice cream maker into an outlet, and make sure it's working. Remove ice cream canister from the freezer, and quickly add it to the base. Immediately pour in ice cream mixture. Churn according to manufacturer instructions. (Mine churns for approximately 18 minutes.)

While ice cream is churning, line a 9 × 5 × 3-inch loaf pan with parchment paper, leaving approximately 1 inch overhanging the sides.

(continued on page 327)

CHOCOLATE CHIP COOKIE DOUGH:

1½ cups raw cashews

15 to 16 pitted medjool dates, (1½ cups)

¾ teaspoon vanilla extract

¼ teaspoon baking soda

¼ teaspoon sea salt

1 tablespoon melted butter (Vg DF P sub vegan butter or coconut oil, melted)

½ cup semi-sweet chocolate chips (Vg DF sub vegan chocolate chips)

ICE CREAM:

1½ cup raw cashews

1 15-ounce can full-fat coconut milk

⅓ cup maple syrup

1 teaspoon vanilla extract

¼ teaspoon sea salt

2 tablespoons vodka, whiskey, or bourbon (optional)

½ batch Chocolate Chip Cookie Dough

DESSERTS

When mixture is finished churning (mine starts to sound weird because it's too solid to keep mixing), remove mixing paddle from the ice cream canister, and fold cookie dough balls into ice cream. Scrape ice cream out of canister into the pan, and spread in an even layer. Wrap tightly with plastic wrap or aluminum foil, and freeze for at least 8 hours.

Allow ice cream to sit at room temperature for at least 15 minutes before attempting to scoop. It may take closer to 30 minutes, and this will depend on how cold your freezer is, the temperature of the room, and whether you used alcohol in the recipe.

Ice cream will keep tightly sealed in the freezer for 1 month.

Ideas for
CHOCOLATE CHIP COOKIE DOUGH BITES

With the leftover half batch of Chocolate Chip Cookie Dough, make bite-size morsels to enjoy on their own. Once you've made the dough following the instructions above, place it in a large mixing bowl. Form dough into balls using approximately 1½ tablespoons for each (you can make them larger, if you like), and place on a baking sheet. Refrigerate at least 1 hour before enjoying. I like to microwave them for 10 to 12 seconds so the chips get a little melty.

Leftovers will keep tightly sealed in the refrigerator for 1 week or in the freezer for 6 months.

Double Chocolate Decadence Ice Cream

  HANDS-ON TIME: 20 min | **TOTAL TIME:** 50 min, plus 8 h freezing and overnight soaking

YIELD: 8 servings ❄ 🌢 **OPTIONS:** 🆅🅶 🆅🅵

I asked and y'all answered! I put out my feelers on Instagram for what flavors of ice cream you wanted to see in this cookbook, and "anything chocolate" was one of the most popular responses. As if I needed more reasons to love you! So I happily obliged with this utterly decadent melt-in-your mouth (okay, that was a shoo-in) ice cream. Ripe for all sorts of add-ins and variations, this recipe serves as a chocolate-y base for all of your cool and creamy dessert dreams! I recommend chopped roasted pecans, marshmallows, and chocolate chips for a "Rocky Road" version. Look for marshmallows that don't use corn syrup, like Dandies brand.

Make sure your ice cream canister has been frozen for at least 24 hours.

Use the short- or long-soak method to soak cashews (see page 44). Drain and rinse.

Using a double boiler or my homemade version (see page 43), melt chocolate chips, constantly stirring. Remove from the heat when there are barely some lumps of chocolate left, and continue to stir until completely smooth. Alternately, microwave on high in 20 seconds increments, stirring in between, until melted. (This takes approximately 80 seconds for me.)

Add ingredients to a high-powered blender in the following order: coconut milk, soaked cashews, cocoa powder, coconut sugar, vanilla, salt, and alcohol, if using. Pour in melted chocolate. Blend until completely smooth and creamy.

Plug the base of your ice cream maker into an outlet, and make sure it's working. Remove ice cream canister from the freezer, and quickly add it to the base. Immediately pour in chocolate mixture. Churn according to manufacturer instructions. (Mine churns for approximately 18 minutes.)

While ice cream is churning, line a 9 × 5 × 3-inch loaf pan with parchment paper, leaving approximately 1 inch overhanging the sides. When mixture is finished churning (mine starts to sound weird because it's too solid to keep mixing), scrape it into the pan, and spread in an even layer. Wrap tightly with plastic wrap or aluminum foil, and freeze for at least 8 hours.

Allow ice cream to sit at room temperature for at least 15 minutes before attempting to scoop. It may take closer to 30 minutes, and this will depend on how cold your freezer is, the temperature of the room, and if you used alcohol in the recipe.

Ice cream will keep tightly sealed in the freezer up to 1 month.

1½ cups raw cashews

½ cup semi-sweet chocolate chips (🆅🅶 🆅🅵 sub vegan chocolate chips)

1 15-ounce can full-fat coconut milk

6 tablespoons Dutch processed cocoa powder

6 tablespoons coconut sugar

1½ teaspoons vanilla extract

¼ teaspoon sea salt

2 tablespoons vodka, whiskey, or bourbon (optional)

NOTES

Goodies you could swirl in after churning: almond or peanut butter, chocolate chips, chopped nuts, coconut flakes, dried cherries, and crumbled cookies.

Adding 2 tablespoons vodka, whiskey, or bourbon to your ice cream makes it even creamier and easier to scoop.

Ideas for
LEFTOVER LIQUOR

Don't usually keep booze around? If you buy some for this recipe, use leftovers in my Bourbon Balsamic Skillet Mushrooms (page 170), Maple Bourbon Baked Pears (page 321), or Roasted Red Pepper Pasta alla Vodka (page 261).

DESSERTS

Cantaloupe Lemon Sherbet Popsicles

V GF DF P | **HANDS-ON TIME:** 15 min | **TOTAL TIME:** 15 min, plus 6 h freezing

YIELD: 10 popsicles | ❄ | **OPTIONS:** Vg

As much as I tend towards chocolatey and nutty desserts, there's nothing I crave more on a hot Tennessee day than a fruit popsicle—especially one with a little bit of coconut creaminess and bright zesty lemon thrown in. That said, the real star of the show here is cantaloupe, which has been my snack addiction during the last few summers. When purchasing cantaloupes, look for ones that feel heavy, smell like the fruit when you sniff the stem, and give a little when you press the base. When you get the hang of finding good ones, there's nothing better than a big bowl of chopped cantaloupe sprinkled with a touch of sea salt . . . except maybe these popsicles! That said, if you're more of a watermelon, pineapple, or honeydew fan, they all substitute brilliantly.

Make space in your freezer to put popsicles on a flat surface.

Place all ingredients in a blender, and purée until smooth. Pour evenly into popsicle molds (I fill to within ¼ inch of the top), and add sticks according to your mold's instructions. (With my mold, I find it easier to add the sticks after the mold is already in the freezer with the lid on.) The popsicle sticks might bob up or turn a little sideways when you put them in. After 1 hour of freezing, straighten sticks, and make sure they're pushed all the way in.

Freeze for at least another 5 hours. To serve, run hot water over molds, being careful not to get water on the popsicles, just until loose enough to remove.

To store, stack popsicles between pieces of parchment paper and wrap in plastic wrap. They will keep in the freezer for 6 months.

SPECIAL EQUIPMENT:

Popsicle molds and sticks (about 3-ounce capacity)

INGREDIENTS:

Zest from 1 lemon (1 tablespoon packed)

Juice from 2 lemons (¼ cup)

½ small cantaloupe, rind removed, cut into 1-inch chunks (3 cups)

3 tablespoons honey (Vg sub maple syrup or liquid stevia drops, to taste)

¼ teaspoon vanilla extract

1 cup canned full-fat coconut milk

Ideas for
LEFTOVER CANTALOUPE

Use the leftover cantaloupe half to make Cucumber Cantaloupe Gazpacho (page 290).

NOTE

To prep cantaloupe, slice disks off the top and bottom to expose the flesh. Set the cantaloupe upright on the counter. Hold with your nondominant hand, and use a sharp knife to slice off the peel in vertical strokes. Cut in half, and use a metal spoon to scoop out the seeds.

DESSERTS

Chapter 11

SPICE MIXTURES, SAUCES, DRESSINGS + OTHER BASICS

Even though I created the following sauces, dressings, spice mixtures, and other basics for specific recipes, they deserve their own spotlight. As I always say in my cooking classes, "The magic is in the sauces!" Packed with creative flavor but without the preservatives, MSG, and refined sugar found in supermarket versions, these recipes are worth keeping handy. My hope is that cooking a few dishes "verbatim" from this book will give you confidence in the kitchen, so that you can create the base of your owns meals . . . then just use these recipes to doctor them up!

BBQ Seasoning

V DF GF | HANDS-ON TIME: 5 min | TOTAL TIME: 5 min | YIELD: approximately ¾ cup

Place all ingredients in a small bowl, and whisk to combine, or place in a sealable jar or container and shake.

Seasoning will keep in a tightly sealed container for up to 4 months in a cool dry pantry.

¼ cup coconut sugar (sub 3 tablespoons monkfruit sweetener)

2 tablespoons paprika

1 tablespoon chili powder

1 tablespoon garlic powder

4 teaspoons onion powder

1 tablespoon sea salt (may start with less and add to taste)

1 teaspoon ground cumin

½ teaspoon ground cinnamon

½ teaspoon black pepper

Cajun Seasoning

V DF GF | HANDS-ON TIME: 5 min | TOTAL TIME: 5 min | YIELD: approximately ¼ cup

Place all ingredients in a small bowl, and whisk to combine, or place in a sealable jar or container and shake.

Seasoning will keep in a tightly sealed container for up to 4 months in a cool dry pantry.

1 tablespoon paprika

2 teaspoons garlic powder

2 teaspoons onion powder

1½ teaspoons sea salt (feel free to start with 1 teaspoon if you're salt-sensitive)

1 teaspoon black pepper

1 teaspoon dried oregano

1 teaspoon crushed red pepper flakes (use ½ teaspoon if you're heat-sensitive)

1 tablespoon coconut sugar (sub monkfruit sweetener)

Taco Seasoning

V DF GF | HANDS-ON TIME: 5 min | TOTAL TIME: 5 min | YIELD: approximately ¾ cup

Place all ingredients in a small bowl, and whisk to combine, or place in a sealable jar or container and shake.

Seasoning will keep in a tightly sealed container for up to 4 months in a cool dry pantry.

1 tablespoon coconut sugar (sub monkfruit sweetener)

2½ teaspoons chili powder

2¼ teaspoons paprika

2 teaspoons onion powder

1¼ teaspoons sea salt

1¼ teaspoons ground cumin

1 teaspoon garlic powder

1 teaspoon dried oregano

Sun-Dried Tomato Marinara

V DF GF | **HANDS-ON TIME:** 10 min | **TOTAL TIME:** 10 min | **YIELD:** approximately 3 ½ cups

Place all ingredients in the order listed in a food processor, and purée until smooth. Transfer to a saucepan, and bring to a simmer over medium heat. Cook for 10 minutes, stirring every 1 or 2 minutes. If it's splashing, reduce the heat. Set aside to cool for at least 20 minutes before using in a recipe.

Sauce will keep tightly sealed in the refrigerator for 5 days

- 1 15-ounce can no-salt-added diced tomatoes
- ½ cup firmly packed sun-dried tomatoes in olive oil, plus 1 tablespoon of the oil
- ½ ounce fresh basil (½ cup, packed)
- 5 cloves garlic, roughly chopped (This will have a pretty noticeable garlic flavor. Use 2 to 3 if you don't want that.)
- ½ teaspoon sea salt
- ½ teaspoon dried oregano
- ¼ cup tomato paste (sub ketchup)

"Big Mac" Special Sauce

V DF GF | **HANDS-ON TIME:** 5 min | **TOTAL TIME:** 5 min | **YIELD:** ¾ cup

In a medium mixing bowl, place mayonnaise, mustard, tomato paste, honey, salt, pepper, lemon juice, onion, and pickle. Stir to combine well. Taste for seasoning, and add more salt and pepper if you like.

Sauce will keep tightly sealed in the refrigerator for 5 days.

- ¾ cup mayonnaise
- 2 tablespoons Dijon mustard
- ¼ cup tomato paste (sub ketchup and decrease honey to 2 teaspoons)
- 2 tablespoons honey
- ½ teaspoon sea salt, or more to taste
- ½ teaspoon black pepper, or more to taste
- Juice from 1 lemon (2 tablespoons)
- ¼ cup finely diced white onion
- ¼ cup finely diced dill pickle

Quick BBQ Sauce

V DF GF | **HANDS-ON TIME:** 5 min | **TOTAL TIME:** 5 min | **YIELD:** approximately ½ cup

Whisk all ingredients together in a small bowl.

Sauce will keep tightly sealed in the refrigerator for 5 days.

6 tablespoons ketchup

1½ teaspoons molasses

1 tablespoon maple syrup or honey

1 tablespoon low-sodium tamari

1 tablespoon apple cider vinegar

Grainy Honey Mustard Sauce

V DF GF | **HANDS-ON TIME:** 5 min | **TOTAL TIME:** 5 min | **YIELD:** approximately ¾ cup

Whisk all the ingredients together in a small bowl.

Sauce will keep tightly sealed in the refrigerator for 5 days.

½ cup whole-grain mustard (sub 6 tablespoons Dijon mustard)

3 tablespoons honey

3 tablespoons ketchup

¼ teaspoon onion powder

Pistachio Pesto

V GF | **HANDS-ON TIME:** 10 min | **TOTAL TIME:** 10 min | **YIELD:** approximately 1½ cups | **OPTIONS:** DF Vg

Combine all ingredients except olive oil in a food processor. Pulse until it forms a fine-crumble texture. While machine is running, slowly pour in olive oil until it reaches your desired consistency. If you want to make the pesto creamier, stir in mayonnaise.

Pesto will keep tightly sealed in the refrigerator for 5 days.

2 ounces fresh basil (2 cups, packed)

¾ cup roasted, salted pistachios

Juice from 1 lemon (2 tablespoons)

1 large or 2 small cloves garlic, roughly chopped

¼ cup freshly grated parmesan

cheese (DF sub 2 tablespoons nutritional yeast)

1 teaspoon mild, white miso paste

Pinch black pepper

½ cup extra virgin olive oil

2 to 4 tablespoons mayonnaise (Vg omit for vegan)

Lemony Pistachio Pesto

Vg DF GF | **HANDS-ON TIME:** 10 min | **TOTAL TIME:** 10 min | **YIELD:** approximately ¾ cup

Combine all ingredients except olive oil in a food processor. Pulse until it forms a fine-crumble texture. While machine is running, slowly pour in olive oil until it reaches your desired consistency.

Pesto will keep tightly sealed in the refrigerator for 5 days.

½ cup roasted, salted pistachios

2 ounces fresh basil, stems removed (2 cups loosely packed)

2 tablespoons nutritional yeast

Zest from 1 lemon (2 teaspoons)

Juice from 1 lemon (2 tablespoons)

1 teaspoon mild, white miso paste

¼ teaspoon black pepper

1 to 2 cloves garlic, roughly chopped

½ cup olive oil

Green Tahini Sauce

Vg DF GF | **HANDS-ON TIME:** 10 min | **TOTAL TIME:** 10 min | **YIELD:** approximately 1 cup

Place all ingredients in a blender, in the order listed, and blend until smooth and creamy. Sauce will thicken in the refrigerator. You can stir in a tablespoon or two of water when you use leftovers.

Sauce will keep tightly sealed in the refrigerator for 5 days.

⅓ cup water

¾ ounce fresh basil leaves (¾ cup loosely packed)

Juice from 1 lemon (2 tablespoons)

¼ cup runny tahini (pourable consistency)

1 teaspoon mild, white miso paste

1 clove garlic, roughly chopped

Pinches salt, black pepper, and onion powder

Avocado Ranch Dressing

V GF | **HANDS-ON TIME:** 10 min | **TOTAL TIME:** 10 min | **YIELD:** approximately 1 cup | | **OPTIONS:**

Place 2 tablespoons minced chives and all remaining ingredients in a blender, and blend until smooth and creamy. Transfer to a small bowl, and stir in remaining 2 tablespoons chives.

For a Buffalo version, decrease the almond milk to ⅓ cup and add 2 to 4 tablespoons Frank's RedHot (start with 2 and add more to taste).

Sauce will keep tightly sealed in the refrigerator for 5 days.

- 2 ounces minced chives (¼ cup), divided
- 1 clove garlic, minced
- 1 teaspoon mild, white miso
- 1 medium ripe avocado, mashed (½ cup)
- ½ cup sour cream (sub plain full-fat yogurt; Vg DF sub dairy-free)
- 1½ tablespoons apple cider vinegar
- 1 teaspoon onion powder
- ½ teaspoon sea salt
- ½ teaspoon black pepper
- ½ cup unsweetened almond milk

Basil Caesar Hummus Dressing

V DF GF | **HANDS-ON TIME:** 10 min | **TOTAL TIME:** 10 min | **YIELD:** approximately 1¼ cups |

Place all ingredients in a blender, and purée until smooth and creamy. Refrigerate at least 1 hour and up to 24 hours before serving. Note that the dressing will thicken a bit in the fridge. You can stir in a little more water before serving if you like.

Dressing will keep tightly sealed in the refrigerator for 5 days.

- ¼ cup water
- ½ cup plain hummus
- 2 tablespoons tahini
- Juice from ½ lemon (1 tablespoon)
- ¾ ounce fresh basil, roughly chopped (¾ cup, packed)
- 1 clove garlic, roughly chopped
- ½ teaspoon onion powder
- ½ teaspoon black pepper
- ¼ teaspoon garlic powder
- ¼ teaspoon sea salt
- 2 teaspoons Dijon mustard
- 1 teaspoon low-sodium tamari
- 1 teaspoon mild, white miso paste
- 1 to 2 teaspoons maple syrup (start with 1 and add to taste or sub liquid stevia drops to taste)

Italian Dressing

 HANDS-ON TIME: 5 min | **TOTAL TIME:** 5 min | **YIELD:** approximately 1 cup | **OPTION:**

Place all ingredients in a blender, and purée until smooth and creamy.

Dressing will keep tightly sealed in the refrigerator for 5 days.

½ cup extra virgin olive oil

⅓ cup white balsamic vinegar

2 cloves garlic, minced

¾ teaspoon sea salt (feel free to start with ½ teaspoon and add more to taste)

½ teaspoon black pepper

1 teaspoon dried oregano

½ teaspoon onion powder

2 tablespoons freshly grated parmesan (DF sub nutritional yeast)

2 teaspoons maple syrup or honey

Lemony Vinaigrette

 HANDS-ON TIME: 8 min | **TOTAL TIME:** 8 min | **YIELD:** approximately 1 cup |

Combine all ingredients in a glass jar with a lid or other sealable container, and shake until smooth and creamy.

Dressing will keep tightly sealed in the refrigerator for 5 days.

½ cup avocado oil

Zest from 1 lemon (1 tablespoon loosely packed)

Juice from 2 lemons (¼ cup)

1 teaspoon Dijon mustard

2 tablespoons finely minced shallot

¼ teaspoon sea salt

1 tablespoon maple syrup

Miso Maple Dressing

 HANDS-ON TIME: 8 min | **TOTAL TIME:** 8 min | **YIELD:** approximately ⅔ cup |

Place miso and vinegar in a small bowl. Use a fork to break up the miso, and whisk until smooth. Whisk in maple syrup, salt, pepper, and onion powder. While whisking continuously, slowly pour in avocado oil until dressing is a uniform consistency. Alternately, double the batch, and purée all ingredients in a blender (one batch is too small to blend).

Dressing will keep tightly sealed in the refrigerator for 5 days.

1 tablespoon mild, white miso paste

2 tablespoons apple cider vinegar

2 teaspoons maple syrup (sub 2 drops stevia or to taste)

¼ teaspoon sea salt

¼ teaspoon black pepper

¼ teaspoon onion powder

6 tablespoons avocado oil

Grainy Mustard Dressing

V DF GF | **HANDS-ON TIME:** 5 min | **TOTAL TIME:** 5 min | **YIELD:** approximately ½ cup

Combine all ingredients in a small bowl, and whisk until creamy.

Dressing will keep tightly sealed in the refrigerator for 5 days.

¼ cup extra virgin olive oil

1½ tablespoons apple cider vinegar

1 tablespoon mayonnaise

1 tablespoon whole-grain mustard (sub 2 teaspoons Dijon mustard)

¼ teaspoon sea salt

¼ teaspoon onion powder

Pinch garlic powder

1 drop liquid stevia, or to taste (sub honey or maple syrup, to taste) (optional)

Ginger Tahini Dressing

V DF GF | **HANDS-ON TIME:** 8 min | **TOTAL TIME:** 8 min | **YIELD:** approximately ¾ cup

Combine all ingredients in a mixing bowl, and whisk until creamy and incorporated (start with 2 tablespoons water). You can also purée everything in a blender. Add more water as you like to achieve desired consistency. (I use 4 tablespoons total.)

Dressing will keep tightly sealed in the refrigerator for 5 days.

¼ cup tahini (pourable consistency)

¼ cup avocado oil

Juice from 1 large or 2 small limes (3 tablespoons)

1½ teaspoons mild, white miso paste

1-inch piece ginger, peeled and grated (sub ¼ teaspoon ground ginger)

2 cloves garlic, finely minced

1 tablespoon honey

2 to 6 tablespoons filtered water

Pinch salt

SPICE MIXTURES, DRESSINGS, SAUCES + OTHER BASICS

Caramelized Onions

(V) (DF) (GF) | HANDS-ON TIME: 20 min | TOTAL TIME: 1 h | YIELD: 2 cups |

Turn on exhaust fan. Heat a large saucepan over medium-high heat, and add avocado oil. When oil moves quickly around the pan and is shimmering, add onions. Allow to cook without stirring until it looks like the onions are burning, 4 to 6 minutes. Add ½ cup water to deglaze, scraping up any brown bits from the bottom of the pan. (Be careful as this will cause hot steam.) Stir onions briefly, reduce heat slightly, and repeat burning and deglazing process once more, using the remaining ½ cup water (another 4 to 6 minutes).

Reduce heat to medium-low (you can turn off the exhaust fan), and cook onions, stirring every 5 minutes or so, until they are a dark and jammy consistency, approximately 35 minutes. Feel free to add splashes of water to prevent sticking or burning as they cook.

Onions will keep tightly sealed in the refrigerator for 5 days.

1 tablespoon avocado oil

2 medium yellow onions, sliced into ¼-inch half-moons

1 cup water

NOTE

It's important to cut the onions into even slices to ensure that they all cook at the same rate.

Fluffy Shallot Rice

(V⁵) (GF) | HANDS-ON TIME: 35 min | TOTAL TIME: 55 min | YIELD: 3 cups |

In a small saucepan, place 2 cups of water and bring to a boil over medium-high heat. While water is coming to a boil, place 1 tablespoon butter in a separate medium saucepan, and heat over medium heat. When butter is melted and moves quickly around the pan, add rice and salt. Cook, stirring continuously, until rice has a toasted fragrance and is leaving some sticky residue on the bottom of the pan, 3 to 4 minutes. Pour boiling water over rice, then bring to a simmer over low heat. Cover with a lid, and cook for 18 minutes. Resist the temptation to look at the rice while cooking.

While rice is cooking, use the pan you used for boiling water to cook shallots. Place the remaining 1 tablespoon butter in the pan, and heat over medium-low heat. When butter has melted and moves quickly around the pan, add shallots. Cook, stirring every 30 seconds or so, until softened and translucent, 4 to 5 minutes. Set aside.

When rice has simmered for 18 minutes, remove from the heat, and allow to sit another 10 minutes with the lid on. After 10 minutes, uncover and fluff with a fork, then stir in shallots.

Rice will keep tightly sealed in the refrigerator for 5 days.

2 cups water

2 tablespoons butter, divided

1 cup medium-grain white or arborio rice

½ teaspoon sea salt

1 medium shallot, minced (⅓ cup) (sub ¼ medium red onion, diced into ¼-inch pieces)

Fluffy Shallot Quinoa

(V) (DF) (GF) | **HANDS-ON TIME:** 15 min | **TOTAL TIME:** 10 min | **YIELD:** 3 cups |

Place quinoa in a fine-mesh sieve, and rinse under running water until there are no small foamy bubbles and the water runs clear, approximately 1 minute. Drain well. Place quinoa in a 2-quart saucepan. Cook over medium heat, stirring, until quinoa has a nutty fragrant and starts to stick, 4 to 5 minutes. Stir in shallots and water. Bring to a boil, then reduce heat to the lowest possible setting. Cover saucepan with a lid, and simmer until the liquid has evaporated (you can peek but do it quickly), 15 to 20 minutes. Remove from the heat, but keep covered. Allow to sit 5 minutes, then uncover, and fluff with a fork.

Quinoa will keep tightly sealed in the refrigerator for 5 days.

- 1 cup dried quinoa
- 1 small shallot, minced (¼ cup)
- 2 cups water

Vegetable Stock

 (DF) (GF) | **HANDS-ON TIME:** 30 min | **TOTAL TIME:** 1 h, 30 min | **YIELD:** 4 ½ cups |

Heat a stockpot or large soup pot over medium-high heat, and add avocado oil. Cut the corn cobs in half crosswise. When oil moves quickly around the pot, add corn cob halves, onions, carrots, fennel, garlic, and jalapeño. Cook, stirring every minute or so, until veggies begin to soften, 6 to 8 minutes. Add water, and use a firm spatula or wooden spoon to scrape any brown bits from the bottom of the pan into the liquid. Bring to a boil, then reduce heat to low, and simmer for 1 hour, uncovered.

Carefully strain stock through a large fine-mesh sieve into a large heatproof bowl. (I gently press the veggies to get a little more liquid out, then let the strainer sit a full minute before removing.) If you only have a small fine-mesh sieve, you can strain the stock in batches, discarding or composting the leftover veggies as you go.

Stock will keep tightly sealed in the refrigerator for 5 days.

- 2 tablespoons avocado oil
- 4 ears of corn, husks removed, kernels cut off and saved for use another use
- 1 medium sweet or Vidalia onion, unpeeled and roughly chopped into 1½-inch pieces
- 2 medium carrots, peeled and roughly chopped into 1½-inch pieces (1½ cups)
- 1 fennel bulb with fronds, rinsed and roughly chopped into 1½-inch pieces (including fronds)
- 1 head garlic, unpeeled and sliced in half crosswise
- 1 medium jalapeño, seeds removed and chopped into ½-inch pieces
- 7 cups water

Condensed Coconut Milk

 | **HANDS-ON TIME:** 10 min | **TOTAL TIME:** 1 h, 20 min | **YIELD:** 1¼ cups |

Pour coconut milk into a saucepan, and bring to a boil over medium-high heat. Watch closely; as soon as milk starts to boil, reduce heat to low, and stir in maple syrup or coconut sugar. If you're not watching it closely, it will bubble over and cause a mess!

Bring to a simmer, and cook until mixture is reduced by approximately half and is thickened significantly, 35 to 40 minutes. Stir in vanilla and salt. Pour into a heatproof bowl, and refrigerate for at least 30 minutes before using.

Condensed milk will keep tightly sealed in the refrigerator for 5 days.

1 15-ounce can full-fat coconut milk

¼ cup maple syrup or coconut sugar (the latter is my preference for a caramel flavor, but the color will be darker)

¾ teaspoon vanilla extract

⅛ teaspoon sea salt

Cream Cheese Frosting

 | **HANDS-ON TIME:** 10 min | **TOTAL TIME:** 10 min | **YIELD:** 3 cups | | **OPTIONS:**

Combine all ingredients in the bowl of a stand mixer or in a mixing bowl, if using a hand-held mixer. Start on the lowest speed, and mix until ingredients are mostly incorporated. You might need to stop and scrape the mixer once or twice if the ingredients are clumping. Increase speed to high, and beat until soft and fluffy, approximately 1 minute. Set aside until ready to use. Don't refrigerate, or it will be too hard to spread.

Dairy-Free Frosting: If you want to replace traditional cream cheese with a vegan cream cheese, the result tends to be runnier in texture. You can also use coconut oil instead of the butter. You can add one tablespoon of arrowroot starch at a time until it thickens to desired consistency.

16 ounces cream cheese, straight from the refrigerator (Vg DF sub vegan cream cheese)

½ cup (1 stick) butter, softened (Vg DF sub coconut oil)

¾ cup coconut sugar (K sub 10 tablespoons monkfruit sweetener)

APPENDICES

Stocking Your Pantry

with NUTRIENT-DENSE WHOLE FOODS

Healthy Proteins:

- Beans and legumes
- Beef, 100% grass-fed, pasture-raised
- Eggs from pasture-raised poultry
- Lamb, pasture-raised lamb
- Nuts and seeds
- Pork, pasture-raised pork
- Poultry, pasture-raised
- Shellfish and fish, wild- and sustainably caught
- Tempeh, organic non-GMO
- Tofu, organic non-GMO, sprouted if available

Healthy Fats:

- Avocado oil, 100 percent cold-pressed
- Avocados
- Bacon fat from pasture-raised pork
- Butter, grass-fed
- Coconut oil, 100 percent organic extra virgin
- Nuts and seeds
- Olive oil, 100 percent extra virgin first- cold-pressed

Grains:

- Arborio rice
- Farro
- Quinoa
- Rice, long- and medium-grain rice
- Rolled oats
- Wild rice

Spices and Dried Herbs:

- Basil, dried
- Black pepper
- Cayenne pepper, ground
- Chili powder
- Cinnamon, ground
- Cumin, ground
- Curry powder
- Garlic powder
- Ginger, ground
- Nutmeg, ground
- Onion powder
- Oregano, dried
- Paprika
- Parsley, dried
- Red pepper flakes
- Sea salt, fine-ground
- Turmeric, ground

Fresh Herbs:

- Basil (refrigerate)
- Chives (refrigerate)
- Cilantro (refrigerate)
- Mint (refrigerate)

Fiber:

- Allium vegetables: garlic, onions, scallions, leeks, shallots, and chives
- Cruciferous vegetables
- Fruit
- Leafy green vegetables
- Non-starchy colorful vegetables
- Starchy vegetables

Canned, Jarred, or Bottled Goods:

- Almond butter, unsweetened, unsalted
- Applesauce, unsweetened
- Artichoke hearts
- Black beans
- Cannellini or great northern beans
- Chickpeas
- Coconut butter
- Coconut milk, full-fat and light
- Frank's RedHot
- Kidney beans
- Lentils
- Mayonnaise, avocado oil–based
- Olives: Kalamata and green
- Pickles: dill and sweet relish
- Pumpkin purée, unsweetened
- Roasted red peppers
- Salsa, low-sodium
- Stocks, low-sodium chicken, beef, and vegetable
- Sun-dried omatoes in olive oil
- Tahini
- Tomato paste
- Tomatoes, diced, no salt added
- Tuna and salmon, canned, wild-caught, boneless and skinless
- Vinegars: white balsamic, aged balsamic and apple cider vinegar
- Water chestnuts

Dried and Packaged Goods:

- Almond milk, unsweetened
- Apricots, unsulphured
- Burrito wraps, whole-wheat or gluten-free
- Coconut: shredded and unsweetened flakes
- Coffee
- Espresso powder
- Figs
- Medjool dates
- Noodles: whole-wheat or gluten-free or lentil- or chickpea-based
- Nutritional yeast
- Nuts, raw: cashew, pecans, and walnuts
- Nuts, roasted and salted: macadamia and pistachios
- Raisins
- Tea: Chai and chamomile
- Tortillas, Non-GMO corn or whole-wheat

Refrigerator Staples:

- Butter, grass-fed
- Cheeses
- Coconut water
- Cream cheese
- Fruit juices: orange and grapefruit
- Hummus
- Ketchup, organic
- Kimchi
- Lemons and limes
- Miso paste, mild white
- Mustard: Dijon and whole-grain
- Pizza dough, whole-wheat
- Prepared horseradish
- Sour cream
- Sriracha
- Tahini
- Tamari, low-sodium
- Yogurt

Freezer Staples:

- Blueberries
- Cauliflower rice
- Corn
- Green beans
- Pineapple
- Potatoes, shredded
- Raspberries
- Spinach

Flours and Baking Supplies:

- Almond extract
- Almond flour, blanched
- Arrowroot starch
- Baking powder
- Baking soda
- Bourbon
- Cacao nibs
- Chickpea flour
- Chocolate: dark and semi-sweet chips
- Cocoa powder, Dutch process
- Coconut flour
- Chia seeds
- Cornstarch
- Maple extract
- Oat bran
- Oat flour
- Vanilla extract

Sweeteners:

- Honey
- Coconut sugar
- Maple syrup, grade A
- Molasses
- Monkfruit sweetener
- Stevia, liquid

Sources for NUTRITIONAL *and* DIETARY INFORMATION

Almond Milk

Swati Sethi, S. K. Tyagi, and Rahul K. Anurag, "Plant-Based Milk Alternatives an Emerging Segment of Functional Beverages: A Review," *Journal of Food Science and Technology* 53, no. 6 (September 2016), 3408–23, https://www.ncbi.nlm.nih.gov/pmc/articles/PMC5069255/.

Avocado Oil

Lana Barhum, "Eight Benefits of Avocado Oil for the Skin," Medical News Today website, April 19, 2018, https://www.medicalnewstoday.com/articles/321543.php.

"Health Benefits of Avocado Oil: Is It Healthier Than Coconut Oil," Wellness Mama website, April 18, 2019, https://wellnessmama.com/123677/avocado-oil/.

Chickpea Flour

Paul Nestel, Marja Cehun, and Andriana Chronopoulos, "Effects of Long-Term Consumption and Single Meals of Chickpeas on Plasma Glucose, Insulin, and Triacylglycerol Concentrations," *American Journal of Clinical Nutrition* 79, no. 3 (March 2004): 390–5, https://academic.oup.com/ajcn/article/79/3/390/4690125.

Tanja Kongerslev Thorning et al, "Milk and Dairy Products: Good or Bad for Human Health? An Assessment of the Totality of Scientific Evidence," *Food & Nutrition Research* 60 (November 2016). https://www.ncbi.nlm.nih.gov/pmc/articles/PMC5122229/.

Chives

Winston J. Craig, "Health-Promoting Properties of Common Herbs," *American Journal of Clinical Nutrition* 70:3 (September 1999), 491–99, abstract, https://academic.oup.com/ajcn/article/70/3/491s/4714940.

Coffee

Ann Gulland, "Scientists Wake Up to Coffee's Benefits," *BMJ* (November 22, 2017), https://www.bmj.com/content/359/bmj.j5381.

Dairy

Charles M. Benbrook, et al., "Enhancing the Fatty Acid Profile of Milk Through Forage-Based Rations, with Nutrition Modeling of Diet Outcomes," *Food Science & Nutrition*, February 28, 2018, https://onlinelibrary.wiley.com/doi/full/10.1002/fsn3.610.

Charles M. Benbrook et al., "Organic Production Enhances Milk Nutritional Quality by Shifting Fatty Acid Composition: A United States–Wide, 18-Month Study," *PLOS One* 8, no. 12 (2013): e82429, https://www.ncbi.nlm.nih.gov/pmc/articles/PMC3857247/.

G. Butler et al., "The Effects of Dairy Management and Processing on Quality Characteristics of Milk and Dairy Products," *NJAS* 58, no. 3–4 (December 2011): 97–102, https://www.sciencedirect.com/science/article/pii/S1573521411000212?via%3Dihub.

Maria Kechagia, "Health Benefits of Probiotics: A Review," *ISRN Nutrition*, January 2, 2013, https://www.ncbi.nlm.nih.gov/pmc/articles/PMC4045285/.

Nissim Silanikove et al., "The Interrelationships Between Lactose Intolerance and the Modern Dairy Industry: Global Perspectives in Evolutional and Historical Backgrounds," *Nutrients* 7, no. 9 (September 2015): 7312–31, https://www.ncbi.nlm.nih.gov/pmc/articles/PMC4586535/.

University of Minnesota, "Forage-Based Diets on Dairy Farms Produce Nutritionally Enhanced Milk: Markedly Higher Levels of Health-Promoting Fatty Acids Reported," *Science Daily* 28 (February 2018), https://www.sciencedaily.com/releases/2018/02/180228085349.htm.

Ana M. Valdes et al., "Role of the Gut Microbiota in Nutrition and Health," *BMJ*, June 13, 2018, https://www.bmj.com/content/361/bmj.k2179.

Farro
P. R. Shewry, "Wheat," *Journal of Experimental Botany* 60, no. 6 (April 2009), 1537–53, abstract, https://academic.oup.com/jxb/article/60/6/1537/517393.

Gerry K. Schwalfenberg and Stephen J. Genuis, "The Importance of Magnesium in Clinical Healthcare," *Scientifica* (2017): 4179326, abstract, https://www.ncbi.nlm.nih.gov/pmc/articles/PMC5637834/.

Frank's RedHot (capsian)
Mustafa Chopan and Benjamin Littenberg, "The Association of Hot Red Chili Pepper Consumption and Mortality: A Large Population-Based Cohort Study," *PLoS ONE* 12:1, e0169876, abtract, https://journals.plos.org/plosone/article?id=10.1371/journal.pone.0169876.

Mark F. McCarty, James J. DiNicolantonio, and James H O'Keefe, "Capsaicin May Have Important Potential for Promoting Vascular and Metabolic Health," *Open Heart* 2:1 (2015), e000262, abstract, https://www.ncbi.nlm.nih.gov/pmc/articles/PMC4477151/.

Kimchi
Bohkyung Kim et al., "Anti-Aging Effects and Mechanisms of Kimchi During Fermentation Under Stress-Induced Premature Senescence Cellular System," *Food Science and Biotechnology* 20, no. 3 (June 2011), 643–49, abstract, https://link.springer.com/article/10.1007/s10068-011-0091-9?&utm_medium=9354.

Myung-Sunny Kim et al., "Effects of Kimchi on Human Health: A Protocol of Systematic Review of Controlled Clinical Trials," *Medicine* (Baltimore) 97, no. 13 (March 2018), e0163, https://www.ncbi.nlm.nih.gov/pmc/articles/PMC5895381/.

K. Y. Park et al., "Health Benefits of Kimchi (Korean Fermented Vegetables) as a Probiotic Food," *Journal of Medicinal Food* 17, no. 1 (Jan. 2014), 6-20, abstract, https://www.ncbi.nlm.nih.gov/pubmed/24456350.

Macademia Nuts
J. D. Curb, et al., "Serum Lipid Effects of a High-Monounsaturated Fat Diet Based on Macadamia Nuts," *Archives of Internal Medicine* 160, no. 8 (April 24, 2000): 1154-8, abstract, https://www.ncbi.nlm.nih.gov/pubmed/10789609.

Emilio Ros, "Health Benefits of Nut Consumption," *Nutrients* 2, no. 7 (July 2010): 652–82, https://www.ncbi.nlm.nih.gov/pmc/articles/PMC3257681/.

Miso
H. S. Gill and F. Guarner, "Probiotics and Human Health: A Clinical Perspective," *Postgraduate Medical Journal* 80 (2004), 516–26, https://pmj.bmj.com/content/80/947/516.

Hiromitsu Watanabe, "Beneficial Biological Effects of Miso with Reference to Radiation Injury, Cancer and Hypertension," *Journal of Toxicologic Pathology* 26, no. 2 (June 2013), 91–103, abstract, https://www.ncbi.nlm.nih.gov/pmc/articles/PMC3695331/.

Soy and Tofu

"The Nutrition Source: Straight Talk About Soy," Harvard T. H. Chan School of Public Health, accessed July 1, 2019, https://www.hsph.harvard.edu/nutritionsource/soy/.

Akimitsu Takagi, Mitsuyoshi Kano, and Chiaki Kaga, "Possibility of Breast Cancer Prevention: Use of Soy Isoflavones and Fermented Soy Beverage Produced Using Probiotics," *International Journal of Molecular Science* 16, no. 5 (May 2015): 10907–20, https://www.ncbi.nlm.nih.gov/pmc/articles/PMC4463682/.

Kaufui V. Wong "Tofu and Soy for Health Benefits," *EC Nutrition* 7, no. 22 (2017): 58–60, https://www.ecronicon.com/ecnu/pdf/ECNU-07-0000225.pdf.

Jie Yu et al., "Isoflavones: Anti-Inflammatory Benefit and Possible Caveats," *Nutrients* 8, no. 6 (June 2016): 361, https://www.ncbi.nlm.nih.gov/pmc/articles/PMC4924202/.

Stevia and Monkfruit

Margaret Ashwell,"Stevia, Nature's Zero-Calorie Sustainable Sweetener A New Player in the Fight Against Obesity," *Nutrition Today* 50, no. 3 (May 2015): 129–34, https://www.ncbi.nlm.nih.gov/pmc/articles/PMC4890837/.

L. A. Barriocanal, "Apparent Lack of Pharmacological Effect of Steviol Glycosides Used as Sweeteners in Humans: A Pilot Study of Repeated Exposures in Some Normotensive and Hypotensive Individuals and in Type 1 and Type 2 Diabetics," *Regulatory Toxicology and Pharmacology* 51, no. 1 (June 2008): 37–41, https://www.ncbi.nlm.nih.gov/pubmed/18397817.

R. Di, M. T. Huang, and C.T. Ho, "Anti-Inflammatory Activities of Mogrosides from Momordica Grosvenori in Murine Macrophages and a Murine Ear Edema Model," *Journal of Agricultural and Food Chemistry* 59, no. 13 (July 2011): 7474–81, https://www.ncbi.nlm.nih.gov/pubmed/21631112.

Kauko K. Mäkinen, "Gastrointestinal Disturbances Associated with the Consumption of Sugar Alcohols with Special Consideration of Xylitol: Scientific Review and Instructions for Dentists and Other Health-Care Professionals," *International Journal of Dentistry*, October 20, 2016, https://www.ncbi.nlm.nih.gov/pmc/articles/PMC5093271/.

Midori Takasaki et al., "Anticarcinogenic Activity of Natural Sweeteners, Cucurbitane Glycosides, from Momordica Grosvenori," *Cancer Letters, Science Direct* 198, no. 1 (July 30, 2003): 37–42, https://www.sciencedirect.com/science/article/pii/S0304383503002854.

I. C. Munro et al., "Erythritol: An Interpretive Summary of Biochemical, Metabolic, Toxicological and Clinical Data," *Food and Chemical Toxicology* 36, no. 12 (December 1998): 1139–74, abstract, https://www.ncbi.nlm.nih.gov/pubmed/9862657.

Q. Xu et al., "Antioxidant Effect of Mogrosides Against Oxidative Stress Induced by Palmitic Acid in Mouse Insulinoma NIT-1 Cells," *Brazilian Journal of Medical and Biological Research* 46, no. 11 (November 2013): 949–55, https://www.ncbi.nlm.nih.gov/pmc/articles/PMC3854338/.

Y. Zhou et al., "Insulin Secretion Stimulating Effects of Mogroside V and Fruit Extract of Luo Han Kuo (Siraitia Grosvenori Swingle) Fruit Extract," *Yao Xue Xue Bao* 44, no. 11 (November 2009): 1252–7, abstract, https://www.ncbi.nlm.nih.gov/pubmed/21351724.

Low-Carb and Low-Sugar Diets

A. Dregan et al., "Chronic Inflammatory Disorders and Risk of Type 2 Diabetes Mellitus, Coronary Heart Disease, and Stroke: A Population-Based Cohort Study," *Circulation* 130, no. 10 (September 2014): 837-44, https://www.ncbi.nlm.nih.gov/pubmed/24970784.

Concepción Peiró, "Inflammation, Glucose, and Vascular Cell Damage: The Role of the Pentose Phosphate Pathway," *Cardiovascul Diebelogoy* 15 (2016): 82, https://www.ncbi.nlm.nih.gov/pmc/articles/PMC4888494/.

Intuitive Eating

Kara N. Denny et al., "Intuitive Eating in Young Adults: Who Is Doing It, and How Is It Related to Disordered Eating Behaviors?" *Appetite* 60, no. 1 (January 2013): 13–19, https://www.ncbi.nlm.nih.gov/pmc/articles/PMC3511603/.

Cheryl Harris, "Mindful Eating—Studies Show This Concept Can Help Clients Lose Weight and Better Manage Chronic Disease," *Today's Dietitian* 15, no. 3: 42, https://www.todaysdietitian.com/newarchives/030413p42.shtml.

Ingrid Elizabeth Lofgren, "Mindful Eating: An Emerging Approach for Healthy Weight Management," *American Journal of Lifestyle Medicine* 9, no. 3 (May 1, 2015): 212–16, https://journals.sagepub.com/doi/abs/10.1177/1559827615569684.

Raquel de Deus Mendonça, "Ultraprocessed Food Consumption and Risk of Overweight and Obesity: The University of Navarra Follow-Up (SUN) Cohort Study," *American Journal of Clinical Nutrition*, 104, no 5 (November 2016): 1433–40, https://academic.oup.com/ajcn/article/104/5/1433/4564389).

Patrick Webb et al., "Hunger and Malnutrition in the 21st Century," *BMJ* (June 13, 2018), https://www.bmj.com/content/361/bmj.k2238.

Special Occasion Menus

Summer BBQ/Picnic
- Blueberry Peanut Butter Crumble Bars
- 5-Ingredient Kimchi Coleslaw
- Best Potato Salad
- Picnic Macaroni Salad with Italian Dressing
- Cucumber Cantaloupe Gazpacho
- Finally Banana Pudding

Kid's Birthday Party
- PB&J Swirl Banana Bread
- Pigs in a Blanket with Grainy Honey Mustard
- Oil-Free Broccoli Cheddar Pasta
- Sweet Potato, Peanut & Black Bean Burgers
- 5-Layer Magic Bars
- Cantaloupe Lemon Sherbet Popsicles

Baby or Bridal Shower
- Raspberry "Pop" Pies
- Tahini Brussels Sprouts with Pistachios & Dates
- Carrot & Zucchini Ribbons with Lemony Pistachio Pesto
- Macadamia & Sesame Crusted Tuna
- Classic Egg Salad My Way
- Lemon Almond Pound Cake

Holiday Dinner
- Bourbon Balsamic Skillet Mushrooms
- Sour Cream & Onion Cauliflower Risotto
- Perfect Pork Chops with Peach Honey Jam
- Orange Balsamic Beef and Farro Stew
- Grain-Free Java Pecan Pie
- Maple Bourbon Baked Pears

Game Day
- Buffalo Cauliflower Hummus
- "Hot" Honey Cheddar-Stuffed Sweet Potato Skins
- Sticky Cajun-Spiced Chicken Wings
- French Dip Calzone
- Buffalo Chicken Dip
- Hungry Girl Chocolate Chunk Cookies

Vegan
- Maple Tahini Date Shake
- Cashew Kimchi Lettuce Cups
- Caramelized Onion & Chive Dip
- Tomato & Spinach "Ricotta" Lasagna
- Roasted Romaine with Basil Caesar Hummus Dressing
- Chocolate Chip Cookie Dough Ice Cream

Vegetarian
- Sun-Dried Tomato & Walnut Paté
- Broccoli Gorgonzola Salad with Miso Maple Dressing
- Artichoke, Leek & White Bean Gratin
- French Onion & Kale Lentil Soup
- Finally Banana Pudding
- Spiced Pear Sour Cream Loaf

Keto-Friendly
- Pistachio Pesto Crab Cakes
- Smoked Salmon, Olive & Pecan Spread
- Steak Bites with Balsamic Cream Sauce & Roasted Asparagus
- Buttery Lemon Pepper Leeks
- Bacon-y Cabbage & Onions
- Easiest Peanut Butter Macadamia Drop Cookies

LL's Favorites
- Creamy Cashew Iced Coffee
- B.E.C. Freezeritos
- Oil-Free Apple Cinnamon Oatmeal Bars
- Double Chocolate Avocado Blender Muffins
- Honey Walnut Shrimp
- Creamy Corn & Chive Farro
- Sheet Pan Sesame Tofu & Bok Choy
- Apple Sausage Breakfast Bake
- LL's Sweetgreen Order Salad
- Pumpkin Spice Cake with Cream Cheese Frosting

Index

Note: Page numbers in *italics* indicate photos separate from recipe text.

About the Author

Laura Lea is a Certified Holistic Chef, and she runs her business, Laura Lea Balanced, from her hometown in Nashville, Tennessee. She graduated from the University of Virginia in 2008 and moved to New York City, where she worked in legal and finance jobs for four years. She soon found herself disillusioned by New York corporate culture, which seemed to reward output at the expense of personal health, as well as the social cycle of overindulging and undersleeping. She began studying holistic health and cooking fresh, produce-focused meals. She quickly marveled at the profound improvement to her physical and emotional state, particularly her ability to cope with stress and anxiety, and became determined to make a career out of sharing this simple but forgotten connection. In 2012, Laura Lea discovered the Natural Gourmet Institute in Chelsea, New York. The program focuses on cooking with whole, mostly plant-based foods, and includes nutrition and healing courses. That September, she quit her job at a hedge fund and enrolled in the program.

After graduating a year later, Laura Lea returned home to Nashville and begin sharing her knowledge of holistic wellness with her community. The goal of LL Balanced is to increase awareness about the relationship between food and mental, emotional, and physical health, so that people can live their most vibrant, productive, and happy lives. Through LL Balanced, Laura Lea provides her clients and readers with easy, family-friendly, and, of course, healthy recipes. Her dishes are often remakes of Southern-influenced comfort food, with the intention of having the best of both worlds. She also contributes articles and recipes for *MindBodyGreen*, *StyleBlueprint*, *Well + Good*, *Shape Magazine*, *Greatist*, *Southern Living Online*, *Women's Health Online*, *Food Republic* and more. She has made regular appearances on *Today in Nashville* and *Pickler & Ben*, where her cookbook was selected by Faith Hill as one of her top Christmas picks. Laura Lea also teaches cooking classes out of her studio in Nashville.

When not tweaking a favorite new recipe or honing her food photography skills, Laura Lea can be found relaxing in her studio with a pencil and drawing pad. Her most frequent subjects to draw are, of course, food.

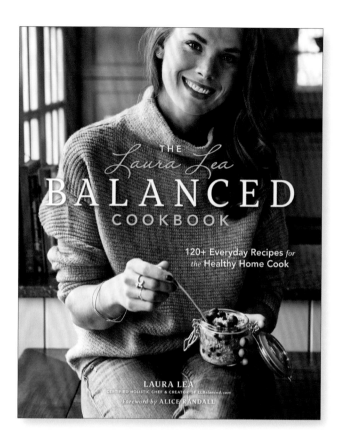

The Laura Lea Balanced Cookbook

978-1-951217-00-6 | $35.00 | 368 Pages

For more of Laura Lea's delicious and healthy recipes,
look for *The Laura Lea Balanced Cookbook* at your favorite
bookstore, specialty retailer, or online at www.bluehillspress.com.

BLUE HILLS
— PRESS —

For more information about Blue Hills Press, email us at info@bluehillspress.com.